Praise for Peter Fisk's previous books:

Marketing Genius

'... truly inspiring book ...' *Brand Strategy*

'... exceptional writer ...' bubblewrap

'... fascinating read ...' *Irish Enterpreneur*

'... spot on ...' *Simon Wakeman Journal*

Business Genius

'I loved this book, it is jam-packed with energy, ideas and inspiration ... you will find something of real value here.' Employer Brand Forum

'... it simply can't fail to be one of the best business books of the year!' BusinessOpportunitiesAndIdeas.co.uk

customer genius

customer genius

Becoming a customer-centric business

peter fisk

CAPSTONE

First published in 2009 by Capstone Publishing Ltd (a Wiley Company)
The Atrium, Southern Gate, Chichester, PO19 8SQ, UK.
www.wileyeurope.com
Email (for orders and customer service enquires): cs-books@wiley.co.uk

Other Wiley Editorial Offices

John Wiley & Sons Inc., 111 River Street, Hoboken, NJ 07030, USA
Jossey-Bass, 989 Market Street, San Francisco, CA 94103-1741, USA
Wiley-VCH Verlag GmbH, Boschstr. 12, D-69469 Weinheim, Germany
John Wiley & Sons Australia Ltd, 42 McDougall Street, Milton, Queensland 4064, Australia
John Wiley & Sons (Asia) Pte Ltd, 2 Clementi Loop #02-01, Jin Xing Distripark, Singapore 129809
John Wiley & Sons Canada Ltd, 22 Worcester Road, Etobicoke, Ontario, Canada M9W 1L1

Wiley also publishes its books in a variety of electronic formats. Some content that appears in print may not be available in electronic books.

Library of Congress Cataloging-in-Publication Data

A catalogue record for this book is available from the British Library.

ISBN : 978-1-84112-788-0

Typeset in Agfa Rotis Sans Serif by Sparks, Oxford – www.sparkspublishing.com
Printed and bound in Great Britain by TJ International Ltd, Padstow, Cornwall

Substantial discounts on bulk quantities of Capstone books are available to corporations, professional associations and other organizations. For details telephone John Wiley & Sons on (+44) 1243-770441, fax (+44) 1243 770571 or email corporatedevelopment@wiley.co.uk

Contents

PART 1 THE CUSTOMER WORLD   1

Track 1:   Hello!   3

Track 2:   My world ... people and their passions   9
   2.1   Wonderful people   10
     Insight 1: Facebook   13
   2.2   Global village   16
     Insight 2: Air Asia   18
   2.3   Customer tribes   19
     Insight 3: Banyan Tree   25

Track 3:   My agenda ... what matters most to me   29
   3.1   Emotional world   30
     Insight 4: Baidu   33
   3.2   Customer kaleidoscopes   34
     Insight 5: Stenders Soap Factory   40
   3.3   The customer agenda   43
     Insight 6: Camper Shoes   48

Track 4:   My terms ... power to the people   53
   4.1   Customer power   54
     Insight 7: Livestrong   57

	4.2	Pull not push	59
		Insight 8: Progressive Insurance	61
	4.3	Outside in, inside out	64
		Insight 9: Zipcars	68
Track 5:		**My business ... the customer business**	71
	5.1	The customer-centric business	72
		Insight 10: Amazon	74
	5.2	Customer value, business value	78
		Insight 11: Best Buy	81
	5.3	Ten dimensions of the customer business	84

PART 2 THE CUSTOMER BUSINESS — 89

Dimension 1: Customer vision — 89

	1.1	Customer purpose	92
		Insight 12: Lego	96
	1.2	Customer brand	98
		Insight 13: Aveda	101
	1.3	Customer alignment	103
		Insight 14: Cemex	106

Dimension 2: Customer strategy — 109

	2.1	Customer profitability	110
		Insight 15: Nike Women	115
	2.2	Customer segmentation	117
		Insight 16: Club Med	120
	2.3	Customer management	121
		Insight 17: Tata	127

Dimension 3: Customer insights   131

  3.1 Customer intelligence   132

      Insight 18: Dove   140

  3.2 Customer immersion   142

      Insight 19: H&M   145

  3.3 Customer insights   147

      Insight 20: Harrah's Casinos   151

Dimension 4: Customer propositions   155

  4.1 Customer context   156

      Insight 21: Whole Foods Markets   160

  4.2 Customer propositions   162

      Insight 22: Oxfam Unwrapped   168

  4.3 Customer conversations   170

      Insight 23: Jimmy Choo   174

Dimension 5: Customer solutions   177

  5.1 Customer collaboration   178

      Insight 24: Heinz Tomato Ketchup   181

  5.2 Customer innovation   183

      Insight 25: Smart USA   187

  5.3 Customer solutions   189

      Insight 26: Boeing 787 Dreamliner   191

Dimension 6: Customer connections   195

  6.1 Customer communication   196

      Insight 27: Wumart China   201

  6.2 Customer networks   203

      Insight 28: Zopa   207

6.3   Customer gateways   209
      Insight 29: Quintessentially   212

Dimension 7: Customer experiences   215
7.1   Customer journey   216
      Insight 30: Nintendo Wii   221
7.2   Customer theatre   222
      Insight 31: Vom Fass   228
7.3   Extraordinary experiences   229
      Insight 32: Build a Bear Workshop   232

Dimension 8: Customer service   237
8.1   Customer delivery   238
      Insight 33: Disneyland   243
8.2   Individualized service   245
      Insight 34: Singapore Airlines   247
8.3   Service recovery   250
      Insight 35: Ritz-Carlton   254

Dimension 9: Customer relationships   259
9.1   Customer partnerships   260
      Insight 36: Harley-Davidson   265
9.2   Customer communities   267
      Insight 37: The Co-operative Group   272
9.3   Customer advocates   274
      Insight 38: New Balance   279

Dimension 10:Customer performance   283
10.1 Value drivers   284
      Insight 39: Enterprise Car Rental   286

10.2	Customer metrics	288
	Insight 40: First Direct	292
10.3	Business impact	294
	Insight 41: GE	300

PART 3	**THE CUSTOMER CHAMPIONS**	**305**

Track 6:	**Leadership ... leading a customer revolution**	307
6.1	Inspiring people	308
	Insight 42: Eczacibasi	313
6.2	New business leaders	316
	Insight 43: P&G	318
6.3	Customer champions	321
	Insight 44: MAC Cosmetics	324

Track 7:	**Culture ... creating a passion in people**	327
7.1	Engaging your people	328
	Insight 45: Pret A Manger	330
7.2	Aligning people and customers	332
	Insight 46: Innocent	335
7.3	Structures, symbols and stories	337
	Insight 47: Toyota	342

Track 8:	**Transformation ... the journey to customer-centricity**	347
8.1	Creating a customer revolution	348
	Insight 48: Avon	352
8.2	Making change happen	354
	Insight 49: Skoda	359
8.3	Virgin inspiration	361

APPENDIX THE GENIUS LAB   **365**

  The customer business roadmap   366

    •   *10 dimensions*

    •   *30 essential tools*

    •   *150 practical actions*

  More genius   377

    •   *Genius LIVE*   377

    •   *Genius WORKS*   378

    •   *Genius BOOKS*   379

Credits   381

About the author   385

Index   387

PART 1

The customer world

In 'the customer world' we will explore what it means to be a customer business and why it is a better way to do business. We explore how customers are changing, what they want, and how they want it. We describe how business can embrace these new expectations, work in new and exciting ways, and what impact it will have on your market and commercial performance.

Hello!

I am your customer.

Yes, a real person, a human being.

I have my needs and wants, to get through the day, and to achieve what I must. But I also have my hopes, dreams and ambitions.

For too long you have treated me as a name or number.
You group me into what you call a segment, or sometimes just a mass market.

But I'm not prepared to tolerate that any more.

I am me. Don't treat me like somebody else.

Sometimes I might be very similar to others,
but I can also be very different and discerning.

In the old world, I realize I didn't have much choice.
I needed you more than you needed me.

But things have changed.

Now I have the power. Now I'm in control.
You need me more than I need you.

It's time you started doing business on my terms.

In fact, why are you actually in business?
Just to make as much money as you can, from whatever you can?

Or to make a difference, to make my life better?

Why don't you learn a bit more about me? Come and listen to what I really want.

I'd love to tell you what I'm really trying to achieve.
Not just whether or not I want your latest gadget, gizmo or gumption.

Why don't we get together and find a way to really solve my problem?
I'd even be happy to pay more if you can really help me find the right solution.

Start thinking about my world.

Don't sell me travel tickets, help me explore the world.
Don't sell me running shoes, help me to run a personal best.
Don't sell me potted plants, help me to create a magical garden.

Stop telling me what you want to sell.

I have got a life, you know. I will buy things, but in my own time, on my terms.

Worst of all are all those unsolicited mail shots and phone calls.
They interrupt me and frustrate me.
And eventually make me hate you.

When I do want something, I expect it to be easy.

Come to me, or to places convenient for me.
And at times to suit me.

I expect what I've seen online to be in your stores or to be available by phone. And to be able to take it back to any of your places if I don't like it.

But I want you to be open and honest about what the deal is.
None of those hidden clauses or additional costs.

If I can get any book or music delivered to my door in 24 hours, why shouldn't I expect a new car, a new washing machine and new home to be just as quick?

And if you treat me with the best service when I'm a big cheese at work, then I don't expect to come back later and be treated like trash as an individual.

Treat me well as an individual and I will tell all my friends how good you are.
I might even switch to you as a corporate customer too.

I know you get rewarded for satisfying me. But frankly I expect much more than that. I demand 100% satisfaction and 100% delight too.

Every time I talk to your people. Every time I experience anything to do with you. It should be right, it should be excellent, it should be perfect.

However, I don't want the same every time. Life's too short and a bit boring.
To be honest, I'd sometimes like you to surprise me!

Which brings me to loyalty.

Whether I really want to come back again. And do. And buy more. And tell others. So you give me a plastic card. With something like a 1% discount.

Hmmm. To be honest, I think loyalty is something that has to work both ways. If you trust me, then care for me and do more for me; I might just do likewise.

I don't really want a relationship with a big anonymous company. I'd much prefer to get to know other people who share my passions.

For travelling. Or running. Or gardening. Real people like me.

The best thing you could do is help me build relationships with other people in my world. Help us to share our ideas and interests, and to do what we love most.

I'm then happy to buy your products. And delighted to be part of your community. And you might even find the things I say and share are valuable to you too.

I know you're a real person just like me.

But when you go to work you put your blinkers on. You restrict yourself to some artificially defined sector. Whilst I see a bigger, more exciting, more connected world.

You follow conventions and prejudices of your own making. Whilst for me, everything is possible.

It's simple, really.

You've just got to see my world. Do business from the outside in. Not the inside out.

Start with me, and everything else follows.

We can be real people together. Happy supporting each other. With so much more opportunity.

And more fun.

Together we can do extraordinary things.

My world ... people and their passions

> *Do you see the world like I do?*
>
> *When I go out for a drink, I go to enjoy the company of my friends, to celebrate a birthday, or maybe to meet somebody. As much as you might like it, I don't go on a mission to find a certain drink or spend time searching out your brand. The drink is an enabler, a consequence, a small part of why I am there.*
>
> *For you it might seem the main thing. You probably spend millions on researching the deep motivational triggers that drive my brand preferences. The reality is that they matter, but not very much. If you can help me to achieve what I really want to achieve, I'd be much more grateful.*
>
> *You probably go out for a drink yourself, just like me. But when you go to work, you seem to put those business blinkers on. Your world is suddenly restricted to the world you are in – the drinks industry, where you think of your competitors as other drinks companies rather than other ways in which I spend my money. You work to your own timeframes, whilst I want things now.*
>
> *That's not my world. My world has far more opportunities for you. My world is genuinely exciting. And I'd have a real passion for anything you can do to make my world better.*

2.1   WONDERFUL PEOPLE

Imagine just over one hundred years ago – without cars and aeroplanes, phones or satellite TV – when people lived their whole lives in the same local communities, locked on their Pacific Islands, remote in their Andes hilltop villages, isolated tribes in the Amazonian jungle. Life stayed the same, traditions were strong, values were consistent, fashions did not change, futures were predictable, ambitions were limited and people were much more similar.

Of course there were travelling communities, too: the nomads travelling across deserts, the warrior tribes seeking to conquer new kingdoms, the explorers searching for new lands. They brought exotic foods and cultures with them, and introduced new ideas and beliefs. Life became influenced by a much bigger and diverse world connected to different cultures, religion, trends and fashions, opening their minds to bigger opportunities.

Today, people live eclectic, transient lives. Although many have their roots, families and friends in one place, they travel the world for leisure and work, and may live in many different countries during their lives. They are in touch with the world through 24-hour satellite TV.

Technology, in particular, has connected our world. People communicate unhampered by time or location: do business on the beach with your BlackBerry, call your mum whilst climbing Mount Everest, order your favourite food from a different continent, chat for hours to your best friends (who you may never have even met physically) by Skype at no cost.

Life is now a fusion of whatever we want. Our influences are limitless, our boundaries undefined. And as a result, people think and behave more differently. We think more. We dream more.

- We are more different.

- We expect more.

- We want more.

We cannot be averaged by market research. We are not predictable by data analysis. We are not engaged by the same messages and incentives as the next person. We do not perceive the same value in propositions as others. We are not prepared to accept standard products and service.

By 2050 India will be the most populous nation in the world

The world top billionaire cities are New York, London, Moscow, Beijing and Istanbul

87% of Italians say sleeping is their greatest pleasure

25% of Silicon Valley start-ups are created by Indian or Chinese entrepreneurs

The average walking speed in cities has increased by 10% in last decade.

73% of people say that a smile is the simplest pleasure.

The probability of a 25-year-old American getting divorced is 52%

40 million Chinese men are unlikely to find a wife. Ever.

1 billion are overweight. 800 million don't have enough to eat.

6.5 billion people in the world, rising to 9 billion by 2050.

If Facebook were a country it would have the 11th largest population in the world

Customers make purchase decisions in an average 2.6 seconds

Young people can do 5.3 things at one time. Adults only 1.7 (and men less).

83% of US children aged 8-18 own a video game player

17% of PlayStation users are over 50

The average US home has more TVs (2.73) than people (2.55)

70% of US children have a TV in their bedroom. 20% families eat every meal watching TV.

51% of US households now use organic products.

44% of people in the UK still live in the area where they were born

Whilst 52% would prefer to live somewhere else

79% of Poles say sweets are their favourite purchase

44 million people visit a Starbucks coffee shop every week.

68% of Americans trust Starbucks, 35% of the British, 12% of the French.

WONDERFUL PEOPLE: CUSTOMERS AROUND THE WORLD

Business needs to treat people more personally.

- Better to know a few customers well rather than many anonymously.

- Better to have some deep insights rather than lots of numeric averages.

- Better to meet the real emotional desires rather than lots of rational needs.

This creates a fundamental dilemma for business. Unless you are, uniquely, a business for one person, you have to manage the dilemma of sufficient size and scale to make money whilst retaining intimacy. You need to balance customization and standardization, wanting more customers, and serving the existing ones better.

Our challenge is to redefine the business's purpose, scope, activities and impact through a customer's eyes. The customer's point of view is broader and richer, it typically requires a wider range of products and services over time, enabling cross-selling and relationship building, but more importantly requiring more listening, more thoughtful solutions and more human support.

Richard Reed never talks about customers. Richard is the visionary and youthful co-founder of Innocent, the great little company that makes the world's most natural and tastiest drinks. He talks, with great passion, about 'those wonderful people who buy and drink our smoothies'.

When was the last time you called your customer a wonderful person?

Indeed, the whole notion of what to call the people you seek to attract, serve and do more with is confusing.

Call them 'customers' and every consumer goods company thinks that we are talking about their wholesalers and retailers, not the people who ultimately buy their products, whom they call consumers. Too many of those companies still have a blinkered obsession with these intermediaries (who pay them and stock them) and not the people who they seek to reach and engage (the people who use them and, over time, hopefully grow to love them).

Call them 'consumers' and every business-to-business company feels alienating, deciding that consumers are a different species of human being from what they might instead call business 'clients'. Of course, engaging a small number of clients with large-volume transactions might be different from mass markets, but it might just be a better way. And the reality is that we are still talking about real people, with a brain and a heart.

For the purpose of this book, we refer to 'customers' as the wonderful people who buy products and services, in whatever type of business you happen to be.

Insight 1: FACEBOOK

You can poke and chest bump, play Scrabble or throw a sheep, tell the world all about you, and share your most intimate moments.

Facebook.com was established by a 20-year-old Harvard psychology undergraduate, Mark Zuckerberg, in 2004. This was not his first venture; he had already developed Synapse, a software device that generated music playlists based on users' previous listening behaviours and for which Microsoft had a big $2 million. At Harvard he created a site called facemash.com, which allowed students to vote on the relative attractiveness of their peers and was quickly closed down by the university's management.

He turned his attention to replicating the physical 'Facebook', which all new students regarded as the essential guide for getting to know people when they first arrive at college. Each student spent hours perfecting their profiles – personal details, previous schools and experiences, hobbies and interests, favourite bands and movies, and the all-important photos of themselves. Surprisingly, nobody had created an online version or connected colleges and universities together.

In February 2004 Zuckerberg launched thefacebook.com, which later became facebook.com. Within three weeks he had 10,000 registered users, and within another two weeks he had opened up the site to the likes of Yale and Stanford. By June, Facebook had spread across 30 universities and had 150,000 obsessed student users, checking each other out and getting connected. All of this was achieved for $85 per month, the cost of renting one server. Perhaps unsurprisingly, Zuckerberg dropped out of his psychology studies, with more lucrative paths to follow.

The business grew rapidly beyond its original purpose. Within a year it had five million active users as it was opened up to other colleges and high schools across the US and then around the world. By 2006, non-students had jumped on the social networking bandwagon. Although 75% of its registered users were in the 25–34-year-old group, significant numbers of older users were joining up too. Within another year, the website had 10 million users and was challenging MySpace to become the world's largest online social networking site.

Communities within the registered users grew rapidly, users joining together with work colleagues to form employee groups or sharing a common social interest or physical location, or supporting a common lobbying point. They can be open or closed groups and these, more than anything, activated people into making more connections, logging on more frequently to see what people were doing and expressing their own views to their chosen worlds.

On 24 May 2007, Zuckerberg surprised the technology world by announcing that he was opening the site to third party developers, giving them instant access to its huge youthful, desirable networked audience. The media called it the birth of 'the Facebook economy'. For users it meant a huge choice of rich interactive content as developers fought to gain a presence.

It transformed Facebook from a popular online meeting place to a technological platform on which anybody could instantly do business. Within nine months of 'opening up', more than 14,000 applications from third party developers were live on Facebook – from online Scrabble, which could be played across the globe by 15 million people, to new virtual economies where people bought and sold their names and relationships. The applications don't simply serve individuals but are typically designed creative ways to embrace and encourage connections.

Robert Metcalfe, founder of 3Com, once estimated that the power of a network is proportional to the square of its users. So as the users grew, the effect grew much faster. Record companies set up fan groups and pre-launched new releases to this highly influential community; market researchers strove to enrol target audiences to learn more about them; rivals looked in awe at the speed of exponential growth.

By mid-2008, with almost 125 million active users (up 160% on the previous year), Facebook was handling around one billion searches and more than 50 billion page views every month. It had become the fifth most popular website in the world and in some countries (such as Turkey) was even more popular than Google. People upgraded their mobile phones and BlackBerries because they couldn't bear to be away from Facebook for a few hours.

Many expected Facebook to be snapped up by one of the leading technology players who were now recognizing the impact of social networks when previously they had missed the importance of search engines. Microsoft invested $240 million for a small share, but Zuckerberg said he was not selling out, merely investing to make his embryonic site even better.

Wharton marketing professor Peter Fader describes Facebook as 'like the qwerty keyboard – there's nothing particularly special about it, but it came along at the right time and place. At some point that standard just becomes locked in'.

However, previous social networking sites have been inherently unstable. Five years ago, everyone was talking about Friendster; then MySpace became the people's choice. When Facebook became the place to go, everyone migrated across. Facebook has much better connections and content, and is simpler and more secure to use, but it is still in its infancy.

Maybe Facebook will define the standards for the networked economy, a decade after it was first trumpeted. How a social network will coexist alongside commercial enterprises is still unclear, as is whether this will become the platform for achieving it.

Zuckerberg, is continuing to innovate. The twentysomething Harvard drop-out has already created a business valued at $15 billion, which really is nothing to throw a sheep at.

2.2   GLOBAL VILLAGE

As the Olympic flame rose up over Beijing's Bird's Nest stadium in the summer of 2008, the world woke up to the enormous, exciting, energetic opportunities of the East. They have long been talked about as 'emerging' economies – markets for the future. However, many people had perceptions of poor and suppressed people, disconnected from the vibrant high-technology world.

This is, of course, a completely false picture. These economies have grown rapidly and will soon outshine the traditional powerhouses of North America and Western Europe. China and India will drive the markets of the future, with billions of customers who already demand the coolest brands and next technologies. In many respects they have always been leaders, particularly in adopting technologies and new ways of working.

C.K. Pralahad describes them as the riches at the 'bottom of the pyramid'. That of course depends on the dimensions of your pyramid. If it's based on wealth, sophistication or power, then the pyramid is rapidly inverting. Its broad base is rapidly becoming the driving force in global economies, and its customers the most important.

Of course it's not just China and India, although these two nations alone will undoubtedly change the world. There are others, too: south-east Asia and South America, for example. In Eastern Europe there is more consumerism than in Western Europe: Russians, Czechs, and Romanians want the plasma screens and fast cars, whilst the British, French and Swedish seek quieter, more natural lifestyles. And then there are the opportunities of Africa, hoping to leapfrog a generation of approaches and mindsets, to enable these markets and their people to trade their way into a new world order.

Imagine a 'global village' where 100 people represent the population of the world:

57 Asians, 21 Europeans, 14 Americans, 8 Africans. 52 women and 48 men. 89 heterosexuals and 11 homosexuals. 30 Caucasians and 70 non-Caucasians. 30 Christians and 70 non-Christians. 6 people would have 59% of the wealth (and all from the USA). 80 would live in poverty, 70 would be illiterate, 50 would be hungry. 1 would own a computer, 1 would have a university degree. 1 would be dying, 1 would be being born.

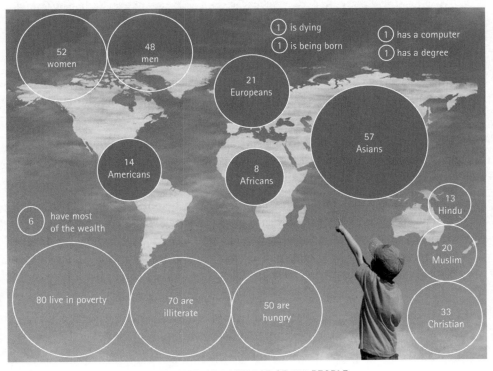

GLOBAL VILLAGE: IMAGINE THE WORLD AS A VILLAGE OF 100 PEOPLE

People are diverse and their motivations and ambitions differ hugely. However, it is easy to lose perspective of our world, the make-up and collective power of its customers. Whilst most business has focused on a minority of these people, it is now waking up to the needs and ambitions, and business opportunities, of the majorities.

Insight 2: AIR ASIA

'There's a new girl in town: twice the fun, half the price.'

The newspaper ads taunted Singapore Airlines and their famed Singapore Girl cabin crew, but were actually launching Air Asia's latest route between Bangkok and Singapore – just another PR blitz from Tony Fernandes, who paid one ringgit (around 25 cents) to buy the airline.

The former music executive cashed in his AOL Time Warner stock options and bought the ailing Kuala Lumpur-based carrier with two old planes and $12 million debt in 2001 when it was on the brink of collapse. Within a year he had engineered a turnaround, launching new routes with new aircraft.

Today Air Asia is one of the world's fastest growing and most profitable airlines. With some of the lowest operating costs in the industry and fares as low as $3, it runs a flying 'bus service' between the bustling and fast growing capitals of South-East Asia. Whilst fares are designed to break even, profits come from additional revenue streams such as food and drink, onboard retail and gaming, and third party car hire and hotel bookings.

The airline succeeds by serving the most populous markets of the world, but it also has one of the most innovative business models. Air Asia is in fact a co-branded collection of several airlines, enabling it to establish hubs in Thailand and Indonesia as well as Malaysia. It has even added a hotel range, Tune Hotels, to its growing business portfolio.

In 2008, Air Asia did what other low-cost carriers such as Easyjet and Southwest had not dared to do – to fly long-haul. It added flights to Australia, with the booming markets of China and India to follow. The low-cost strategy is enabling millions of people to take to the skies for the first time and it is quickly establishing itself as the airline of the people.

Richard Branson, who has established Virgin-branded low-cost airlines across the world, was so impressed that he took a 20% stake in Air Asia X, the long-haul division of the airline. Describing what he would add to the Fernandes vision, Branson promised 'the best entertainment system in the world at the lowest prices, to the world's biggest marketplace'.

Whilst Fernandes stays focused on improving his proposition – constantly finding innovative ways to further reduce costs, offer the best prices, deliver the best service and fund expansion – to the millions and potentially billions of customers, Air Asia is a symbol of the new entrepreneurial opportunities of south-east Asia and beyond.

2.3   CUSTOMER TRIBES

Whilst people are more different, they still want to connect. Individuals come together in new ways.

Instead of being forced together by circumstance – with similar physical attributes in terms of location, occupation, family, wealth – people now come together by choice: similar attitudes, beliefs, lifestyles and aspirations. Today, you are more likely to build friendships with people you meet at your chosen holiday destination than you are with your next door neighbours.

These are the new tribes, driven by values, driven by broader influences, driven by bigger dreams.

New tribes might be defined by a common passion: people who enjoy gardening, support the same political ideas, share a religious faith, love the same music, follow the same football club. These tribes are unrestrained by geography, background or wealth, and form virtual and physical communities to share their passion. They form loyalties to the structures that bring them together and to each other.

Tribes are the new communities that we want to belong to and participate in: market niches that businesses must understand and decide which ones they will align themselves to – to reflect through their brands, attract as customers and serve over time.

The business that attempts to be for everybody will end up being special for nobody.

The business that is obsessed with maximizing its market share of an industry sector or local geography would find it much easier and more profitable to align itself to the ways in which people want to come together – to target a smaller slice of a bigger world.

There are many tribes that your business can choose to serve. The more specific your selection, the more relevant you can be for those people and the more closely you will be able to connect with them.

Small tribes are typically bound more closely together by more specific interests or beliefs – a specialist sport like fell running, for example, or a specific political idea such as human rights. Tribes form when there is a focus for a passion and a way of connecting with each other. Since the number of interests is unending and the connections are easy, there is no limit to the number of such groups today.

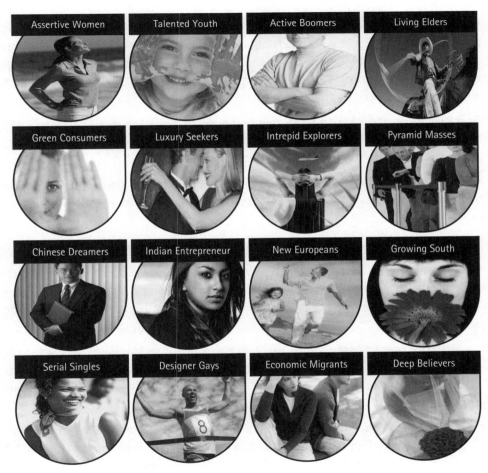

Assertive Women | Talented Youth | Active Boomers | Living Elders

Green Consumers | Luxury Seekers | Intrepid Explorers | Pyramid Masses

Chinese Dreamers | Indian Entrepreneur | New Europeans | Growing South

Serial Singles | Designer Gays | Economic Migrants | Deep Believers

CUSTOMER TRIBES: PEOPLE COME TOGETHER IN NEW WAYS

They are more connected and influence each other – not necessarily by formal associations, but by word of mouth or informal friendships and networks. They have high trust and loyalty to each other and want to share information and ideas. They have more definable needs and wants but are often less well-served. However, they will love a brand that understands them, is designed for them and wants to support them.

From Beijing to Buenos Aires, from those with a conscience (caring about environmental, social and ethical issues) to those who love luxury (the mass market who aspire to luxury brands), people come together to redefine local and global markets.

'Global' is no longer about importing and exporting but the natural starting point for doing business. Similarly, 'local' is no longer about distance, but about the tribes emotionally closest to you.

Some of the fast-growing global tribes are illustrated in the 'global village':

- **Active boomers**: The baby boomers – the 1950s and 1960s kids who are now in their prime, heading towards the end of their first careers. They are fit and wealthy, and ready to explore the world. Retirement is their new beginning and they want to enjoy life to the full.

- **Assertive women**: As the primary decision-makers in 92% of food purchases, 84% of car purchases, women now drive the customer agenda and, increasingly, the business agenda too. They are more assertive and aesthetic, happy to multi-task, and not prepared to compromise.

- **Chinese dreamers**: The world's biggest and most diverse market is hungry for success. The 2008 Beijing Olympics symbolized the reawakening of an economic dragon, with 1.3 billion people emerging from years in the economic wilderness.

- **Deep believers**: From fundamental beliefs to spiritual enlightenment, faith has become more important in people generally, as well as reshaping the world's politics and security. People increasingly seek an anchor to hang onto, values to live their life by.

- **Designer gays**: Having sorted out their morality, businesses now recognize the 'pink dollar' as a crucial and definable market to target – typically more aesthetic and discerning, wealthier, and fashionable, gays and lesbians are asserting their customer power.

- **Economic migrants**: Attracted by the thought of a better life, many cities represent new ethnic mosaics, bringing new skills as well as their own cultural needs. In London, for example, Polish shops are on many high streets and advertisers develop Polish ads.

- **Green consumers**: They want to do the right thing for themselves and for the world – to consume but in a way that is in sympathy with 'green' issues – from organic food to global warming, local communities to human rights.

- **Growing south**: With the majority of the world's population, from Australia to Brazil, Borneo to South Africa, the southern hemisphere is the dark house of future growth. Africa leapfrogs technologies, southern Asia is the new design shop and South America grows fastest.

- **Indian entrepreneurs**: Another huge, diverse market that is set to leapfrog China as the world's most populous nation by 2050, with 1.75 billion people, India is more practical and technical in nature, often well-educated and highly entrepreneurial. They work hard, study hard and are already the backbone of academic and research organizations around the world.

- **Intrepid explorers**: The world is the oyster of many more people, young and old, exploring it in high speed packages or spending a lifetime shifting continents. People are more transient and cultured, fusing many traditions and practices that they carry with them to other markets.

- **Living elders**: The world's population of over-60-year-olds will triple in the next 20 years. More people than any nation, they are increasingly wealthy and healthy, living longer and richer lives, with wisdom and time to contribute more and enjoy life to the full. However, they also need more care and support, a business sector that will boom.

- **Luxury seekers**: Gucci handbags, Porsche 911s and Burberry coats were the exclusive icons of the rich and glamorous. But now, despite the prices, everybody wants one, prepared to sacrifice essentials for the premium symbols of progress.

- **New Europeans**: A new generation of Central and Eastern Europeans knows little of a previously divided world and have formed the most ambitious, entrepreneurial, disciplined and hard-working businesses anywhere. They want a better life and are making it happen for themselves quickly.

- **Pyramid masses**: C.K. Pralahad described it as the fortune at the bottom of the pyramid. Companies such as Baidu and Tata understand the opportunity As others blindly target the few wealthiest customers, they forget that a different proposition could be even more profitable in the huge mass markets of the low-paid and developing economies.

- **Serial singles**: The majority of all households are now singles, be they young or old, or in between. By choice or circumstance, there are more single adults than ever, challenging the convention of family units. They are relatively wealthier, with fewer people to support, and bigger spenders.

- **Talented youth**: The young people who have grown up with Bart Simpson, Google, MTV and PlayStations. They live and think in a globally connected way, where unlimited knowledge is online and culture comes by satellite. They have high expectations and want rich experiences – speed, thrills and instant success.

Insight 3: BANYAN TREE

Imagine that you have just gone to dinner. You start with a fusion of local dishes and then a lightly spiced vegetable soup, followed by red snapper caught that morning and the chef's speciality. You celebrate with champagne. The cool breeze is refreshing after a day on the dazzling white sand. It seems like you are lost in the charm of this tropical island.

You finish with a wonderful dark chocolate mousse that melts in your mouth and is washed down with the last of your bubbles. Your waitress hopes that your dinner was perfect and wishes you a great evening with her ever-gracious smile. Time for a good night's sleep, you think.

Whilst you have been dining, your room has been transformed.

You walk across the small bridge to your glass-walled private villa. The scent of the bougainvillea and hibiscus trees is enhanced by one hundred candles that light your path. Silk drapes now cover the glass walls and the bed in the centre of the room has been remade with silk sheets, scattered ornate cushions and flower petals. On your balcony, an outdoor bath is bubbling, with more champagne and essential oils by the side. The ultimate in intimacy and luxury.

At Banyan Tree, it is all part of the guest experience. Here, the hotel is a stage, a place for treasured moments. The staff can set the stage, either at your request or sometimes by surprise, leaving it for you to create your own story.

Banyan Tree Hotels and Resorts are not for everyone, targeting a wealthy and globetrotting elite. Led by its charismatic founder, Ho Kwon Ping, the group launched its first hotel in Phuket in 1994 and has since won many accolades for its business, service and environmental practices. The mission statement says:

> 'We want to build a globally recognized brand which by inspiring exceptional experiences among our guests, instilling pride and integrity in our associates, and engaging both the physical and human environment in which we operate, will deliver attractive returns to our shareholders.'

In Hindu religion, the banyan tree is considered sacred, representing eternal life because of its ever-expanding branches. The Banyan Tree group now owns, develops and manages 23 resorts and hotels across Asia Pacific, and extending the experience are retail galleries, 65 spas and two golf courses. Resorts are typically small, with between 50 and 100 rooms, and command the highest prices.

The resorts are not just opulent and beautiful; the attitude and attention of their people make this a different experience. Staff are encouraged to be 'creative within a framework', addressing guests by their first names, facilitating whatever the guest seeks from their stay and combining their natural Asian style and hospitality with the multicultural expectations of guests.

Staff are encouraged to see their role from the customer's perspective – to participate in it, with passion and pride. And there are two brand managers; one making the promise through marketing and the other operationally making sure that it becomes a reality. Before a new resort opens, everyone comes together for a pre-opening party. There are exchange programmes to help employees experience different resorts around the world.

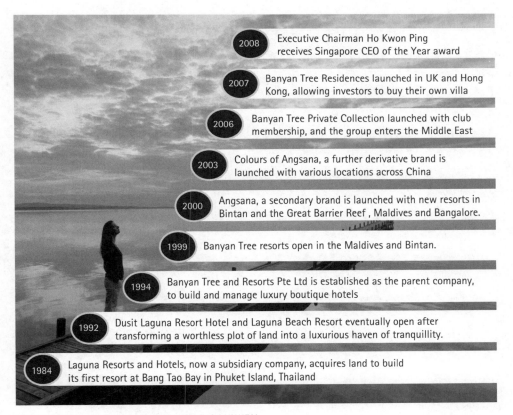

2008 Executive Chairman Ho Kwon Ping receives Singapore CEO of the Year award

2007 Banyan Tree Residences launched in UK and Hong Kong, allowing investors to buy their own villa

2006 Banyan Tree Private Collection launched with club membership, and the group enters the Middle East

2003 Colours of Angsana, a further derivative brand is launched with various locations across China

2000 Angsana, a secondary brand is launched with new resorts in Bintan and the Great Barrier Reef , Maldives and Bangalore.

1999 Banyan Tree resorts open in the Maldives and Bintan.

1994 Banyan Tree and Resorts Pte Ltd is established as the parent company, to build and manage luxury boutique hotels

1992 Dusit Laguna Resort Hotel and Laguna Beach Resort eventually open after transforming a worthless plot of land into a luxurious haven of tranquillity.

1984 Laguna Resorts and Hotels, now a subsidiary company, acquires land to build its first resort at Bang Tao Bay in Phuket Island, Thailand

BANYAN TREE: EXPERIENCE THE EXOTIC LUXURY

My agenda ... what matters most to me

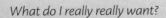

What do I really really want?

Of course lots of things matter to me and my priorities change regularly too – life's a juggling act, constantly making trade-offs. But it's also about principles, beliefs, ambitions and dreams. Please don't prejudge me – don't put me in a box alongside hundreds of other people. We're all different, and anyway it's hard to articulate what we really want, so don't assume that your existing words are sufficient to describe it. My priorities change at home and work, and depending on whether I'm thinking about myself or others, and whether we're talking reality or aspirations. Or maybe you could help me to connect them?

Of course all the usual things matter – quality, service, convenience, value – but they are my basic expectations. Everybody offers that today, don't they? I expect 100% satisfaction on these things.

But I want more. The small things matter and can make a big difference to me, even if they can seem trivial to you. And of course I love it when you remember me, go the extra mile for me. It's great when you exceed my expectations. It shows me how good you can be. But I also care about what your products do for me and my family, what impact your business has on the world around me, and how together we make the world a little better.

3.1   EMOTIONAL WORLD

Emotion stimulates the mind 3000 times faster than rational thought.

Many people say we live in a rational world, but nothing could be further from the truth. Although rational thoughts drive knowledge and skills, emotions drive our attitudes and behaviours. Rational thoughts lead to customers being interested but it is emotions that sell.

Emotions turn inventions into innovations. People have most of what they need – just look in your wardrobe! – but they have a thirst for wanting more.

Research by Anthony Damasio, author of *The Feeling of What Happens: Body and Emotion in the Making of Consciousness*, reminds us that whilst 83% of all information is visual, there are many other ways to engage people. He found that improving people's moods depended on their exposure to different sensory stimuli:

- Positive smells improve your mood by 75%.

- Positive sounds improve your mood by 65%.

- Positive images improve your mood by 46%.

- Positive touch improves your mood by 29%.

- Positive tastes improve your mood by 23%.

He goes on to explain how we are able to construct feelings about the future based on past experiences. When these secondary emotions, or 'somatic markers', are linked to future outcomes, they can act as powerful incentives to act in certain ways – for example, in driving brand preference and purchase decisions.

- Lynx found that its most popular anti-perspirant for young men was chocolate-fragranced – not because it mattered to the men, but because it engaged the girls they sought to attract.

- Mercedes created a personalized, de-bossed supple leather envelope for its direct mailed brochure, reflecting the luxury of its new CL-class interiors.

- Nokia constructs its retail stores with image walls so that the whole interior can change from green to pink or cityscape to tropical island within seconds.

Damasio compares the 40 billion neurons in the brain to a corn field. Walk through the field once and the corn is likely to spring back with little trace of the route for others to follow. However, if you walk through it several times, following the same path, the corn will stay flat. The more frequently that the connections between neurons in the brain are activated, the stronger their memory becomes. When more senses are used to make different connections within the brain (equivalent to more paths across the cornfield), there are stronger and more lasting impressions.

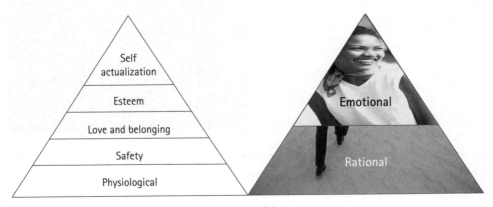

EMOTIONAL POWER: MASLOW'S HIERARCHY OF NEEDS

If we want to buy a new car, we can check the specifications, do test drives and visit price comparison websites, but will ultimately choose to pay a little more for the car we dream of. We look for the perfect houses, considering the floor space, bedrooms, taxes and schools, but then fall in love with the cottage by the sea. Customers think emotionally, but business continues to try to understand and engage them in rational, monochromatic ways.

Rational	Emotional
Needs	Wants
Objectives	Ambitions
Products	Solutions
Features	Benefits
Consistency	Personalization
Transactions	Experiences
Rewards	Relationships
Information	Education
Automation	Human
Maintenance	Enablement
Satisfaction	Surprise
Completion	Achievement

Customers are emotional not rational beings. They engage with people and ideas, more than processes and logic.

Insight 4: BAIDU

The name 'baidu' was inspired by a Song Dynasty poem written 800 years ago by Xin Qiji that compared the search for a retreating beauty amid chaotic glamour with the search for one's dream whilst confronted by life's many obstacles:

> '... Hundreds and thousands of times, for her I searched in chaos, suddenly, I turned by chance to where the lights were waning, and there she stood.'

'Baidu' means 'hundreds of times' and represents the persistent search for the ideal.

China is now the world's largest online society, with more than 210 million users out of its 1.3 billion population, and around six million more logging on for the first time every month. The rapid growth of the Internet in China has fuelled an online nationalism not seen elsewhere, bringing together people like never before who want to share content and transact in their own language and culture too. In China, Alibaba is larger than eBay, and Google (a word which means the number 1 with a million zeros, by the way) is nowhere compared to Baidu.

In the summer of 1998 at a picnic in Silicon Valley, Eric Xu, a 34-year-old biochemist, introduced his shy, reserved friend Robin Li to John Wu, then the head of Yahoo's search engine team. Li, 30 at the time, was a frustrated staff engineer at Infoseek. Wu says what most impressed him was that despite all of the pessimism surrounding search in his own business, Li was passionate about search.

'The people at Yahoo didn't think search was all that important, and so neither did I,' says Wu, who is now the chief technology officer at Alibaba, the Chinese online business-to-business exchange. 'But Robin seemed very determined to stick with it.'

A year after the picnic, Li founded his own search company in China and named it Baidu. In exchange for letting censors oversee its website, Baidu has sealed its dominance with support from the Chinese government (which regularly blocks Google and imposes strict rules and censorship on other foreign Internet companies).

With around a 60% share of online searches, Baidu is more customized to its audience in terms of language, search algorithms and advertising. It is the most popular site in China and the third largest search engine in the world, with a 6% share.

Baidu went public in August 2005 at $27 a share. When trading ended that day, shares closed at $122, up 354%, the biggest opening on the Nasdaq since the dotcom peak in 2000. Suddenly, Baidu was a $4 billion company and Mr Li held stock worth more than $900 million. But many analysts said that by almost every measure Baidu's stock was ridiculously over-valued – it eventually tumbled to as low as $44 before rebounding.

Co-founder Rin Li is convinced that Baidu will soon 'become bigger than Google'. The company recently launched a Japanese search engine, a mobile search engine in Chinese and an advertising-funded streaming music service. There is also Post Bar, where users can exchange questions and answers, and Baidu Knows, which gives points for the best answers.

Today it has a market value of more than $3 billion and operates the fourth-most popular website in the world. With China's fast-growing market, and Li's continued innovation, Baidu looks likely to be a growing force in the virtual world.

Or as a Chinese philosopher once said, 'a beauty in the chaotic glamour'.

3.2   CUSTOMER KALEIDOSCOPES

'Coolhunters' sit in the pavement cafes of Manhattan's Tribeca district, the La Ramblas in Barcelona or Tokyo's Kappabashi Dori, camcorder in one hand, double-shot skinny latte with cinnamon in the other. They seek to capture what's hot, what's happening and what's next.

Observing a trend is like staring at a lump of rock and trying to see the trillions of atoms inside it, all moving about at incredible speeds. It's impossible to see trends. They are directional shifts invisible to our eyes. They happen over time. We frequently see temporary and largely directionless fads, and fashions that are more enduring and with more coherent direction.

Trends emerge over time. However, there is more science to it than reading a crystal ball. Magnus Lindkvist, the Swedish futurist describes trendspotting as 'pattern recognition' – making sense of multidirectional fads and directional fashions, understanding the underlying drivers and influences, and how they will shape future attitude and aspirations.

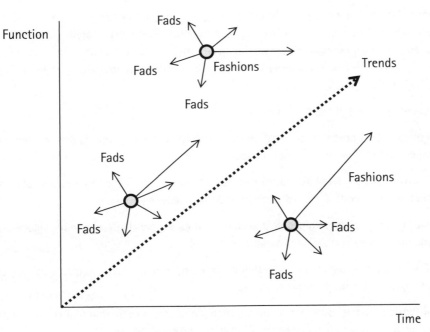

DIRECTIONAL TRENDS: FADS, FASHIONS AND INVISIBLE CHANGE

customer
genius

Reinier Evers from the Netherlands is another futurist. He has a network of 8000 trendspotters all around the world and aggregates their observations and foresights at trendwatching. com. Reiner defines a trend as 'a manifestation of something that unlocks or newly services an existing (and hardly ever changing) customer need, desire, want, or value'.

This definition assumes that human beings, and therefore customers, don't change that much. Their deep needs remain the same yet can be unlocked or newly serviced. Driving this can be anything from changes in societal norms and values to a breakthrough in technology or rise in prosperity.

Abraham Maslow described the different levels of core human needs – from the essentials of food, water, sleep and sex to the energizers such as creativity, morality, confidence and achievement. As an example, a core human need is to be in control or at least to have the illusion of being in control. No wonder that the online world is so addictive – after all, it firmly puts the individual in the driver's seat.

What are the drivers of the customer's world?

Technology is the most fundamental driver of change, changing what is possible and raising the expectations of what customers expect:

- *Digitalization* – the ability to store and access, share and shape vast amounts of information, such as iPods, DVDs, satellite TV and the BlackBerry.

- *Networks* – connecting people and communities, supply chains and marketplaces, crossing boundaries and sharing knowledge.

- *Convergence* – the coming together of fixed and wireless technologies, communication and entertainment, home and workspaces.

- *Robotics* – whilst automation increasingly dominates production and service, sophisticated artificial intelligence enables intuition and consistency.

- **Speed** – fast-changing structures, short product lifecycles, rapid imitation, fast interactions and instant decisions.

In response, market structures have morphed to become more global and fragmented, reflecting the greater individuality and interdependence of customers:

- **Globalization** – more connected, fewer borders, more interdependence. Never before has a butterfly flapped its wings and caused a hurricane so strong elsewhere.

- **Fragmentation** – same but different, with people able to assert their individuality and differences, making markets more complex and diverse.

- **Competition** – there are no limits to competitors. They come across seas and sectors, easily accessible with a search and a click.

- **Regulation** – whilst national entities have become private property, new regulation grapples to cope with the fast and dispersed nature of new technologies.

- **Corporations** – the largest companies are truly global: the likes of GE, Microsoft, Samsung and Toyota have more presence and power than most nations.

Businesses, large and small, have struggled to respond to, survive and exploit this new world order. They too influence the perceptions and behaviours of customers:

- **Consolidation** – combining forces to achieve more influence and efficiency, more powerful and broader solutions, reducing choice or simply trying to survive.

- **Transparency** – everybody can find out anything about your business, driving more openness and information, and responsible and ethical behaviours.

- **Intangibles** – the value of business is no longer in hard things, but in the soft stuff – brands and relationships, ideas and capabilities.

- *Investment* – changing ownership from long-term owners and investors to short-term private equity companies and hedge funds seeking a quick buck.

- *Resources* – securing the most important resources, energy and minerals, partners and people, and of course, the best customers.

Each of these factors shape the customer's world directly and indirectly – how they live and work, what they need and want, how they interact and buy, what influences and drives them.

However, the Internet stands above all else in driving change in the customer's world.

In fifteen years, the Web has changed human society so profoundly that historians have begun comparing the Internet Age with the Renaissance and the Industrial Revolution. It now connects more than a billion people and is the backbone of the global economy and, increasingly, our own daily lives.

Tim Berners-Lee, who established the World Wide Web as a simple, intuitive way to navigate the military and technology-driven Internet, was somewhat disappointed at the way in which the Web was initially used in the late 1990s as little more than online shops. He dreamt of a much more powerful world that is now becoming reality. The Web's second coming, often referred to as Web 2.0, is all about networking and collaboration, shared knowledge and global communities.

Conventional wisdom was that groups delivered less good results than expert individuals. Everyone knew that a camel was a horse designed by committee. Social networking has changed all that. Whilst the early focus has been on the aspects of sociability, the real opportunity comes in terms of working. A new mode of learning, production, distribution, communication and relationship has been born.

If you can make the world's largest and most regularly updated encyclopedia, Wikipedia, via social networking and collaboration, then what else could you do?

- Boeing co-created the 787 Dreamliner with thousands of partners, customers and suppliers around the world, each contributing their ideas and skills.

- Current TV is a profitable digital television channel where all the content, chosen scheduling and even advertising is user-generated.

- Zopa is a peer-to-peer lending network where you lend money to and from each other at better interest rates than banks could ever offer.

Business is moving from the physical labour of production to the intelligent creation of environments where people can collaborate. Find a purpose for people to interact, create a platform where they can come together and sit back and watch your customers do the work, willingly and in their millions – and potentially, make you money too.

James Surowiecki's best-selling and thoughtful book *The Wisdom of Crowds* proposes that crowds have an intelligence that exceeds that of traditional experts, illustrating how a long-lost submarine wreck was located underneath the North Atlantic by the mass contributions of thousands of amateurs who individually had much less idea than the military's own experts, yet solved the problem first.

Similarly, *The World is Flat* by Thomas Friedman describes a new world order of globally located, digitally integrated smart crowds who are 'highly connected and can do wondrous things'.

At the recent European Marketing Conference in Istanbul, Don Tapscott – who co-authored *Wikinomics: How Mass Collaboration Changes Everything* – described to me how 'the Internet, mass collaboration and open-source technologies transform the basis of competition. The winners are those who can embrace business models as diverse as eBay and Wikipedia, MySpace and Linux in order to bring together people and their content'.

As Barry Libert and Jon Specter, authors of the inspirational co-created book *We Are Smarter Than Me* profoundly state, 'the power of the collective we is nearly unfathomable'.

Insight 5: STENDERS SOAP FACTORY

'There is a land which, since ancient days, has been home to strong men and beautiful women. They were known to gather herbs, flowers and buds and to prepare healing ointments and salves that were used to help skin regain its glow and become rejuvenated.

'The most well-known of all sages was a man by the name of Stenders. In his recipes the herbs and flowers had come to a second life with all the force and charm of nature that they possessed. Through generations, his wisdom has been retained to the present day and is now the source of amazing bath and body cosmetics, which give a glow to the skin and bring joy back to the heart.

'Rumour has it that one of the Stenders recipes contains the secret of eternal youth ...'

Stenders was a dream of two young Latvians, Zane Berzina and Janis Berzins, who in 2001 began making soaps from traditional recipes over their single kitchen stove. Their dream was a shop where people could immerse themselves in the multi-sensory experience of fresh herbs, dried flowers, natural soaps and essential oils. Their first shop in Riga was initially a success and the business grew rapidly.

Zane describes the Stenders Soap Factory experience as being 'all about feelings – feelings of beauty, of harmony, of passion, of love ... It's the emotions set into each and every product created by our masters'. She describes her target customers as 'women who want to buy either gifts for themselves or those close to them. She is confident, lives a healthy lifestyle, every now and then wants a bit of a romance and has a definite taste for design.'

The traditional products are seen as antidote to today's world.

BALTIC HERITAGE: THE TREND FOR AUTHENTICITY (REPRODUCED WITH PERMISSION OF STENDERS

'Our mission is to give people the opportunity to learn to know themselves better and to seek out values that uniquely complement them, to seek and find peace and beauty in the relationships. We encourage people to always keep their eyes and ears open, to learn about their own culture and about traditions from elsewhere. We emphasize the warmth of relationships among people, to revive the age-old tradition of people actually enjoying meeting each other, and the value of a harmonious life style in an age characterized by haste and superficiality.'

In many ways this mission reflects the paradox of this small Baltic nation – re-emerging as an independent country, rediscovering its own traditions and culture, whilst enthusiastically embracing brands and technology. It has become one of the fastest-growing nations in the EU.

However, Stenders does not only reflect its own heritage in its skin and body care ranges:

'The notion of East conjures up mysterious, ancient fragrances ... The South is fiery and passionate as topless dancing, it smells of spices, sun and adventures ... The whirlwind of bright city lights, high-heeled shoes characterize the West ... a tenacious life force that cools off a heated mind, strong feelings hidden deep inside, and untamed beauty from the North.'

Stenders achieves its mission by creating an environment that brings back memories of the olden days 'when beauty prevailed over functionality', where people could reflect and talk, a place where 'details are important and things are made to nurture the soul'. They make natural products using plant-based ingredients and old recipes gleaned from local as well as world traditions. The also create a culture of distinctive customer service, 'highlighting the importance of relationships among people and helping customers to discover those most appropriate things they just can't afford not to have'.

In 2007 the business grew by almost 40%, generating revenues of 3.35 million lats, largely through international growth. A franchise model that builds on its Baltic traditions in a relevant way for local customers around the world underpins this: 'we have found out that local people can feel their market much better and provide much more for the local customer, within our basic guidelines. This approach also allows us to keep the personal touch in each and every of our 160 shops worldwide.'

Janis and Zane are careful not to forget their original customers:

'Our brand is interesting for new markets where it is relatively easy to gain new customers. However our first priority is to loyal customers in existing markets, constantly seeking to do more for them, and rewarding their ongoing loyalty and relationships. We care for each and every customer as if they were the only one. We live with our products, we breathe with them and dream about them.'

3.3 THE CUSTOMER AGENDA

The impact of this changing world on customers is profound.

At one level, customers are more individual, and in some ways more self-centred, than ever before – they care about themselves and their families first. They care about health (or well-being, to look at it more positively), education and wealth, as well as more emotional factors such as happiness, enjoyment and friendships.

At another level, customers are more collective and selfless than ever before. They care about their local communities, the social fabric itself not just their favourite people within it, and about broader national and global issues – such as the environment, poverty, fairness and justice.

These motivations can be clustered around three intersecting worlds: me, my world and the world. The 'me' trends are about individuals, caring more about themselves. 'My world' means engaging more with families, friends and communities. 'The world' is more about the role we play in the wide world and its broader issues.

Within these clusters a number of strong trends are identified. Although everybody has some connection with each world, they align most closely with one of them.

'Me' trends are about individuality, what people trust and seek to achieve. They are particular strong motivations for younger customers, and in emerging markets.

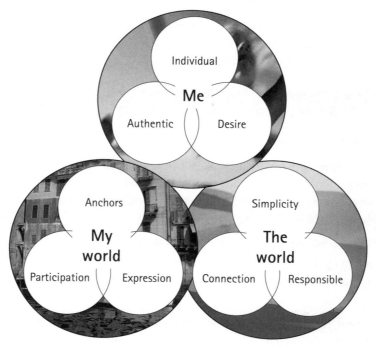

CUSTOMER WORLDS: ME, MY WORLD, THE WORLD

- *Trend 1: Individual*

  - Achievement: I want to achieve more in my professional and personal life.

  - Control: I want to do business on my terms – when, where and how I want it.

  - Myself: I want to be uniquely me – different, personal and special.

  - Privacy: I want my own space, to do what I want without interruption or fear.

  - Well-being: I want to healthy and happy – eat the right stuff, stay fit, enjoy life.

- *Trend 2: Authentic*

  - Genuine: I want the original, real thing – no cheap imitation of questionable origin.

  - Lifestyle: I want to improve my quality of life and income, and what it enables.

  - Spiritualism: I want to find more purpose and meaning, be it religious or in other ways.

  - Natural: I want fresh, local, organic food, nothing synthetic or with additives.

  - Trust: I want to trust you, to believe that you will keep your promise and are on my side.

- *Trend 3: Desire*

  - Aspirations: I want to achieve my dreams, things I never thought possible.

  - Doing more: I want you to go the extra mile – educate me, guide me, entertain me.

  - Enabling: I want your help – don't just sell it me, help me to use it and achieve my goals.

  - Luxury: I want premium brands, the status symbols that say what I want to be.

  - Surprise: I want you to wow me – to do the unexpected, to make me laugh and smile.

'My world' trends are about engagement with others, being part of a community. New parents and older customers typically have a strong affinity with these factors.

- *Trend 4: Anchors*

  - Belonging: I want to have a place I belong to – to feel wanted and at home there.

  - Community: I want to be part of a local community where people like me and are nearby.

  - Families: I want to be with those I care for, to be close and do more for them.

  - Predictable: I want to know you and you to know me – familiar and friendly.

  - Safe and secure: I want to feel that I am protected, that nobody can get me.

- *Trend 5: Participation*

  - Activism: I want to be active not passive, to make a difference, to shape my world.

  - Collaborative: I want to work with you and others, co-creating and co-working.

  - Involvement: I want to be listened to and consulted, to have a say or even a vote.

  - Reflective: I want you to reflect my values and aspirations, to be my kind of brand.

  - Tribal: I want to do things with others – to play in teams and act together.

- *Trend 6: Expression*

  - Confirmation: I want you to reflect my personality – the kind of person I am or want to be.

  - Fashion: I want to be with it, cool and contemporary, or even surprising.

  - Identity: I want to be recognized, to be known, to establish myself in the big world.

- Opinion: I want to express my opinion about issues, to debate and influence others.

- Sharing: I want to tell the world about me – what I've been thinking and doing.

'The world' trends are about participating and being responsible for the broader world. These can be most relevant to customers who travel more, and more aware of global issues.

- *Trend 7: Simplicity*

  - Clearer: I want everything to be obvious and intuitive, to edit my choices and talk my language.

  - Easier: I want it to be incredibly easy to find, compare, buy, install or use.

  - Enabling: I want you to make my world simpler, so that I'm in control, in touch, on top.

  - Faster: I want it now – instant quotes and customization, fast delivery, and fast operation.

  - Supporting: I want you to be on my side, sticking up for me, championing my cause.

- *Trend 8: Connection*

  - Accessible: I want to connect anywhere, anytime, anyhow – to anybody in the world.

  - Interactive: I want to interact with anyone in the world – talk, learn, share, design, do.

  - Finding: I want to find the people, knowledge and activities that are special to me.

  - Searching: I want to explore the world and find anything I want, wherever it may be.

  - Time and place: I want to connect at the right moment, when and where I need it.

- ***Trend 9: Responsible***

  - Care: I want to make a difference, to my world, my community and the people I love.

  - Environment: I want to reduce my impact on the natural world, particularly the climate.

  - Ethics: I want to work with people who do the right thing and are honest and trustworthy.

  - Fairness: I want to ensure fairness in my world and for people around the world.

  - Legacy: I want to leave behind a better place for my children and future generations.

Each customer will engage differently with the factors in the customer agenda. Each business must understand which matter most to each of its customer segments. They are unrelated to the specific products or sectors, because they are about people – customers of any business large and small, in consumer or business markets. Separately and collectively, the appropriate factors give every business a diverse range of opportunities to innovate, differentiate and engage more deeply with its customers.

Insight 6: CAMPER SHOES

In Catalan, 'camper' means 'peasant'.

You will find the whole story of the company and its value inside every pair of colourful, quirky and distinctive Camper shoes. The shoe company from the beautiful Spanish island of Majorca likes to do things differently. In some styles, left and right shoes are intentionally mismatched; in others, there are philosophies and quotations on the soles.

What are the drivers of change in the customers' world?	The Customer Agenda	What are the implications for a customer-centric business?
People are more different, in their needs and wants, attitudes and ambitions	**Individual**	Engage each customer in more individual and intuitive ways
Interactions are remote, automated and impersonal with little to engage people	**Authentic**	Find a more compelling social and human purpose for your business
People expect more from you, and want to achieve more for themselves	**Desire**	Do more for people, addressing their broader issues and ambitions
Security and safety, fragmenting communities and dispersed families	**Anchors**	Bring like-minded people together, creating a place where they feel they belong
Security and safety, demise of old institutions and order, and low trust in brands	**Participation**	Build a reputation for being open, fair , and on the customer's side
People want to be heard, to establish their own identity and express their own views	**Expression**	Enable people to assert their identity, to collaborate in creating personal solutions
Technology and business are complex, continually changing and intimidating	**Simplicity**	Make complexity simpler, be the customer's guide and educator
Convergent technologies mean customers expect everything instantly	**Connection**	Work with networks and partners to be accessible anywhere, anytime
Environmental crisis, poverty, justice, human rights and ethics matter more to people	**Responsible**	Be more responsible, put environment, social and ethical issues at your core

CUSTOMER AGENDA: DRIVERS, TRENDS AND IMPLICATIONS

The shoes are rustic and authentic, unlikely to be called fashionable. They are inspired by the unique culture and traditions of the tiny Mediterranean island where they are still designed and many of them manufactured. Most people of the island worked on the land, so they wanted tough, durable shoes that could withstand the extremes of weather.

'Imagination walks', goes the advertising slogan.

The story inside the shoes tells you that the business was founded in 1877 by a shoemaker called Antonio Fluxa. The Camper brand was introduced by his grandson Lorenzo 98 years later. In an interview with *Fast Company*, Lorenzo said that 'when people call us a fashion brand it offends me. We don't like the fashion world at all. We're trying not to take ourselves too seriously.'

Not fashionable or serious, maybe, but certainly popular. Camper's sales reached almost €100 million in 2007, making it a market leader in Spain, and it continues to grow rapidly with more than 250 stores across the world.

The brand is much more than the shoes, becoming a lifestyle that challenges conventions. 'Camper Together' stores are designed in partnership with local artists and architects to offer customers far more than a shoe shop. In Barcelona, for example, the store is inspired by Jaime Hayon, one of Spain's most provocative graphic artists who designs furniture and toys. The bright and bold store is as much a quirky art gallery as a place to buy comfortable shoes. In Paris, the store seems to be still waiting for a designer, encouraging visitors to draw on the walls and express their own feelings and creativity.

There are Camper hotels and restaurants too. Casa Camper offers 25 simple but stylish bedrooms in the heart of Barcelona, but also with free WiFi and DVD players in every room. It has a help-yourself 24-hour snack galley, a vertical garden, a recycling centre and free bikes to explore the city. Down the street you can eat at FoodBall, Camper's vegetarian restaurant that specializes in microbiotic foodballs made of rice and numerous natural and surprising ingredients. Sit on the floor cushions, listen to the karma music and drink the local organic beer too.

The website allows you to do this in a virtual world. 'Take a walk' enables you to test-walk the Camper shoes: as you walk down the Barcelona street, you might pass a Camper Together store, pop into FoodBall for some new recipes, and then arrive at Casa Camper, where you can book your real accommodation and pay for your new shoes too.

Brands such as electronic gadgets are designed to support or encourage the frenetic pace of our lives. Yet experience and expression are increasingly valued above money and materialism. Camper is a brand at peace with itself, its purpose to enjoy living life, rather than anything with numbers attached. Sebastian de Grazia captured the attitude of the Catalan shoemakers in his book *Of Time, Work, and Leisure*, saying 'perhaps you can judge the inner health of a land by the capacity of its people to do nothing – to lie abed musing, to amble about aimlessly, to sit having a coffee. Whoever can do nothing, letting his thoughts go.'

My terms ... power to the people

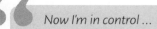

Now I'm in control ...

I used to travel miles to get your place. I used to take time off work because I wanted to. I used to be prepared to queue, to tolerate your slow deliveries, to be grateful for any choice. I used to be happy to tell you all my details and pay more for a personal service. I even used to enjoy seeing your adverts on television and waiting for the money-off coupons to come through the door.

I really don't need to play by your rules any more – to go to the locations most convenient for you at the times when you want to be open, to be pushed from department to department, to repeat information time after time. And quite frankly, I probably know more about what I'm seeking to buy than you do. I checked it all out online – I know the options and how much your competitors are selling it for. I know how much I'm prepared to pay and if you don't do me a deal, I have plenty more choices. I'm the customer. I'm in control, and don't forget it.

Power has fundamentally shifted from companies to customers. However, companies still try to operate on their own terms – to push products at customers, to arrogantly expect customers to buy, listen and do what is convenient to the corporate drive.

We are individuals, different and discerning.

Customers demand, expect and know more. One experience conditions what we expect of another – having experienced a Banyan Tree hotel resort, I expect much more from my local swimming pool; if Amazon can deliver a book or washing machine the next day, why does it take a car retailer three months to get you a new car or your local store eight weeks to deliver some new furniture?

Emotions drive customer attitudes and behaviours like never before. At the same time that more choice and broader experiences have driven higher expectations, falling trust in business has led to significant decline in customer loyalty. Business transparency and media focus on the negative aspects of business have fuelled this decline in trust in brands, whilst the abundance of choice and speed of innovation accelerates the promiscuity of customers.

Customer satisfaction has, in general terms, not increased. Indeed, in this hyperactive, emotional world, it is the extremes of emotion that can stir customers inside. As Jonas Ridderstrale, author of *Funky Business*, is fond of saying – today 100% satisfaction is expected, as is 100% delight … today, in a world of sameness, hyper-efficient processes and standard experiences, surprise is what customers want.

Customers now call the shots.

The availability of information, unlimited reach of the Web and strength of recommendations between friends means that customers are more knowledgeable and able than ever before.

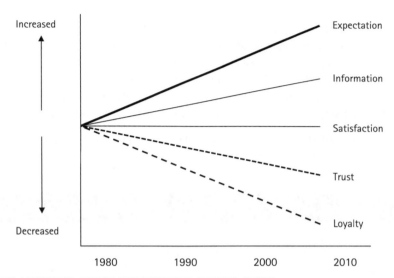

CUSTOMER ATTITUDES: RISING EXPECTATIONS, FALLING TRUST

They probably know about the item they seek to buy than the shop assistant could ever know about every item in their store.

In the past there was surplus demand – now there is surplus supply. As borders fall and competition intensifies, there is no shortage of choice for customers – and therefore they have the stronger hand. Companies need customers more than customers need companies.

Their power might be subtle or it might be exerted more overtly. From eBay to Priceline, customers are becoming accustomed to setting their own prices in terms of the perceived value to them. And once one company sets a standard for free delivery in 24 hours and the ability to customize an order or request additional services, then customers expect – and demand – the same service levels from any other company too.

Customers assert their power in less direct ways too: most simply by just shifting their custom to one of your competitors, but more dangerously to expressing their view to everyone else. In the past, a particularly unhappy customer was thought to tell around ten to twelve other people – think of the way people love to tell tales of misfortune or annoyance round a dinner table – whereas now they get online and give you a negative review, write a blog or add a comment to somebody else's site, where hundreds and maybe thousands of people can instantly share their unhappiness.

The 'promise gap' evaluates the gap between a brand's promise and reality – between the expectation of quality and service that it has set in the customer's mind, and the experience the customer has.

Brand	Image	Experience
Google	7.62	8.46
Jaguar	7.21	8.23
Honda	7.20	7.86
KFC	5.27	5.08
Fiat	5.15	4.74
McDonalds	4.78	4.55

(Source: UK Promise Index 2007, ranked by experience level)

Whilst there is obviously delight, maybe even surprise, when the experience goes beyond a customer's expectation, the implications of failing to live up to your promise are much more significant. The speed and impact of negative publicity is huge – a brand's reputation can be shattered in hours, not years – and the higher you project your image, your claims of quality and being on the customer's side, then the further you can fall.

One faulty product in 100,000 or one bad service experience in 10,000 might not seem unreasonable. But just imagine if that one customer decides to feature their unhappiness on a YouTube video that is then watched by thousands of others or writes a damning review on Amazon that is then read by virtually every other potential customer.

Insight 7: LIVESTRONG

At the age of 25, Lance Armstrong was one of the world's best cyclists. He proved it by winning the World Championships and multiple stages of the Tour de France. He seemed invincible and his future looked bright.

Then he was told he had cancer.

At first, his single-mindedness meant that he ignored the warning signs and never imagined his condition could be serious. But then the implications of testicular cancer were explained to him. It would spread and he would die.

Then his dedication to excellence, physical conditioning and survival instinct took over. He declared himself a survivor, not a victim. He learnt everything he could about the condition, underwent aggressive treatment and, as his own fate hung in the balance, started talking about how others could survive too.

He created the Lance Armstrong Foundation, dedicated to educating others about the condition and supporting those who were living with cancer. In time he beat the disease and dedicated his life to helping others, famously saying that 'unity is strength, knowledge is power, attitude is everything'.

However, he was not finished as a sportsman. He started training again and became one of the best cyclists the world had ever seen: his six consecutive Tour de France victories from 1999 to 2005 were awe-inspiring to even the healthiest sportspeople. The sight of the yellow jersey-wearing Armstrong storming down the Champs-Elysées year after year to win one of the toughest sporting challenges was phenomenal.

To mark his final Tour, he joined forces with his long-time sponsors Nike and their advertising agency Wieden and Kennedy to create a symbol of his real challenge: to lead the fight against cancer, support others like him and ensure victims became survivors – to live strong.

The 'livestrong' wristband is a yellow silicone bracelet that was launched in May 2004. It raises funds for the Lance Armstrong Foundation to support cancer research, raise awareness and encourage people to live life to the full. It was sold individually for $1 each from Nike's retailers around the planet, as well as in packs of ten to 1000. It was meant to raise $25 million but achieved this in the first six months. Almost 100 million wristbands have now been sold.

The yellow band became extremely popular worldwide. Everyone from movie stars to presidential candidates, news anchors and royalty wore it. A temporary version, make out of paper and sticky tape, even appeared in an edition of the television show *The Office* when a character felt he was at risk of skin cancer.

The wristband became a global fashion statement, showing how quickly a trend – and a cause – can spread and engage people across ages, beliefs and geographies. Other wristbands have since imitated the campaign, each with a worthy cause in mind, whilst other types of events – such as the Red campaign supporting HIV and AIDS victims, and Live 8's crusade against global poverty – have changed attitudes and driven action using sophisticated marketing techniques.

Icons, endorsements and symbolism are incredibly powerful forces in mobilizing people.

4.2 PULL NOT PUSH

Doing business on customers' terms requires a fundamental inversion in the way you do business. It changes the starting points, reverses the dynamics and transforms the roles of people. Business moves from hunter to gatherer, from aggression to assertion, from doing things when and how it wants, to when and how the customer wants.

It used to be about push.

Businesses used to be powerful. They used to 'push' themselves on customers, persuading them to buy their products whether they needed them or not, enticing them with advertising and special offers, forcing them to come to locations of their choosing and then trying to sell as much as possible when they got there. Not only this, but they might seek to 'upsell' you a more premium option or 'cross-sell' you additional products and services.

Customers played along with this because they had limited choice, there was a limit to other sources of the products and the lower prices might not be around for long. They grudgingly accepted that this was what businesses did.

Businesses became even more aggressive, with more commercial breaks interrupting your favourite TV programmes and movies, or buying lists of target customers and then mailing them constantly in the hope of winning their attention by power of doormat deluge. Other bought lists of customers and called them at all hours – at home at meal times, when they are most likely to be there, or on their mobile phones too. The same happened with emails and text messages.

Customers resented this intrusion.

They were no longer prepared to accept such forms of 'interruptive' marketing. They created campaigns against these bullying practices. In the USA, the majority of households registered their details at donotcall.com and responsible companies then pledged not to call people who had stated they didn't want to receive unsolicited calls. In response to customer lobbying governments introduced stricter data protection laws restricting companies from making unsolicited approaches.

It also showed how uncreative and downright lazy, many companies and their marketers had become. Charities, strangely, are some of the worst offenders – glance at the amount of unsolicited mail and you will find that much of it comes from not-for-profit organizations. Not only do they bombard you, but they add in free gifts to try to make you feel obliged to respond, or unrequested Christmas cards asking you to then send payment.

Customers started to realize there were more options – they need not support these organizations because there were better ones with better ways of working out there. In particular, the online world opened the eyes of customers. Enlightened companies realized they needed to fundamentally change the way they do business.

Now it's about pull.

Customers will not be pushed around any more. They want to work with you, and others, but on their terms. They have the awareness and intelligence to know what they want and to explore where they can get it. They have the means to research and evaluate their options in terms of comparing specifications or finding the best price.

They are more likely to engage you (rather than you engage them) if you can act on their terms – easy to access whenever and however they want, responsive when they do contact you, able to meet their needs and aspirations. They expect you to be loyal to them rather than the other way around.

Of course you still need to be visible, to have presence and a brand that is known and well regarded. Reputation is best achieved through word of mouth. Image is best achieved through sponsoring events that target audiences want to be part of, endorsed by experts or celebrities who people trust and aspire to be like. Similarly, the direct marketing backlash has promoted the concept of permission marketing, gaining people's authority to contact them in advance of doing so.

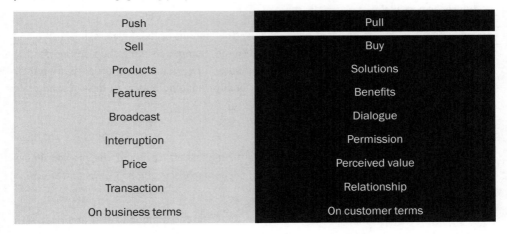

Push	Pull
Sell	Buy
Products	Solutions
Features	Benefits
Broadcast	Dialogue
Interruption	Permission
Price	Perceived value
Transaction	Relationship
On business terms	On customer terms

However, this is not just a marketing challenge. It affects every part of the customer experience and includes sales, customer service, operations and customer support. As such, it affects strategy, decision-making, suppliers, distributors, finance and human resources too.

Insight 8: PROGRESSIVE INSURANCE

'It's about you. And it's about time' proclaims Progressive, recognizing the need to rethink financial services, particularly the emotional world of insurance, from a customer's perspective.

Progressive is the third-largest car insurance firm in the US, founded in 1937 by Jack Green and Joe Lewis and based in Mayfield Village, Ohio. It has also become a rare beacon of customer-centricity in the notoriously product-driven world of financial services.

Progressive's purpose is all about customers and 'to reduce the human trauma and economic costs associated with automobile accidents with the aim to get their lives back in order again as quickly as possible'.

Anybody who has had an accident will recognize the amount of helplessness, heartache and hassle that it can create. In a market where 98% of customers simply shop around for the cheapest price – regarding insurance as a commodity, a necessary evil in order to drive their car – Progressive offers a distinctive and emotionally engaging reason to look beyond price and make a positive choice.

Progressive is driven by its five core values:

- *Integrity*: We revere honesty. We adhere to the highest ethical standards, provide timely, accurate and complete financial reporting, encourage disclosing bad news and welcome disagreement.

- *Golden Rule*: We respect all people, value the differences among them and deal with them in the way we want to be dealt with. This requires us to know ourselves and to try to understand others.

- *Objectives*: We strive to communicate clearly Progressive's ambitious objectives and our people's personal and team objectives. We evaluate performance against all these objectives.

- *Excellence*: We strive constantly to improve in order to meet and exceed the highest expectations of our customers, shareholders and people. We teach and encourage our people to improve performance and to reduce the costs of what they do for customers. We base their rewards on results and promotion on ability.

- **Profit**: The opportunity to earn a profit is how the competitive free enterprise system motivates investment to enhance human health and happiness. Expanding profits reflect our customers' and claimants' increasingly positive view of Progressive.

The $14.7 billion company employs 27,000 employees, was voted by *Fortune* magazine one of the United States' top 20 best companies to work for and is also a favourite of iconic investor Warren Buffett. Progressive has a history of pioneering innovation in the world of car insurance:

1937	First insurer with a drive-in claims office.
1956	First insurer to offer a safe driver plan.
1990	First insurer to serve customers at the accident scene.
1994	First insurer to provide 24/7 customer service by phone.
1995	First insurer to launch a website.
1997	First insurer to offer online real-time purchase.
2003	First insurer to introduce a concierge-style claims service.
2004	First insurer to launch a usage-based plan.

Most eye-catching of all these innovations was the ability to be reach the site of an accident, mediate between parties still affected by the incident and sort out the claim instantly. Progressive claims that its Immediate Response Vehicles will be at the scene of any accident within ten minutes.

In 2008, Progressive went beyond its narrow focus on insurance, seeking to make a bigger difference to the lives of car owners. It launched the Progressive Automotive X Prize, which invites teams from around the world develop viable, super fuel-efficient vehicles that 'give people more car choices and make a difference in their lives'.

4.3 OUTSIDE IN, INSIDE OUT

The customer business works from the 'outside in' rather than 'inside out'. It thinks like a customer, not like a product salesman. It helps customers to buy, rather than just trying to sell. It works on customers' terms and then finds a way to be competitively and commercially successful. It pulls more than it pushes.

Imagine if every aspect of business started from the outside in rather than the inside out. Imagine if business decisions were in this order:

- 'What do our target customers really want?'

- 'How can we do this for the customer better than anyone else?'

- 'How can we do it in a way where we can also maximize our own profit?'

Imagine if everything started with customers and, more broadly, the marketplace and environment where you do business – the outside.

This would be in stark contrast to most businesses today. They start with what they do and seek to do more of it. They start with what they have and try to sell them faster. They start with their existing performance and seek to make it a little better each year.

But this assumes that the world never changes – that your capabilities and products will always be in demand. It assumes that markets are in a steady state, competition and prices don't change much, most customer needs and wants are already well-defined, innovation is incremental, and that the only way to gain customers is to take them from a competitor.

Doing business from the outside in is different.

It assumes the opposite. It recognizes that markets are constantly changing, that competition is constantly evolving, that customers' wants and aspirations continually change and grow. It therefore knows that the past is a poor guide to the future – that success is found by moving with markets with most profitable growth rather than hanging on to outdated capabilities. It recognizes that more radical innovation is possible, and similar leaps in results.

Of course there is a balance – between doing everything for customers and being distinctive and profitable, between being responsive to external change and driving change internally, between doing business from the outside in and from the inside out. But the balance has shifted and continues to move towards the 'outside in' business.

Ask yourself these questions:

- Does your brand define your target customers and their ambitions or arrogantly talk about your business or product and what it does?

- Is your research still centred on average statistics or existing prejudices, or does it listen to and explore more deeply the real needs and wants of individuals?

- Do you still subject all customers to blanket communication campaigns, trying to sell what you want, when and how you choose, not them?

- Are your distribution channels chosen for your convenience and efficiency rather than your consumers'?

- Does your pricing model play at the margins of your direct competitors rather than being based on the perceived value relative to the customer's view of their alternatives?

- Do you still try to persuade customers to have 'relationships' with your company when they'd thank you much more for connecting them with other people like them?

The 'Customer Power Profiler' enables you to profile your business, externally and internally, in terms of where your balance lies today and where you want it to lie in the future. Do you do business more from the outside in, or from the inside out?

Do you engage customers **inside out?**	External **Customer Power** Profiler ™	Do you engage customers **outside in?**
Attract all customers, and regard all as good and of equal importance	⬭⬭⬭⬭⬭	Attract best customers based on their potential loyalty and long term value
Brands define the function of the business or products and services	⬭⬭⬭⬭⬭	Brands articulate the aspirations of customers in distinctive ways
Propositions are individual products available to everyone	⬭⬭⬭⬭⬭	Propositions capture benefits to each target customer segments
Communications builds awareness through 'push'-based campaigns	⬭⬭⬭⬭⬭	Communications engage customers through 'pull'-based dialogue
Standard products and services sold and delivered separately.	⬭⬭⬭⬭⬭	Products and services brought together to solve customer problems
Distribution channels designed and chosen for business efficiency	⬭⬭⬭⬭⬭	Customers buy from trusted partners – when, where, how they want
Prices are standard and based on manufacturing costs and competition	⬭⬭⬭⬭⬭	Prices are based on each customer's perceived value of benefits
Consistent and standardized service delivery to all customers	⬭⬭⬭⬭⬭	Service is delivered in a personal style, flexible to each customer
Transactional focus based on more on purchase than usage experience	⬭⬭⬭⬭⬭	Total experiences that educate, entertain, enable people to do more
Seeking to build relationships between customers and the brand	⬭⬭⬭⬭⬭	Bringing customers together in relationships with others like them

CUSTOMER POWER PROFILER: WHAT DRIVES YOUR EXTERNAL ACTIVITIES?

Do you manage your business **inside out?**	Internal **Customer Power** Profiler ™					Do you manage your business **outside in?**
Strategy is driven by optimizing the value of existing capabilities	○	○	○	○	○	Strategy is driven by the best market opportunities for value creation
Patents, processes and property are the most important business assets	○	○	○	○	○	Customers, brands and ideas are the most important business assets
Decisions are made from a finance perspective first, customer second	○	○	○	○	○	Decisions are made from a customer perspective first, finance second
Growth is managed through portfolios of businesses and products	○	○	○	○	○	Growth is managed through portfolios of markets and customers
Innovation is focused on products, making them scientifically better	○	○	○	○	○	Innovation of every part of business in collaboration with customers
Employees are recruited primarily for their specialist skills	○	○	○	○	○	Employees are recruited for their attitude, and skills developed later
Culture is serious and conventional, hierarchical and functional	○	○	○	○	○	Culture is energizing and innovative, flexible and collaborative
Structure is aligned to products, with profits measured by category	○	○	○	○	○	Structure is aligned to customers, with profits measured by segment
Leadership is directing, controlling and managing delivery	○	○	○	○	○	Leadership is inspiring, connecting and empowering people
Key results are volume and market share, short-term revenues	○	○	○	○	○	Key results are satisfaction and advocacy, long-term profitability

CUSTOMER POWER PROFILER: WHAT DRIVES YOUR INTERNAL ACTIVITIES?

Robin Chase and Antje Danielson were sitting in a Berlin café, excited about a car-sharing concept they had observed in the German city in late 1999. Cars were parked around the city in dedicated bays, ready to be driven by the hour by members of the scheme.

They thought it was an obvious idea, particularly in the crowded cities of the US. They returned home, putting a high-tech spin on the idea by using wireless technologies to track and open the cars, and launched their own service the following year.

From an initial fleet of a dozen Volkswagen Beetles, the company now has more than 3000 cars positioned around the streets of key cities in the US, the UK and Canada. Each one is distinctive with its bold green 'Z' along the side.

The philosophy is sound. Owning a car in a city comes at a high price, never mind the damage to the environment. Of course, sometimes a car is the best solution, giving you the freedom to get where you want, whenever you want, letting you carry high luggage and large families, or simply allowing you to enjoy the feel of the road. But for most of us, particularly city dwellers, these days are infrequent.

Imagine if you could have the car of your choice – perhaps even better and newer than you could normally afford – waiting for you around the street corner, available whenever you want it. But at all other times you don't need to worry about or pay for it – 'wheels when you want them', as Zipcar puts it, with particular focus on hip, young, thoughtful audiences.

They have particularly targeted college students, partnering with universities to secure the best parking spaces on campus, seeking to sign them up before they ever get into the cycle of car ownership. The biggest cultural challenge has been the ingrained aspiration of youth towards car ownership as a sign of maturity and achievement, and so getting to people before this takes hold has been important for the future. Forty per cent of new members either sell their existing cars or choose not to buy one once they have experienced car-sharing.

There is a touch of Apple in its marketing strategy, targeting niche but influential customer segments that then become and influence the mainstream.

Zipcars actively promotes a youthful image in everything from its website design to its brand promotions, locations and pricing. Building communities of like-minded members is also a significant feature – sharing news and advice on places to go and things to do at the weekend.

Becoming a 'Zipster' is easy, and major car hire companies such as Avis and Hertz have been slow to recognize the disruptive innovation but are now starting to imitate the new business model. Meanwhile, Zipcars recently merged with its rival Flexcar to become the dominant player. The company now has almost 200,000 members paying an average $50 each year, delivering around $100 million revenue in 2008.

The ambitions of CEO Scott Griffith are much greater: he is targeting two million members and $1 billion revenues, followed by an IPO. He is looking at other congested, highly populated cities around the world, thinking about the city-to-city market, and ultimately sees Zipcars as a lifestyle brand. He sees high oil prices and environmental concerns as only helping his business grow, although he will continue to focus on flexibility and freedom as the most important benefits to his target customers.

Zipcars thinks and works from the outside in, with an innovative model for car usage in a world where congestion and carbon emissions matter more, but having the freedom and prestige of a car still matters.

My business ... the customer business

I want to work with a business that really understands me, one that shares my ambitions and reflects my values. I want to do business with a company that really is ready when I am and is happy to work on my terms.

Most of all, I need somebody who can really solve my problems, bring together the right solution for me and help me to do things that I would not be able to do myself. I don't want a business only interested in selling me stuff. I don't want a business obsessed with itself.

Of course I want the company to succeed – that's how it can invest in even better solutions for me. We both know what the score is. So don't patronize me or try to bribe me into being what you call loyal. Let's work together – but treat me as an equal and I'll do likewise.

5.1   THE CUSTOMER-CENTRIC BUSINESS

Doing business on the customer's terms is obvious and essential.

Peter Drucker was one of the first to suggest that the sole purpose of a company is to create and retain customers. He reasoned that since the customer alone pays for the product or service, the customer is the most important entity within the business. Indeed, in recent years, from the 1980s bandwagon of total quality management to the 1990s obsession with customer relationship management, organizations have sought to align themselves to customers.

However, some argue that a blind obsession with customers has a destructive impact on competitive advantage: the focus on competitors is last, as every company seeks to meet the same needs of the same customers. This, they argue, leads to falling customer satisfaction as they face a large number of relevant but commoditized products and services. It also misses the stimulus for innovation, meeting the unarticulated needs of customers and finding better ways to solve their problems.

Companies have succeeded with both strategies – Courtyard by Marriott, for example, was a business traveller hotel concept designed entirely by analysis-based customer research, focusing on the priority needs of this target audience. Meanwhile companies such as Chrysler have succeeded through innovation – their groundbreaking minivan, for example has defined and shaped an entire market despite customer research saying that customers did not want it.

The reality is that a successful business does both – these approaches do not conflict. Having a customer orientation is not about blindly obeying the customer but about working with them so that you both understand their needs and ambitions, whether they are articulated or not. Similarly, an innovation orientation is not about product obsession – increasingly, customers are partners in the innovation process and all innovations ultimately need customers to embrace them.

Companies realize that they need to meet the existing and emerging needs of their customers, but also drive innovation and differentiation. Indeed, they realize that a customer orientation is not just about bowing to the declared needs of customers, but being selective about which customers to work with and then collaborating to understand their real issues and aspirations. They also realize that competitive advantage stems from having the better insights and customers, thereby driving better innovation and growth.

Perhaps it comes down to words and meanings – early approaches to 'customer focus' were largely cultural and superficial, achievable despite being driven by products and internal priorities.

'Customer focus', 'customer-intimate' or 'customer-driven'? These initiatives tended to focus on attitudes and behaviours, and mainly those at the 'customer interface' – a term that implied that the rest of the business was not connected to customers. They were largely about nice words and soft focus, but when it came to the crunch, it was still business first, customer second – how to gain and grow profits first, satisfy and retain customers second.

So what's different?

A 'customer business' starts with the customer. It works from the outside in, and then balances this inside out. By starting from the outside in, the business is fundamentally inverted – its priorities are different and its performance better.

No longer can businesses see the best opportunities, engage the best customers or compete most effectively by standing inside and looking outwards. Products and processes, strategies and systems, rewards and relationships must start and revolve around the customer.

'Customer-centric' is probably the best adjective, if you need one.

Insight 10: AMAZON

Amazon seeks to be 'the most customer-centric business on Earth'. That's a bold ambition from the world's largest bookstore, and retailer of much more, but with a compelling logic.

Amazon believes that in a fast-changing world, customer-centred rather than competitor-focused strategies are more effective. Customer needs change more slowly than competitive actions – therefore, investments have more time (and more chance) to make an impact. Competitors are easy to follow, imitating their successes and avoiding their mistakes. But if you want to be a leader in markets today, competitors will hold you back – or once ahead, you get complacent. Addressing the priorities of customers is a never-ending challenge and the source of your revenues too.

Amazon wanted to be a leader, to shape the market like nobody else, so chose customers as its guide. However, it all started more analytically. Indeed, founder Jeff Bezos demonstrates how a left-brained strategist and analyst can only succeed with right-brained insight and imagination.

In the early 1990s, Bezos was an investment analyst with a New York hedge fund, excited by the potential of the Internet, not just for his clients but also as a personal opportunity. He looked across industry sectors for what he felt would be a sweet spot; he watched the early dotcom start-ups and their relative successes. Then he stumbled across the concept of an online bookstore, a business that he felt could really have an advantage online.

In 1994 he named his start-up online bookstore cadabra.com, as in abracadabra, and realized the potential when his first sale came in the form of the book *Fluid Concepts and Creative Analogies: Computer Models of the Fundamental Mechanics of Thought*. How many physical stores or even mail order companies would bother to stock that? The diversity of customers and books lay at the heart of his business plan.

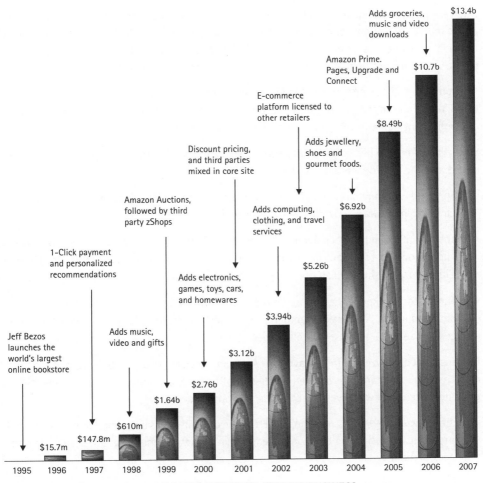

$13.4b

Adds groceries, music and video downloads

$10.7b

Amazon Prime. Pages, Upgrade and Connect

E-commerce platform licensed to other retailers

$8.49b

Adds jewellery, shoes and gourmet foods.

Discount pricing, and third parties mixed in core site

$6.92b

Amazon Auctions, followed by third party zShops

Adds computing, clothing, and travel services

$5.26b

1-Click payment and personalized recommendations

Adds electronics, games, toys, cars, and homewares

$3.94b

$3.12b

Jeff Bezos launches the world's largest online bookstore

Adds music, video and gifts

$2.76b

$1.64b

$610m

$147.8m

$15.7m

1995 1996 1997 1998 1999 2000 2001 2002 2003 2004 2005 2006 2007

AMAZON: CREATING THE WORLD'S MOST CUSTOMER-CENTRIC BUSINESS

75

One year later, amazon.com was launched, the new name reflecting the size and complexity of the market and supply chain that he sought to connect with a click of a mouse. His initial financial projections were unusual in that they did not expect to return a profit for at least four or five years, unlike the many other wild dotcom projections at the time.

As promised, the business grew steadily, much to the frustration of some shareholders, and when 'the bubble' burst in 2000, he persevered and finally delivered a profit in 2002 – the small but significant figure of $5 million on revenues now in excess of $1 billion.

Since then, Amazon has continued to show a knack of spotting the best opportunities before others and the confidence to seize them.

- The product range has diversified to include music and video, electronics and computing, clothing, homeware, downloads and groceries.

- The global reach has been achieved by online affiliates with other websites and retailers, and regional distribution centres across the world – initially in Europe and Japan, and then China through the acquisition of joyo.com.

- The customer experience has grown richer, now including customer ratings, personal recommendations, 'look inside' sampling, 'one-click' purchasing, wish lists, delivery tracking, customized books and self-publishing.

Perhaps most controversial (and brave) was Amazon's decision to open up the website to third-party retailers. To many this seemed a self-defeating idea, letting your strongest competitor pitch up, potentially with even lower prices, on your prime estate.

Its initial concepts, Auction and zShops, were unsuccessful. It was only when third-party retailers were listed alongside the Amazon price for each item that Amazon and third parties found a successful model.

Although that might seem crazy to some people, Amazon thought long and hard about the pros and cons of doing it. Eventually it decided that by giving the customer more choice, they were more likely to come to Amazon; by being more transparent about the competitive alternatives, customers would trust them more. Bezos describes that some decisions are just too difficult analytically and at these times he turns to the customer, asking what it best for them.

In an interview with *Harvard Business Review*, Bezos surprised many with his very honest description of what guides him and his business decisions: 'It helps to base your strategy on things that won't change. People ask me what is going to change in the next five to ten years, but I rarely get asked what's not going to change.' He argues that investing in these factors will deliver the longest-term returns, even if they sometimes take time to make a difference.

Customer insights tell him the aspects that will change least, he believes. 'Our customers want selection, low prices and fast delivery. I can't imagine that in ten years from now, customers are not saying that they wish we could deliver products more slowly, or that our prices were a little higher. If we keep putting energy into these flywheels, ten years from now it'll be spinning faster and faster.'

Another fundamental belief is about transparency – that there is more information around than ever before and customers are more intelligent and informed. It is therefore smart to align yourself with the customer, rather than against him. 'In the old world you devoted 30% of your attention to building a great service and 70% to shouting about it, in the new world that inverts.' If you deliver a great customer experience, customers will tell others – particularly online.

According to Bezos, the foundation of great service is culture. The customer-centric behaviours of Amazon are rooted in practical actions – every employee, for example, has to spend a number of days every year in the fulfilment centres or on the telephones. Bezos leads by example, describing it as the most fun part of his job and the place where he learns most, too.

Culture emerges out of these principles and practices, and is obviously shaped particularly by those who initially set the business up. Cultures become surprisingly stable, argues Bezos, describing how many new recruits remark on Amazon's customer obsession more than anything else. They also become naturally selecting, drawing people to them who have a similar mindset and ejecting people who find their beliefs lie elsewhere. The distinctive culture drives an equally distinctive type of customer experience and becomes a competitive advantage that is hard to copy. It also becomes a foundation on which strategy is built and must align.

In delivering great customer service, Bezos has not lost his left-brain liking for analytics, focusing on process as much as the softer stuff. 'Defect reduction' is an enduring passion of the business, seeking to minimize the number of errors that occur in the system, embracing techniques such as Six Sigma and lean manufacturing, and focusing on key quality and consistency metrics.

The important thing, he has found, is to understand the areas that require consistency – the repeatable processes – and the areas that require flexibility, for example in the form of personalization and responsiveness. Amazon might seem like a huge automated machine, yet it has people at its heart, editing choices, responding to customers, making improvements and shaping the future.

> 'Amazon rules – it's that simple. It keeps track of what I buy so I don't end up with duplicates. I find lots of used books that are out of print or that cost way below retail. If it's not the first place I go to shop, it's usually the last, because I've looked at prices elsewhere and realized I can get it cheaper at Amazon. I participate in their Vine program where I test products and write reviews, but I wrote reviews before, just for fun. I check my recommendations several times a week just to see what's new and update my wish lists. I use the gift lists to plan my holiday shopping. I'm saving my pennies so I can hopefully someday buy a Kindle.'

That is the opinion of one fan of Amazon and perhaps an example of why revenues have tripled since 2002 to $13 billion.

5.2 CUSTOMER VALUE, BUSINESS VALUE

Becoming a customer business is not just about passion. It makes commercial sense.

Customer businesses deliver more profitable growth, are more sustainable over time and deliver better returns to shareholders. It can also be a more efficient business, a more flexible organization and a more enjoyable place to work.

At a strategic level, customers are a business's scarcest resource.

It is easy to secure physical resources from suppliers around the world, except in the case of oil, which we all know is running out. It is relatively easy to secure capital, from conventional investors or more recently from private and particularly from ethically motivated sources. It is not so easy to secure the best talent, as knowledge and ideas become more important. Yet the most difficult to secure, and most valuable resource, are the best customers. These are the golden nuggets of today's business.

At a commercial level, customers are the most valuable assets of a business.

Consider the market capitalization of a business – the collective value of all your shares, reflecting the price somebody might pay to buy your business. This value reflects the future profit potential of your business and therefore the assets that make up that figure are most important in driving future profits. Today, 86% of the value of publicly quoted businesses is intangible (according to *Brand Finance*) and the most significant intangible assets are typically brands, relationships and ideas. Two and sometimes all three of these are driven by customers.

At an operational level, the best customers cost less and spend more.

Research, to be considered in more detail later, describes your best customers as those who are prepared to engage in a long-term, profitable relationship. It shows how they will typically stay longer, cost less, buy more, pay more and tell others. Their acquisition costs will be lower, falling to zero when they want to come back of their own accord. Their operational costs will also be low, as they do more themselves. Their perceived value is higher and therefore they may pay more or at least seek smaller discounts. And, best of all, they are great advocates – recommending you to their friends, other people like them, helping you to build a reputation and attract others.

Every business will quote different figures to demonstrate the importance of customers. The numbers and chosen ratios may differ by type of business and market. However, these are some of the most typically quoted statistics, averages and generalizations that help to make the business case:

- 20% of your customers give you 80% of your revenue.

- 10% of your customers give you 90% of your profit.

- A very satisfied customer will tell three other people.

- A dissatisfied customer will tell 12 other people.

- A very dissatisfied customer will tell 20 other people.

- 98% of dissatisfied customers never complain, they just leave.

- 65% of lost customers are due to negative experiences.

- 75% of negative experiences are not related to the product.

- The biggest reason people leave is because they don't feel appreciated.

- It costs three times more to acquire than to retain a customer.

- It costs 12 times more to win back a dissatisfied customer.

- Over five years, a typical company retains 20% of its customers.

- A 5% increase in retention would increase profits by 25–55%.

(Sources: TARP, Bain & Co, ECSW)

Most companies are quick to make claims about delivering superior value to shareholders, driving profitable growth, reducing risks, improving dividends and seeing their share prices rise. Of course they can do this in the short term by 'slash and burn' approaches to cost reduction and aggressively driven sales. But it won't last. The only sustainable route to long-term value creation, profitable growth and lucrative dividends is in creating and delivering superior value to customers.

- **Creating superior value for customers** through deeper insights, more relevant propositions and personal solutions is the foundation of a successful 'customer business'.

- **Creating superior value for shareholders** through sustainable growth, enhanced margins,and reduced risks is the result of a successful 'customer business'.

'Customer value' is therefore the starting point – not the financial value of the customer to us, but the value we create for them, which is obviously a perception that differs by customer rather than an absolute value. But it is the notional value, the philosophy and approach that matter.

Insight 11: BEST BUY

Best Buy has its origins in the heart of Minneapolis, a small but cult 1960s store called the Sound of Music.

As music and technology evolved, it grew and diversified, acquiring many other small rivals on the way – until a tornado hit in 1981 resulting in a 'tornado' sale at the lowest prices around, which then became an annual event. The idea of low pricing caught on and the company was renamed Best Buy. It grew rapidly and within a decade had hit $1 billion annual revenues. Acquisitions continued, first with Magnolia Hi-Fi, the specialist premium electronics, and Future Shop, a Canadian electronics chain. It even launched its own label music and video business.

When Brad Anderson took over as CEO of Best Buy in the summer of 2002, he inherited a company that was flying high: it had reported four quarters of double-digit earnings growth. So it's perhaps not surprising that when Anderson proposed spending $50 million on a new organization strategy, he got a few raised eyebrows. His 'customer-centricity' strategy addressed every part of the business and every one of the group's 650 stores.

He recognized that most retailers think little about their customers, displaying a vast collection of products and not really caring who walks in. Customer-centricity meant a different approach, designing stores, service and product selections around the needs of specific customers.

Based on detailed customer segmentation, he recognized that not all customers were good, going as far as describing some as 'angels' and others as 'devils'. He also identified strong and profitable segments behind which to align propositions, such as 'Barry' the home entertainment fanatic and 'Jill' the busy suburban mother.

Stores were redesigned and new training was developed to focus on one or other of these segments – for example, with personal shoppers for Jill stores, a much greater technical knowledge for Barry locations – as well as different types of in-store layouts, signage, fixtures, lighting and even uniforms. Barry stores focused more on technology and specifications, and

'Angels' are the best existing or potential customers:

- Higher spend
- Lower cost
- Brand affinity
- Loyalty potential
- Positive advocates

Best Buy targets the "angel"

but not the "devil" customers

'Devils' are the worst existing or potential customers:

- Lower spend
- Higher costs
- Limited relevance
- High promiscuity
- Negative influencers

BEST BUY: SOME CUSTOMERS ARE ANGELS, OTHERS ARE DEVILS

included music and movie theatres to sample the products. Jill stores included coffee bars and children's play areas.

'Lab stores' were used to test a particular location's audience types, trial particular themes, profile the likely customer base and customize the store mix to the local needs. Each store conversion would represent an investment of at least $1 million. Best Buy continued to acquire companies to enhance its offer, either in terms of locations or services.

Most famously, in 2002 Best Buy acquired a young rebellious start-up called Geek Squad. Founded by Robert Stephens, the 24-hour computer support business was creating quite a stir in inner cities – particularly with homeworkers who were desperate for help. Robert would rush round and turn up at the door complete in his 'geek' uniform (black shades, white short-sleeved shirt, clip-on black tie, white socks) and 'special agent' badge. This was pure theatre, but it was also great service. And a brand that spread like wildfire around homeworkers in need of help.

Geek Squad set up 'precincts' in Best Buy stores (and also in partnership with Kinko's in order to offer more coverage) where people could bring along their laptops and peripherals to be attended by 'counter-intelligence' officers. Customers bought more complete solutions – multiple products and at higher margins, too.

The board was impressed with the results. Customer-centric stores delivered around twice the growth rate of other stores. By 2006 the business had open or converted 233 stores with a multi-segmented format and 300 with single segment formats.

Clearly the customer-centric approach worked and Best Buy decided to really now push for growth. It trialled new concepts such as knitting and scrapbooking zones, and held demonstrations and in-store evening classes for handicraft-loving Jills. It also recognized that this customer-centricity depended on his people – and Anderson described the internal shift as 'talent powered' and about moving 'from managing products to managing people'. Managers were encouraged to try ideas themselves and were rewarded handsomely for their entrepreneurship.

Indeed, all staff can participate in a shareholding and bonus programme that has turned many store managers into millionaires.

When I asked Anderson at a recent retail conference in London how he really makes decisions about which business to buy, market to enter or services to launch, he is impressively committed to the customer-centric approach:

> 'Anybody can make up a convincing business case based on assumptions about future profits and discount rates – whereas spending time with the customer, understanding what they want, and how you could make things better for them, is a far better guide to decision-making and where your business priorities really lie.'

Best Buy now wants to extend its customer-centric model worldwide. It opened sourcing and retailing sites in China, and acquired the Five Star Appliance chain with 151 stores around Beijing and Shanghai. In Canada it continued to operate 128 stores under the Future Shop brand, and 51 as Best Buy. In Europe it formed a joint venture with the UK's Carphone Warehouse to develop the Best Buy Mobile concept of GSM and broadband services, as well as using the British company's network and experience to start rolling the big blue box, with a customer-centric inside, out across Europe.

5.3   TEN DIMENSIONS OF THE CUSTOMER BUSINESS

Defining a 'customer business' can sound simple and obvious. It sounds like the right thing to do. And this is perhaps why so many organizations, and particularly their leaders, have failed to appreciate the more fundamental differences involved. They have applied the philosophy but not the disciplines that move from a product to customer obsession and turn passion into profit.

We understand now that it is about creating value for customers first, and business second. We are ready to embrace pull rather than push approaches to our markets, and adopt this more holistically in our 'outside in' approach to business. We can also make a strong business case for it based on the significant impacts on profitability and value creation.

But what are the more practical differences? How does it affect the business strategy, performance metrics and our decision-making criteria? What does it mean for how we recruit and manage people, our key operational processes and systems, and organization structure? What does it mean we must stop doing and start doing?

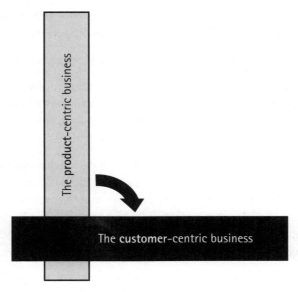

CUSTOMER-CENTRICITY: TURNING THE BUSINESS ON ITS SIDE

Moving from a product-centric to customer-centric business is like flipping the organization on its side. It is about aligning the organization to the customer experience rather than product management. It is about managing your customer portfolio rather than your product portfolio. It is about solutions rather than products and relationships rather than transactions. It is about measuring profitability – with profit and loss reports, budget allocations, performance rewards – by customers and segments rather than by products and business units.

The specific differences between a product-centric to a customer-centric business are shown below. Some of them are obvious; others require more explanation, which will follow later. Some of them challenge ingrained principles or philosophies of business, such as moving from a large catalogue of products to a capability to bring together the right solutions, or replacing 'Percentage of market share' with 'Percentage share of best customers'.

How do you make this happen? What matters most? And where should you start?

Of course every business is different and will already have embraced some aspects of customer-centricity. Fundamental will be the strategic direction, targeting the right performance metrics and giving people the tools to act differently. However, it is the business that combines these many different factors that will be able to realize the real commercial benefits.

The 'ten dimensions of a customer business' must be addressed individually and collectively in order to create a successful customer-centric business. They are based on the analysis and experiences of more than 100 companies and build on similar but less comprehensive models such as the EFQM (European Foundation for Quality Management) Excellence Model. Uniquely, the list connects aspects such as customer strategy and insights with customer propositions and communication, service and experiences, and relationships and performance.

Together they form the 'customer blueprint' that will form the structure of Part 2 of this book, adding the specific tools and approaches to making them happen, and a diagnostic for evaluation and improvement in the Genius Lab at the back of the book.

The product-centric business

Best product
Add value through features
Competitive obsession
Treat customers equally
Wide range of products
Selling and delivering

Short-term transactions
Revenue and volume
% market share
% new products
% satisfaction
New customers, existing products

Sales driven, push
Customers come to us
Connect with intermediaries
Broadcast campaigns
Mass media
Awareness and attraction

Internally focused
Product management
Technological innovation
Product profit centres
Planning and consistency
Left brain, X-type people

The customer-centric business

Best relationship
Add value through service
Customer obsession
Treat customers differently
Personalize solutions
Collaborative and enabling

Long term relationships
Profit and value
% best customers
% wallet share
% advocacy
Existing customers, new products

Buyer driven, pull
We go to customers
Connect with end users
Personal conversations
Experiential
Engagement and retention

Externally focused
Relationship management
Market innovation
Customer profit centres
Agility and responsiveness
Right brain, Y-type people

CUSTOMER CENTRICITY: TURNING THE BUSINESS ON ITS SIDE

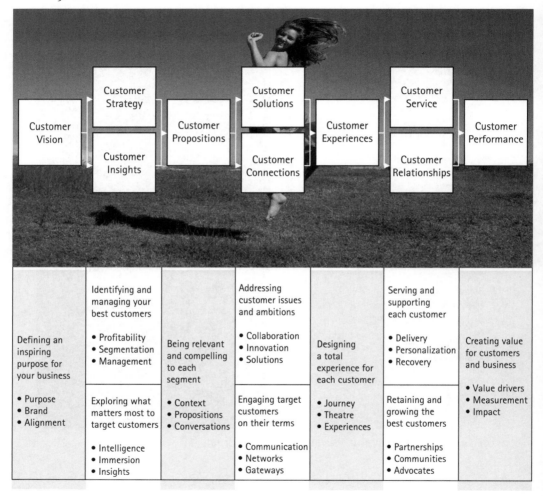

Customer Vision	Customer Strategy / Customer Insights	Customer Propositions	Customer Solutions / Customer Connections	Customer Experiences	Customer Service / Customer Relationships	Customer Performance
	Identifying and managing your best customers		Addressing customer issues and ambitions		Serving and supporting each customer	
Defining an inspiring purpose for your business	• Profitability • Segmentation • Management	Being relevant and compelling to each segment	• Collaboration • Innovation • Solutions	Designing a total experience for each customer	• Delivery • Personalization • Recovery	Creating value for customers and business
• Purpose • Brand • Alignment	Exploring what matters most to target customers	• Context • Propositions • Conversations	Engaging target customers on their terms	• Journey • Theatre • Experiences	Retaining and growing the best customers	• Value drivers • Measurement • Impact
	• Intelligence • Immersion • Insights		• Communication • Networks • Gateways		• Partnerships • Communities • Advocates	

CUSTOMER-CENTRICITY: BLUEPRINT FOR A CUSTOMER-CENTRIC BUSINESS

PART 2

The customer business

The 'customer business' has ten dimensions. Having understood why a 'customer business' is essential and better, we now consider how to make this happen effectively. Each dimension brings a practical 'outside in' approach to business, balancing customer and commercial objectives. The priorities for implementation will differ by business, although the real impact will come the integrated implementation of all ten dimensions in the right way.

Customer vision

Most businesses seem obsessed with money, more interested in sales and profit targets than in me, the customer.

Where do they think their profits come from? Most business leaders seem most concerned about themselves and their companies – growing in size, becoming more famous, achieving success. All I ever hear them talk about is their own goals. I wonder if they even have time to think about their customers?

Imagine a company that exists to serve me, designed to make life better for its customers. That doesn't mean it has to be a charity – I'm happy that it succeeds as long as I get what I want too. Instead of trying to be the world's biggest or best company, it tries to do the right thing for me.

Imagine a company where its purpose and its brand is all about helping me to do things I never thought possible.

1.1   CUSTOMER PURPOSE

Defining the purpose of your business from the 'outside in' means rethinking what you really do for customers, how you add value to society more broadly and what would be missing if you didn't exist.

The arrogant self-interest of most 'mission statements' does little for customers who have lost faith in big companies and their pursuit of money.

Financially obsessed businesses – pursuing more profits, bigger bonuses and executive life-styles – used to offer a positive social image: the pillar of the community, a sign of progress and success. In the US they called it the American Dream.

In emerging economies, people saw brands as symbols of a better life, an end to poverty and repression. We celebrated them and wanted to support these companies, not begrudging them their money for one second.

But then it all went ugly. Business became associated with greed.

Companies and brands, and sometimes even non-profit organizations, were seen as all for themselves and ready to use customers as a means to their ends. The stood for higher prices, lower quality, hard selling, high surcharges, unethical practices, outsourcing jobs, unbelievable bonuses, environmental destruction and moral corruption.

Trust has declined, loyalty has become rare, suspicion is high.

Most companies see profits as their ultimate goal. They relentlessly pursue more, caring less about what they do and how they do it, thinking most about how much they make. Yet if every company blindly pursued profit maximization, they would most likely converge to sameness, their profits diluted. It would feel like a never-ending treadmill and customers would just be a means to this end.

Similarly, most mission statements are based around 'becoming the market leader' and 'maximizing returns to our shareholders'. Such ambitions might seem entirely reasonable in terms of a business strategy, but are they really the broader purpose of business? Is it why the founders started the business? Will this make them any different from all the other companies with similar statements? Is it the only reason why the company now exists?

Customers are much more engaged in a company that is about them. Employees and shareholders are more engaged too, in a business about people.

A 'customer vision' describes a better world for people, where they can achieve more in one way or another, and how the company can uniquely help them to do this. When mobile phone company Orange first launched, it projected a vision of 'a wireless future' where people could work and play, instantly and connected, anywhere and anytime.

A purpose beyond profit, making people's lives better.

However, the vision should not come from an advertising agency. It must be the vision of the people inside the business. It is a fundamental role of leadership to paint a picture of where we are going and then find the words and symbols to bring that to life. Indeed, developing such a vision is an excellent way of bringing together a leadership team, getting them to look upwards together at their collective opportunity rather than downwards at individual challenges.

A 'vision workshop' might include:

- Leaders together taking time out to describe their own visions of a great company, what they'd love to achieve, be famous for and leave behind for others. This is no ordinary strategy session, but fundamentally thinking about why, how and what we do.

- Working with customers in a 'big talk' session, learning how real people describe how a great business might look and feel. Listening to their anger and frustrations about your types of business, together with their hopes and dreams for themselves and you.

- Learning from other successful business across the world, about their visions and how they are achieving success in their industries. And then consider what they would be in your industry – how they would challenge conventions and drive innovation.

- Building a jigsaw of images and ideas, characteristics and attributes. Perhaps using a free-form artist or cartoonist to bring it to life as you talk. And then standing back to consider how the ideas combine more powerfully, and where are the centres of gravity.

- Understanding the sacrifices that this vision might involve, such as changing to strategic focus, no longer charging for customer support, moving out of the corner office. It is just as important to define what you will stop doing as what new things you will do.

- Capturing specific ideas for innovation, products, services, promises or policies that would make the vision tangible. Whilst this is not an innovation workshop, such concepts help to make a vision real for people and would require separate evaluation later.

- Mapping out how the vision might unfold as a series of horizons, making the bold vision more attainable and progressive – with some aspects achievable more quickly and others taking longer, understanding the evolution, with symbols of progress on the way.

The vision can be captured in a 'purpose statement' that explains how the company adds value to people's lives. What is the role of your business in society? What is your challenge, belief, crusade or passion? How does it enable people to do things that they would otherwise not be able to do? And if the business were no longer here, how would the world be a lesser place?

Some organizations continue to call their customer purpose a 'mission' or 'vision'. Others call it a 'promise'. These range from dreams of their founders, such as Bill Gates' 'a computer on every desk and in every home', which seemed incredibly ambitious at the time, to more practical commitments. They capture an attitude, sometimes a challenge, and a set of values to work by:

- Apple believes that 'man is the creator of change in this world. As such he should be above systems and structures, and not subordinate to them'.

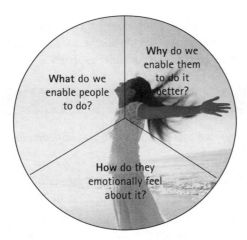

CUSTOMER PURPOSE: WHAT DO YOU ADD TO THE WORLD?

- Disney hopes to create 'the happiest place on earth' through everything from its characters to its movies, its websites to its theme parks.

- Pret A Manger promises 'hand-made, natural food, avoiding obscure chemicals, additives and preservatives common to so much of the "prepared" and "fast" food in the market today'.

- Ritz-Carlton, the luxury hotel chain, describes itself as 'ladies and gentlemen serving ladies and gentlemen'.

- TGI Friday's, the restaurant chain, seeks to 'treat every customer as we would an honoured guest in our home'.

- Wal-Mart exists 'to give ordinary folk the chance to buy the same things as rich people. We can save people money so that they can live better'.

Once the customer purpose is established, it becomes a more inspiring platform on which to develop business strategy and a more sustainable business model. It is also a more distinctive basis on which to build a brand, culture and customer experience.

Insight 12: LEGO

Did you know that there are more than 915,103,765 ways of combining six eight-stud Lego bricks of the same colour?

Lego is an abbreviation of the Danish words 'leg godt', meaning 'play well'. (In Latin it also happens to mean 'I put together'.) Since its creation in 1932 by Ole Kirk Kristiansen, Lego has been one of the world's most popular toys. It has come a long way from a small carpenter's workshop to being voted 'toy of the century' in 2000 by *Time* magazine and the fifth-largest toy manufacturer in the world.

Indeed, the bricks were initially made of wood, and it was not until 1958 that they became plastic and colourful – acquiring its unique interlocking tubes that offer the opportunity to build things only limited by your imagination.

The founder's grandchild Kjeld Kirk Kristiansen now leads the Lego Group, which is based in Billund in Denmark and has 4500 employees. Its purpose is 'to inspire children to explore and challenge their own creative potential' by helping them to 'learn through play' – developing their creative and structured problem-solving, curiosity, imagination, interpersonal skills, and physical motor skills.

For Lego, children are the best source of new ideas and an inspiration for the future. They are persistently inquisitive, unlimited in their creativity and imagination. As Kristiansen urges his people, 'we must stimulate the child in each of us!'

Despite a number of years when profits came under pressure, largely due to the popularity of electronic games and the success of movie-linked branded toys from the likes of Disney and Mattel, the business is profitable again, reaching a $280 million profit in 2007.

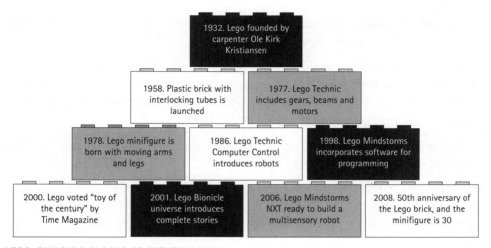

LEGO: BUILDING BLOCKS OF CREATIVE PLAY

Lego is developed to suit all ages of development. The core creative team of more than 100 designers from 15 different nationalities focuses on 'building systems' rather than just bricks. Different sub-brands reflect the systems for each age group:

- **Lego Duplo** is for pre-school children, encouraging them through creative play to use their hands and improve motor skills.

- **Lego creative building sets** contain traditional bricks plus specific parts around themes – from police stations to a medieval castle, a circus or a zoo.

- **Lego Bionicle** develops complete stories, fantasy and adventure, most recently with the Mistika and Vehicles ranges.

- **Lego Technic** brings the constructions to life with power functions – mechanical parts that are computer-controlled.

- **_Lego Mindstorms_** is based around advanced software controls, creating a robot that can see, hear, feel, speak and move.

Lego is co-created with its customers. Online, the Lego Digital Designer will create bricks to individually submitted designs, building competitions stretch imaginations in return for prizes, and 2.4 million children have joined the Lego Club. Members can submit photos online of their creations and view others from members around the world.

In 2008, Lego celebrated the 50th anniversary of the Lego brick. In that time enough Lego bricks have been produced to give each of the world's 6.5 billion people 62 bricks each.

With seven new sets sold each second, children around the world spend five billion hours a year playing with Lego. Or to put it another way, if you built a column of 40 billion Lego bricks, representing 100 bricks for every child and adult who plays with Lego each year, then it would reach the moon.

Think like a child – be inquisitive, creative and imaginative.

1.2   CUSTOMER BRAND

Brands are not about what you do but what you enable people to do. Brands are about people, not products. Brands are about customers, not companies.

A great brand is one you want to live your life by. You can trust and hang on to it when everything around you is changing. It articulates the type of person you are or want to be, and enables to you to do what you couldn't otherwise achieve.

Brands were originally developed as labels of ownership (the 'branding' of cattle with a hot iron showed which farmer they belonged to). They have most typically been used to describe an organization, product or service.

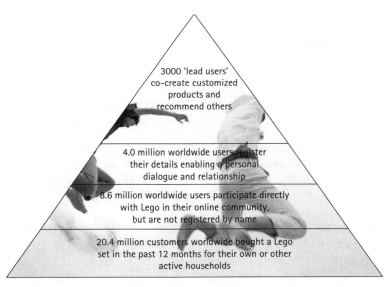

LEGO CUSTOMERS: ADVOCACY PYRAMID (SOURCE: LEGO AT ECSW)

They are factual and introspective: 'the best cosmetics company in the world', 'the most innovative technological solutions', or 'the original hand-made shoe company'. They rely upon their names and logos, articulated through superficial taglines and delivered through generic service.

Just like internally motivated mission statements, this does little to engage customers. It doesn't reach out to them, describe their world, cut through the noise of crowded markets or gain the trust of sceptical customers. It can also be limiting to the business, reducing flexibility and stretch into other markets and applications.

Customers find brands engaging when they are about them, when they reflect who they are or want to be. They define what they do for customers rather than simply what they do. They capture customers' dreams and aspirations, or at least the applications and benefits.

A brand builds on the customer purpose, articulating and visualizing it in a clear and compelling way, standing out from the crowd and touching people more deeply.

Brands can become 'anchors' that customers choose to live their lives around. They represent something familiar and important when everything else in the market or their personal world continues to change. Brands must also evolve with markets and customers, needing portability to move easily into new markets and glue to connect diverse activities.

A great brand is designed for a specific audience. In reflecting these people, the brand is able to build affinity and preference, encourage purchase behaviour, and sustain a price premium. It seeks to retain the best customers, building their loyalty, introducing new services and encouraging advocacy.

The brand identity, communication and experience is designed to reflect the target customer. Look at the typography of the Build a Bear Workshop logo, the layout of its stores, the programme of activities – all designed to be childlike. Consider the design of Apple: its leaders and messages, the black T-shirts of its people, and design of its products all capture modernity, coolness and simplicity.

If a brand seeks to reflect its target audience, it must also be prepared to alienate other people.

As Scott Bedbury, the man who put the 'Just do it' into Nike, and the Frappucino into Starbucks, says, 'a great brand polarizes people – some people will love it, and others will hate it'. FC Barcelona can never be everyone's favourite sports club, but it is everything to its fans. McDonalds is heaven to some, hell for others. Some people adore their Mini Cooper, other people think it is ridiculous.

There are many complex models of brands. However, a brand is fundamentally not about description, but enablement – what it does for people rather than what it is. It then describes this in three components:

- *Rational*: What does the brand enable customers to do? Nike, for example, is not about great sports shoes or apparel, it's about people doing sports.

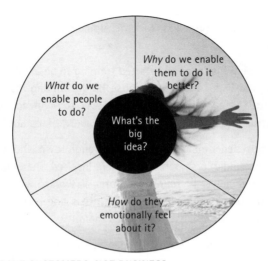

CUSTOMER BRAND: ABOUT CUSTOMERS, NOT BUSINESS

- **Comparative**: Why does it enable them to do it differently or better? Nike is not just about running, it's about running faster or further than you could ever before.

- **Emotional**: How do people feel about the brand as a result? Nike is an attitude to doing more, doing it better, and winning – 'just do it', no finish line.

Connecting these different components at the heart of the brand is the core idea, which should be very similar to the core purpose for a corporate brand but perhaps articulated in a more creative and memorable way.

Insight 13: AVEDA

Horst Rechelsbacher grew up in the Austrian mountains where his mother would spend hours in their kitchen making natural remedies from the Alpine plants and herbs that grew around their home.

He dropped out of school in his teens and started training to be a hairdresser, working in the salons of Manhattan and Paris, and with Brigitte Bardot among his clientele. After being detained in hospital due to a car accident when he moved to Minneapolis in 1965, he set up a chain of Horst of Austria salons across the region. They were an instant hit.

A few years later Rechelsbacher met a yogi passing through town who persuaded him to start meditating. He moved to India in search of meaning. Inspired, the hairdresser turned to his mother's remedies and the power he found in nature. He worked with an Indian herbalist to create a range of shampoos, conditioners, blood purifiers and bowel cleansers that looked uncertain but smelt wonderful. His customers loved them.

In 1978 he rebranded his business as Aveda, meaning 'whole knowledge' and based on the Sanskrit word 'Ayurveda'. He sold the natural products through retailers and salons before eventually setting up his own Aveda stores, with natural environments and holistic beauty and well-being treatments. In 1997, Estée Lauder offered him $300 million for his business: he was interested in accessing the giant's research facilities and distribution network, and letting it take on the boring side of management, which he didn't enjoy.

Aveda is about 'the art and science of pure flower and plant essences', which is reflected in the design and experience you receive at any of the brand's 8000 studios, spas or well-being and beauty experience centres. Aveda's head office, just down the road in Minneapolis from where Horst lived, has a stunning architecture – full of space and natural light, and set in 65 acres of wetlands.

Aveda's philosophy is simple and profound: to offer positive choices for living life in balance – with yourself, each other and the Earth.

Colours in the make-up for face, lips and eyes reflect a palette inspired by nature. Its skincare formulas are plant-packed to infuse skin with radiance and haircare products use nature's power to defy damage. Many of its ingredients are organic and ethically sourced, and it is working towards all of them being so.

The company partners with traditional communities in the remotest parts of the world to find authentic ingredients that offer more effective treatments for customers and a more positive social impact.

Today, Rechelsbacher runs a chain of health businesses called Intelligent Nutrients, focusing on organic food. He still meditates and does yoga, and uses his mother's Alpine remedies. He runs a charitable foundation and loves travelling the world in search of new herbs. He also has a love of expensive fashion, fast cars, good food and fine art. Like his customers, the hippy hairdresser who creates the hip cosmetics sees no problems in combining principles with pleasure.

1.3   CUSTOMER ALIGNMENT

The organization – its people, partners, products and processes – must align around these customer aspirations to ensure coherence and consistency of purpose.

This sounds obvious, yet most companies work in functional silos whilst people work within the limits of their job descriptions – and as you go downwards through the organization, the fractures and chasms become wider in both purpose and behaviour. Customer focus seeks to align people towards a common purpose, to serve customers, yet it can become hidebound by internal structures ('focus on your internal customers' – forget the real ones!).

How do you align every part and every person to think, breathe and be inspired by customers? How do you align their direction as well as their tasks around a common purpose? How do you ensure they also deliver a seamless, consistent experience for customers?

Successful customer businesses ensure that their customer purpose is relevant and anchored in every part of their activities internally and externally. They seek to bring their brand concept alive in every person and action. Through leadership, collaboration, shared insights and shared rewards, the same passion runs through the organization and structures support rather than interfere.

John Lewis is a British retailer owned by its employees – everyone is a partner in the business, with voting rights on key issues, representatives in the boardroom and sharing dividends when their trading results are good. Ask a sales assistant, or rather a partner, in John Lewis for help on something unrelated to his department: they will walk across the store to help you. Ask them if they can waive a certain delivery policy and they have the authority to say yes or no.

However, it is important to understand that a customer orientation does not necessarily mean that customer service is the primary difference in the business. Michael Tracey and Fred Wiersema developed a model known as 'the value disciplines of market leaders'.

They introduce three essential disciplines for market leadership – product leadership, customer intimacy and operational excellence. They argue that any company seeking to be a market leader must be good at all three disciplines but must choose to be special at one.

- Sony, for example, chooses to put disproportionate resources and investment into innovation and design. It therefore aims to achieve success through product leadership and more than anything seeks to offer customers the best product.

- Virgin chooses to put disproportionate resources and investment into service and relationships. It aims to achieve success through customer intimacy and more than anything seeks to offer customers the best service and relationship.

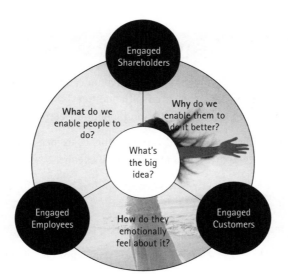

CUSTOMER ALIGNMENT: MANY PEOPLE, ONE VISION

- Toyota chooses to put disproportionate resources and investment into quality and efficient processes. It aims to achieve success through operational excellence and more than anything seeks to offer customers the lowest price.

Toyota is still highly customer-oriented – its 'lean' manufacturing approaches achieve their efficiency by better understanding the prioritized needs of customers and focusing on what matters most, rather than everything. Dell is still highly customer-oriented, enabling customization of your computer, yet its business model enables efficiency from which it can also deliver the lowest price.

Customer visioning, branding and alignment isn't just one way of doing business – it is a platform for all types of successful businesses, whatever their industry and positioning in their market.

Insight 14: CEMEX

Cemex's customers had traditionally bought cement by volume, but placed little value on the cubic metres provided by one company compared with another – they saw it as a commodity and looked for the cheapest price. Lorenzo Zambrano thought differently.

Zambrano became Cemex's CEO in 1985 and turned to his customers, to understand them better. He found that far more important than being a little cheaper than competitors was:

- Whether you could deliver it exactly when needed – a few hours' difference added up to millions of dollars in overall completion date bonuses.

- The mix of the aggregates – different types of building required different mixes.

- Whether it arrived ready-mixed – which could save significant labour costs.

- Where it was delivered – pumping it straight from truck to building was far better than having to store it.

He looked across other industries' delivery models. How did Domino Pizza always manage to deliver within 60 minutes? How did FedEx achieve worldwide parcel deliveries within 24 hours? What did emergency services do to speed up their response times? He learnt much from these sectors; disciplines that had never been dreamt of in the cement world.

Zambrano learned to sequence his response to orders based on their complexity and distance delivered, or divert postponed orders to other customers. He reorganized the distribution points to imitate the 'hub and spoke' operations of FedEx, and even positioned advance response units in the field to meet urgent requests.

He could now deliver building materials within hours – sometimes within minutes. Customers could change their orders at any time and could always rely upon Cemex to meet their unusual and precise requirements. This flexibility helped customers to build more effectively, minimize wastage in materials and time, and improve their own cash flow.

The Mexican company grew rapidly to become a world leader by serving customers better than anyone else, acquiring companies all around the world and converting them to its model. One hundred years after Cemex was founded, its market value was around $30 billion.

The Cemex mission statement, redefined for its centenary, is all about its customers and what they aspire to rather than construction and the materials required:

> 'People are builders. They build to educate, to heal, to shelter and comfort families. They build to connect with each other, to share their art and knowledge for the benefit of humanity. Everything people build requires strength to weather the forces of nature and time. It requires a solid foundation. By helping people to solve their building challenges in communities around the world, we are a vital part of that foundation. Our products are everywhere, from the smallest villages to the largest cities – linking communities, providing shelter, and enabling society's sustainable growth. As a global industry leader, Cemex will continue building a better world for the next 100 years.'

In 2008 *Wired* magazine placed Cemex just behind Google, and ahead of eBay and Microsoft, in a survey of companies reshaping the global economy. People in South America are incredibly proud of the brand that symbolizes the progress of their nations, with its name on the many impressive buildings being constructed in their thriving cities. Interbrand's survey of the world's favourite brands in each region around the world found that people in South America ranked the cement brand as one of their favourites – incredible for a business-to-business brand.

Customer strategy

I want you to treat me appropriately.

I spend lots of my money with you. I want to continue buying from you and I'm prepared to recommend you to all my friends, too. But I want you to work with me, so that if I do more for you, you do more for me. I know that sometimes it's just not possible to give me the deal I want or that somebody else can. On those occasions, let's just agree not to do business.

Don't talk to me like I don't know you or you don't know me.

You should know everything and me, my family and my life by now. Don't try to bribe me with superficial offers and gimmicks. I think we've gone beyond that. And don't try and sell more to me, just because your supervisor has told you. I think you know that I will come back again, when I'm ready.

2.1   CUSTOMER PROFITABILITY

Not all customers are equal.

There are good customers and bad customers – or 'angels' and 'devils' as Best Buy more emotively calls them. No business needs customers, indeed many businesses could be surprisingly more successful with fewer customers – as long as it's fewer *better* ones.

The customer is not 'king'.

Whilst an 'outside in' approach starts with customers, it does not mean every customer is equal. It means making commercial decisions that start with customers. In the same way that a good business strategy starts with the choice of the best markets to focus on, a customer strategy starts with the choice of best customers.

Ask a company if they have unprofitable customers and most would say no. If they do say yes, most will estimate that 80% of their profits come from 20% of their customers, although they are unlikely to know which ones.

In fact, it is likely to be more extreme than this – that 80% of revenue comes from 20% of customers and 90% of profit comes from 10% of customers. Many of the other customers are actually unprofitable, leading to situations where 200–300% of profits come from these best customers and the others simply dilute it.

Even the most profitable companies continue to attract, serve and retain unprofitable customers because they don't know who is good and bad – they can't measure customer profitability or allocate it to individual customers.

Imagine a portfolio of products or businesses or investments. All might generate revenue, some might be profitable and others unprofitable. But once you have considered long-term growth prospects and the need to get an acceptable return on your initial investment, there will probably only be a small number who will create economic value over the longer term.

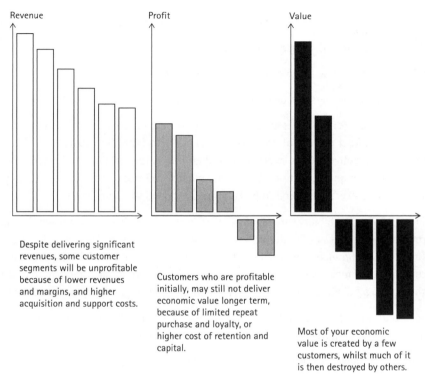

Revenue

Despite delivering significant revenues, some customer segments will be unprofitable because of lower revenues and margins, and higher acquisition and support costs.

Profit

Customers who are profitable initially, may still not deliver economic value longer term, because of limited repeat purchase and loyalty, or higher cost of retention and capital.

Value

Most of your economic value is created by a few customers, whilst much of it is then destroyed by others.

CUSTOMER PORTFOLIO: CUSTOMERS BY REVENUE, PROFIT AND VALUE

Why do companies have unprofitable customers?

- A worthy, but naive belief in treating all customers equally.

- Desire for market share and revenue growth at any cost.

- Focus on customer acquisition rather than retention.

- Sales pressure to close deals, with significant discounting.

- Little knowledge of the cost of other terms, e.g. extended credit.

- Offering same levels of service to all customers.

- Don't know when to be flexible and personalized, and when not.

- Belief that all customers can be profitable eventually.

Measuring customer profitability is not simple, partly because in a service-based business there are many more indirect costs that are harder to allocate to individual customers. Customer experiences are collective efforts internally and therefore harder to allocate functional costs. Yet it is such costs (high acquisition costs of the most promiscuous customers, high support costs of discount-seekers) that tend to make some customers so unprofitable.

Allocating customer profitability can therefore be done at different levels of precision, depending on information available, size of customer base and the variation of spend and experience by customer. This is rarely a problem in business-to-business companies, but harder in large and diverse consumer markets. It may involve a simple allocation of gross profitability relative to customer spend, through to a full allocation of costs using methods similar to activity-based costing.

A practical solution is to allocate all costs that can reasonably be associated with an individual customer through their purchase transaction or ongoing relationship:

Customer profitability = Customer revenue – Customer-related costs

Where customer-related costs might include:

- Production costs, e.g. sourcing, materials, manufacturing, packaging.

- Selling costs, e.g. advertising, promotions, commissions, discounts, channels.

- Service costs, e.g. advice, processing, shipping, installation, support.

- Relationship costs, e.g. account management, CRM, hospitality, rewards.

- Business costs, e.g. administration, offices, staff, research and development.

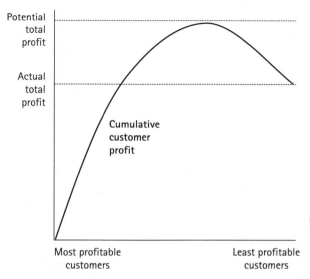

CUSTOMER PROFITABILITY: SOME CREATE IT, OTHERS DESTROY IT

If we illustrate the cumulative profitability of customers, starting with the most profitable, we can observe from the peak of the graph where we start to erode our hard-earned profits by continuing to serve unprofitable customers.

In seeking to manage customers, companies often develop a way of understanding the value of each customer. This is common in airlines, for example, where the pattern of customer purchases is used to predict their future value and therefore how to incentivize and treat such customers.

'Customer lifetime value' (CLV) refers to the future profit potential of a customer.

Of course, the only situations where you are certain of a customer's future profitability are where there is some form of contract – in business markets where a deal is signed over a number of years, or in consumer markets where customers pay by subscription, for example. In other cases, it is about estimating likely future behaviours and the likely profits associated with them.

Mathematically, CLV is the sum of the profits likely to be attained from that customer in future years. This might be significantly more or less than currently, so will require a projection of changes in future purchase behaviour, estimated over the number of years they are likely to remain with you, the likely costs to serve them over this time. This is calculated as a net present value and is therefore factored by the likelihood of this happening.

The 'lifetime value' of an individual customer to the business	=	The future contribution of the customer to operating profits	−	The cost of retaining the customer over the future years

$$CLV_i = \sum_{p=1}^{t_i} \frac{m_{i,p}}{(1+r)^{p/f}} - \sum_{a=1}^{n} \frac{\sum_s x_{i,s,a}\, y_{i,s,a}}{(1+r)^{i}}$$

CLV_i Predicted lifetime value of customer **i**

$m_{i,p}$ Estimated contribution to operating margin of customer **i**, in purchase occasion **p** (in dollars/euros etc)

t_i Estimated number of purchases made by customer **i** until the end of the future period over which you are planning

f Estimated frequency of purchase

$x_{i,s,a}$ Estimated costs of retaining customer **i** through relationship marketing, through channel/programme **s** in year **a**

$y_{i,s,a}$ Estimated number of contacts or activities with customer **i** through channel/programme **s** in year **a**

n Number of years to forecast

r Discount rate of money

(Note: this analysis could be further enhanced by considering the potential of customer to refer other customers. Referral values might even be larger than personal value. This becomes particularly important if the business is focused on advocacy and net promoter scores).

CLV is often misunderstood as the value of customers to date, i.e. a reflection of their past behaviours. This might be useful to acknowledge and may help to indicate future behaviours, but is not where the organization should be focused. CLV should be about the future, not the past. Similarly, it is often measured in terms of revenue – which is better than nothing, but as we have seen, it is not uncommon for high revenues to deliver low profits or indeed none at all.

In a world where the total value of customers (i.e. the sum of their customer lifetime values) approximates to the overall value of a business, the understanding of customer profitability has a fundamental impact on business performance and ultimately on market capitalization. Being selective about who you want to do business with might not seem too customer-intimate, but it drives the economics of a customer business. The challenge is to focus on the value creators and eliminate the value destroyers.

Insight 15: NIKE WOMEN

Nike. The Greek goddess of victory – a fabulous, powerful and beautiful woman. Yet throughout the history of Nike, the company had been about loud, masculine, testosterone-fuelled success.

Phil Knight first met coach Bill Bowerman at the University of Oregon when he was trying to make it as a middle-distance runner. After an MBA at Stanford, Knight returned with an idea to bring low-priced, technically-superior running shoes from Japan. They each invested $500 to establish Blue Ribbon Sports and import running shoes made by Onitsuka Tiger, which later became Asics.

The two men knew what runners wanted, so Knight focused on selling the shoes at local track meets whilst Bowerman constantly worked on ways to make them better. In 1972 their competitiveness drove them to set up their own brand – Nike was born.

They rode the 1970s jogging boom (and in many ways created it) and gradually embraced more sports. With his passion for success and marketing flair, Knight took Nike into basketball, soccer and golf. With the support of the likes of Michael Jordan and Tiger Woods, Nike stormed the world of sport. By the end of 2006 it had revenues of $15 billion and profits of $1.4 billion.

But the business needed to change. People were more sophisticated and discerning in their sporting appearance, wanting technical excellence in their shoes and clothing, but also fashion and style. Long-term rivals Adidas had acquired Reebok and although Nike was still the choice of champions, it was becoming less popular on the street. New CEO Mike Parker recognized that they needed to be closer and more responsive to the changing needs of their customers: 'There is no question that today customers have the power in business,' he said.

Nike's existing structure – with business units focused separately on footwear, apparel and equipment – just wasn't working together. Integration between the units was inconsistent, customer insight was fragmented, and innovation and design were too technical and product-centric. It was only at special moments such as the Olympics or the World Cup that Nike came together.

Parker wanted Nike to align itself to customers and their different needs. He identified six market segments where the business could expect to see 90% of its future growth and would focus its resources, innovation and marketing: running, men's training, basketball, soccer, women's fitness and sportswear. Smaller categories such as golf, tennis and children could be incorporated later. 'Nike Women' was the most remarkable of the new businesses.

To understand Nike's approach, you should watch the movie *What Women Want*. Advertising hotshot Nick (played by Mel Gibson) thinks that he is God's gift to women. After an accident, he discovers that he is suddenly able to hear what women really think. At first Nick is pretty disappointed when he discovers that his macho behaviour makes him undesirable. Then it emerges that the job he has dreamed of is being given to a new team member – Darcy is not only a woman, but a man-eating one, and a very talented marketer too. So Nick decides to sabotage his new boss by reading her thoughts and selling her ideas as his own.

Understanding women and selling their thoughts has made commercial sense for Nike, too. It found that women typically spend around 40% more on sports apparel than men and will pay a higher price for the most fashionable items too. They buy more items, more frequently, and coordination is important too. Nobody wants to be seen with shoes that don't match or in last year's tennis range.

Back at Nike's Beaverton campus, Heidi O'Neill had been pushing for years to get separate functions to work together and offer a more coordinated approach to women. Her cross-functional team had delivered success but had had to compete against the system, challenging processes and leadership, breaking though the silo-driven product-centric profit centres. At last, in January 2007, she became head of Nike's global women's fitness business with a team responsible for everything from product development and operations to marketing and profitability.

With top global athletes such as Maria Sharapova, Nike has been sharpening its focus on women's fitness, emphasizing running, walking, cardio, yoga and fitness dance. Nike Women stores have opened around the world with a very different interior to the noise and adrenalin of traditional Niketowns. The annual Nike Women's Marathon, launched in 2004 in San Francisco, has become one of the largest women's running events in the world. Nike's dance fitness events, such as the globally popular RockStar Workout, and innovative clothing and footwear products such as the Zoom Dansante, have deepened connections with women and driven significant growth.

They maybe didn't realize it back in the 1970s, but Knight and Bowerman chose a good name for their business.

2.2 CUSTOMER SEGMENTATION

Segmentation might also be used for different purposes:

- Strategic prioritization, using segmentation to formulate a customer strategy that understands the value of different customers and how to approach them differently.

- Competitive positioning, using macro-segmentation to ensure that the overall brand and its values are relevant to the target audiences.

- Engaging customers, using micro-segmentation to identify the specific purchase motivations of different customers and thereby shape value propositions.

Customers can be grouped by their profitability but also in others ways – their physical characteristics (ranging from your age to where you live), socio-economic factors (perhaps driven by your wealth and spending profile), and broader motivations (e.g. your general attitudes to life through to your specific needs for a product or service).

You want to target customers who will be profitable, can serve in relevant and compelling ways (maybe differently for different groups of them) and you have some means of accessing – not necessarily their addresses, but at least some idea what they do, watch or belong to.

You can segment your market in each of these ways, but ultimately they need to overlap – you don't need to know how to reach everybody, just the ones who can be profitable. And you don't need to develop propositions and solutions for every motivation, but instead focus on the factors that are most important to these customers.

The use of consumer segmentation is widespread amongst the public and private sectors. Such organizations understand the demographic and lifestyle characteristics of audiences, their values and motivations and even (in the case of geo-demographic classifications) the precise location and neighbourhoods in which they live. This can be used to profile and analyse behaviour, quantify the size of audiences in local areas and to create more tailored communication from which you can optimize response to marketing.

Companies often seek to characterize their target segments with names that help bring them to life to make them easier to visualize and understand. One example is Experian's Mosaic

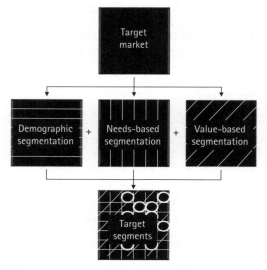

consumer classification that segments the UK population into one of 61 lifestyle types, aggregated into 11 groups.

Group	Group Description	% Households	Type	Type Description	% Households
A	Symbols of Success	9.62	A01	Global Connections	0.72
			A02	Cultural Leadership	0.92
			A03	Corporate Chieftains	1.12
			A04	Golden Empty Nesters	1.33
			A05	Provincial Privilege	1.66
			A06	High Technologists	1.82
			A07	Semi-Rural Seclusion	2.04
B	Happy Families	10.76	B08	Just Moving In	0.91
			B09	Fledgling Nurseries	1.18
			B10	Upscale New Owners	1.35
			B11	Families Making Good	2.32
			B12	Middle Rung Families	2.86
			B13	Burdened Optimists	1.96

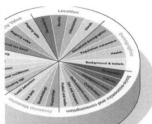

Group A: Symbols of Success | **Group B: Happy Families** | **Group C: Suburban Comfort** | **Group D: Ties of Community** | **Group E: Urban Intelligence**

Rupert and Felicity
9.62% of UK Households
(Types 1 – 7)

Symbols of Success people are well set in their careers and their incomes have risen far into upper income tax ranges. Some work for large corporations in senior management positions; others hold respected roles in professional practices; others have built successful enterprises with their own commercial acumen.

These are people with busy and complex family lives. Their children are now less time consuming, with more independent lifestyles, but with leisure interests that are likely to be more expensive.

This group is mostly white British but is likely to contain significant Jewish, European, Chinese and Indian minorities.

Symbols of Success neighbourhoods are concentrated in economically successful regions, notably London and the South East of England, where a high proportion of the workforce is engaged in 'knowledge' industries. These are typically neighbourhoods of choice housing, whether...

Darren and Joanne
10.76% of UK Households
(Types 8–14)

Happy Families contains people whose focus is on career, home and family. They are mostly young couples, married or living with their partner, raising pre-school and school-age children. This group's educational attainment has enabled them to secure positions in large organisations in either the private or the public sector, with the prospect of future career advancement.

These neighbourhoods consist of modern, purpose-built family housing, either detached or semi-detached, on estates with other young families. These estates are often some considerable distance from major commercial centres but an easy driving distance from many potential workplaces, such as major new industrial or office 'parks'.

Happy Families neighbourhoods are typically found in areas of rapidly expanding employment, around towns such as Swindon, Northampton and Milton Keynes. Some of the new jobs are in locally-grown businesses in new industrial sectors such as information technology, biotechnology or business services. Other jobs are in organisations...

Geoffrey and Valerie
15.10% of UK Households
(Types 15-20)

Suburban Comfort people have established themselves and their families in comfortable homes in mature suburbs. Children are becoming independent, work is less of a challenge and interest, payments on homes and other loans are becoming less burdensome.

These people live in inter-war suburbs and work mostly in intermediate level, white-collar occupations, where they are beginning to plan for approaching retirement. They are likely to be married and most have children, who may be at secondary school or university, or grown up and starting families of their own.

These neighbourhoods consist mostly of houses built between 1918 and 1970 to meet the needs of a new generation of white-collar office workers. Pleasant but homogenous semi-detached houses are set back from the road in generously sized plots with leafy gardens. Such areas were once on the edge of the city but they now often form a no-man's land between the high density Victorian inner city and the more modern family estates further out.

Lee and Noreen
16.04% of UK Households
(Types 21-27)

Ties of Community people live in very established, rather old-fashioned communities. Traditionally, people in this group married young and had manual jobs in industries such as docks and mines. Today, this group has a younger than average population; many are married or cohabiting and bringing up young children. Social support networks are strong, with friends and relations nearby.

These neighbourhoods are often characterised by late nineteenth century housing. Many homes have been improved, and are comfortable if somewhat cramped places to live (usually two rooms and a back extension downstairs, two or three small bedrooms, and a modest rear garden). Originally such neighbourhoods were within short walking distance of local factories and shops, and many still have access to small corner shops, often owner-managed by recently arrived Asian families.

Typically these neighbourhoods are in former coalfield regions, old steel and shipbuilding towns, and places with docks and chemical plants – industries that have been in serious if not terminal decline in recent years. But national initiatives have...

Ben and Chloe
7.19% of UK Households
(Types 28-34)

Urban Intelligence people are young, well educated and open to new ideas and influences. They are cosmopolitan in their tastes and liberal in their social attitudes. Few have children. Many are in further education while others are moving into full-time employment. Most do not feel ready to make permanent commitments, whether to partners, professions or to specific employers. As higher education has become internationalised, the Urban Intelligence group has acquired many foreign-born residents, which further encourages ethnic and cultural variety.

These neighbourhoods typically occur in inner London and the inner areas of large provincial cities, especially those with popular universities. The growth in student numbers has led to their dispersal from halls of residence into older working class communities and the areas of large Victorian houses that typically surround the older universities.

Other inner city areas have also been taken over by recent graduates and young professionals who want to live close to their work and the facilities of the inner city. Demand for flats is outstripping supply.

CUSTOMER PROFILING: DESCRIBING THE TARGET CUSTOMERS
(SOURCE: EXPERIAN'S MOSAIC UK CONSUMER CLASSIFICATION, © EXPERIAN, 2008)

Insight 16: CLUB MED

> 'To dream, to laugh, to play, to contemplate ... what if luxury in our current society was to freely enjoy those small and big joys that pepper our lives?'

These are the words of Henri Giscard D'Estaing, president and director general of Club Méditerranée, the French company that is more commonly known as Club Med. The youthful leader with the famous name is rapidly transforming the business that was founded in 1950 and has for many years focused on premium resorts in the most exotic parts of the world.

'We have continually sought to reinvent the concept of happiness,' claims D'Estaing. 'Today, that happiness is synonymous with enjoying elegance and luxury together. Follow Club Med along the new pathways of your dreams and share a delightfully special experience'.

The company has grown steadily around the world. There are 80 villages worldwide, divided into six concepts or 'pleasures' such as: 'to discover', 'to experience the exceptional' or 'to live life to the full'. Most villages accommodate families, with daytime supervised facilities for different age ranges, whilst a few are dedicated to adults.

Indeed, 60 years ago, founders Gérard Blitz and Gilbert Trigano declared that happiness was the business of Club Med. Having essentially invented the 'all-inclusive' concept, Club Med had for many years thrived on delivering a French style of happiness. Fifty years on, the world had moved ahead: the standards of exclusive luxury, personal service, facilities and entertainment had been surpassed by resorts and cruise lines, particularly catering to the booming US market.

In 2004 D'Estaing set about trying to understand who his target audiences should be, what they really wanted from their visit and how he could ensure that Club Med was different and better at meeting those aspirations.

He described his approach at the recent Brand Finance Forum in London. The company surveyed 165,000 potential customers, who demanded more comfort and services, more clubs for children and particularly for babies and teenagers, and felt that all-inclusive should mean just that – bar and snacking should be included too.

The brand was repositioned from mid-market to upmarket, from couples to families. Building on its original foundations of 'friendliness, conviviality, freedom and multiculturality', it now wants to be 'the worldwide specialist in all-inclusive, upmarket, friendly, multicultural vacations, especially for families'. The transformation was not just about new advertising – it also embraced a €1 billion investment on renovating its villages and introducing more luxurious facilities and services.

Club Med is now the place 'where sophistication meets fun', creating an environment for guests that lets them discover their own happiness, at their own pace and without fuss. There are fewer group activities. Resorts have been rethought to ensure that they are more multicultural, luxurious and personal.

From 2005 to 2007, brand perception indices improved significantly. Perception of comfort increased by 13 points to 75%, for trendsetting and innovation by 14 points to 70% and as a 'one-of-a-kind' destination by 12 points to 51%. In 2008 Club Med launched a new worldwide advertising campaign entitled 'Where happiness means the world'.

2.3   CUSTOMER MANAGEMENT

A customer strategy is about attracting, serving, retaining and growing with the best customers. It is a consequence of the various other strategic approaches in an organization, and similar in terms of its analytical and decision-making approach:

- Business strategy is about choosing which types of business we are in and how to create superior value in them.

- Market strategy is about choosing the best markets to compete in and how to position ourselves for competitive advantage.

- Customer strategy is about choosing the best customers to target and how to attract, serve and retain them profitably.

A customer strategy defines who to target, what their potential is to the business and how to best engage them in the short and long term in order to do the right thing for customers and maximize value to the business.

- What's their long-term revenue potential to the business?

- How much will they cost to attract and retain?

- Do they actually want to work with us over the long term?

- What should we do to attract, retain and grow with them?

- Does this fit with our preferred strategic direction?

- Are there others like them that can be influenced and accessed?

- What is the overall value potential of this customer?

For each target segment, defined in terms of its motivations and value potential, there will be a combination of the five activities that follow, each delivered in different and appropriate ways. The ways in which each segment is treated will depend on what turns them on. The cost and time allocated to this will depend on their potential profitability.

- *Identify* who they are and how to access them.

- *Attract* them with relevant propositions.

- *Serve* them in more personal ways.

- *Retain* them if they are potentially profitable.

- *Grow* their relationship in profitable ways.

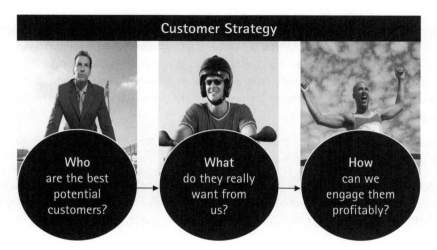

Customer Strategy

Who are the best potential customers?	What do they really want from us?	How can we engage them profitably?
• Build database of details of existing customers	• Understand their problem and/or their ambitions	• Develop value propositions for each target segment
• Evaluate current and future profitability of customers	• Define the context in which you can serve them	• Consider appropriate and relevant customer solutions
• Identify highest potential customers to target	• Segment target customers by different motivations	• Attract and serve across a customized experience
• Develop alternative strategies for other customers	• Understand their prioritized needs and wants	• Retain and grow through a profitable relationship

CUSTOMER STRATEGY: ATTRACTING, SERVING AND RETAINING THE BEST CUSTOMERS

Together these activities form a business strategy for each customer segment, one that will create value for each customer through compelling propositions and appropriate solutions, and collectively managed to ensure that they deliver optimal value to the business. It is the balance and integration of these many different activities, knowing where to focus and allocate resources in a way that is reasonable for customers and the business, that we term 'customer management'.

Customer strategies for each of these customer types will differ in terms of their emphasis and in the ways in which activities are delivered.

- A 'champion and grow profitably' strategy might be based on more specific and compelling propositions for individual customers, more collaboration to understand motivations and triggers, delivering a more personalized service experience, and rewarding their loyalty.

- A 'sustain but more efficiently' strategy might look to retain the customer but migrate them to a more efficient way of doing business – maybe to lower-cost direct channels or a different service package, which for the customer might still meet their needs.

- A 'nurture and change behaviour' strategy might seek to help the customer in whatever they are seeking to do – buying a house, getting a better job – that will improve their profitability. Such education and support would be matched by incentives linked to these changes.

- A 'reduce costs or eliminate' strategy might involve cross selling to more efficient options, more standardized processes, reducing the cost to serve. If the customers cannot be turned profitable, appropriate offers to them are withdrawn or you simply apologize and say no.

	Unprofitable	Profitable	
Future behaviour	**Strategy for future stars:** Nurture and change behaviour	**Strategy for champions:** Reward and grow profitably	**Profitable**
	Strategy for laggards: Reduce costs or eliminate	**Strategy for fading stars:** Sustain but more efficiently	**Unprofitable**
	Current behaviour		

CUSTOMER MANAGEMENT: IMPLEMENTING STRATEGIES FOR DIFFERENT CUSTOMERS

These strategies affect the whole organization – sales and marketing, operations and service, purchasing and finance. Customer strategies become key enabling devices of business strategies, but also inform them of the best opportunities and priorities for implementation.

Much has been written about CRM. Indeed, many organizations were disappointed with the return they received on the investments in huge data management systems, enabling them to track, profile, target and communicate with customers in much more scientific and personalized ways. Unfortunately they were too often used as direct selling machines, with the blinkered pursuit of sales volumes and market shares. Little initial thought went into the broader aspects of customer management.

Similarly, one-to-one marketing has been much promoted over recent years, perhaps most notably in the books of Don Peppers and Martha Rogers. They advocate a more disciplined approach driven by customer profitability, to identify the 'picket fence' between the customers worth treating individually and those where a more general, mass-market approach would be sufficient.

Yet the idea of treating customers individually is not new. Think of the account manager in a business market who knows his client intimately, sits down together to agree plans for the year(s) ahead, develops unique products and services to support it, and business models where both sides can share in the success. Similarly, the owner of your local shop might know everything about you, remember the day your teenage children were born and can anticipate what you want before you even walk in.

Customer management must work at many different levels, all of which are relevant:

- **Markets** – being first sure that the business is focused on the right markets before deciding which customers to target, although following the best customers in their broader needs might equally be a guide to adjacent markets.

- **Segments** – making sense of your chosen markets both in terms of the ability to make money but also of the different types and locations, needs and wants, motives and aspirations of customers.

- **Niches** – deciding whether to be a business for a single or multiple audiences. Niches might seem to limit scale, but targeting a very specific type of customer across the world can still create a significant audience.

- **One-to-one** – targeting the most profitable individuals and building personal relationships with them through a listening dialogue, customized solutions and an ongoing partnership of mutual benefits.

- ***All-to-one*** – recognizing that the whole organization needs to act as one, sharing customer insights and knowledge, and collectively delivering a seamless experience for individuals, aligning and connecting people across functions and partners to achieve this.

- ***One and one*** – collaborating with customers to find the best solutions to their problems or ambitions, learn from them to serve them better and innovate more broadly, and build partnerships of mutual value.

Of course the term 'customer management' is completely wrong. Companies cannot 'manage' or control the minds and actions of customers (and similarly, customer relationship management [CRM] cannot be about enforced relationships). It is about business management from a customer perspective – developing different business approaches for different customers.

Insight 17: TATA

The Ford Model T, the Volkswagen Beetle, the Austin Mini ... and the Tata Nano.

Tata Motors' transformation from an Indian truck maker to a global car business is remarkable. The launch of the Tata Nano (the world's lowest-cost car) followed by the acquisition of Jaguar and Land Rover less than three months later demonstrates its ambition and phenomenal speed at which it intends to achieve it.

When chairman Ratan Tata launched his dream low-priced car at the Auto Expo 2008 in New Delhi in January 2008, *Time* magazine said it would change the rules of car-making. It even included the Nano in its list of 'the dozen most important cars of all time starting from 1908 to the present'. The car, with a price tag of around $1500, has become a symbol for serving the rising billions of increasingly mobile customers across developing markets and an inspiration in how to innovate and design products to serve these masses.

The business had struggled for decades. In the early 1990s, the Indian government began opening up the economy. This left Tata Motors in a very vulnerable position: it was focused on traditional truck-making and lacked the capital and knowledge of new entrants. It struggled to sell the backward trucks internationally.

To get out of this trap, Ratan Tata suggested making small cars for the home market, at which everyone laughed. How could an old truck builder make cars, and who would buy them in India? But his first model, the Indica, was a huge success. Others have followed. The truck business has thrived too, particularly through the acquisition in 2004 of Daewoo's commercial vehicles business from South Korea.

The Nano was developed based on Ratan's vision of a safer transport for middle-class families, which have until now depended on two-wheelers in India. He stayed closely involved in the project, driving and encouraging his team to achieve what at first seemed unachievable. A large cross-functional team was assigned the task of designing 'a very low-cost, four-wheel vehicle' with no compromises on aesthetics, value to the customer, or safety and environment issues.

The team was given a free hand and asked to work without fear of failure. Everything was questioned and every part was designed upward from a zero base. No supplier could produce an engine within the budget, so the team developed one in-house. They managed to reduce costs in every area whilst ensuring that the car did not look too 'cheap'. The interiors had to be spacious and comfortable. The overall effect was style and reliability for a fraction of the price of any other car in the world.

Tata Motors is just one business within the rapidly growing Tata Group, which in 2007–8 gener-ated revenues of $28.8 billion and profits of $2.8 billion, 61% of which comes from business outside India. The Group employs around 350,000 people worldwide and its 27 publicly listed companies have a combined market capitalization of some $60 billion and include steel, power, hospitality and airlines. *Business Week* ranked Tata sixth among the 'World's Most Innovative Companies.'

Tata's 'outside in' approach enabled them to create a car that was affordable to the masses but with the engineering and style to match any in the world.

Customer insights

Do you really know what I want? Have we ever sat down and talked about it?

Sometimes I can tell you exactly what I want. And I want it as quickly and cheaply as possible. But I don't always want the same thing, delivered in the same way. Sometimes I'm not sure what I want because I need your help in solving a problem or in putting together a solution that will achieve what I want. In fact, you are often only one part of a bigger thing I'm trying to achieve, but you probably don't realize or care about that.

You have so much information about me from all the times I've bought something from you, or called up and told your colleagues things, every time I use my credit or loyalty card, and from all those questionnaires you keep asking me to complete. You must know me better than myself. Yet you still treat me like an average, anonymous entity. Some things are so obvious, they're hardly worth mentioning. Some things are incredibly important to me. And other things are just nice, but they make me smile.

3.1   CUSTOMER INTELLIGENCE

Have you ever met the average customer?

The one who is 51% female, drives a silver four-door car, has 2.1 children, lives in a 2.7 bed-room house with 1.2 cats, shops 3.4 times per week, doesn't trust politicians but loves George Clooney (or Angelina Jolie for the minority males)?

Nobody is an average. Very few people want to be an average.

Yet most businesses are focused on the average customer, developing products and service that seeks to satisfy and delight them. They end up delighting nobody, providing mediocrity to everybody.

Doing business from the 'outside in' demands customer information. However, it is what you do with it that matters. Indeed, there is no shortage of customer data in most organizations today – there is often too much:

- Databases full of transactional details that are too immense and most of the information too granular to know where to start.

- Market research reports with reams of statistics that sit on the shelves gathering dust or have been summarized until they lose any sense of meaning.

- Mountains of anecdotes and knowledge stuck inside the heads of the people who talk with customers every day but are unable or have no motivation to share it.

In the same way that research data is averaged, most summaries of customer information are filtered on their way through the organization. The context from which trends can be interpreted is stripped out, the prejudice of middle managers who have been producing the same reports for years is applied to interpretations, diversity is eliminated as data is reduced to normality

The equivalent of tasty, multi-seeded organic bread has become sliced, white and processed.

The search for new insights and opportunities becomes difficult because it is precisely these variations on norms that are suppressed. The summary report that is reviewed by business decision-makers holds little actionable content, unlike their obsession for the minute details of financial results that are actionable.

Add to this one further problem: the lack of connected information. Discoveries, as we know through history, are most commonly achieved by connecting two pieces of common knowledge in new ways. Insights, similarly, are typically achieved by building a mosaic of information, making sense of the unarticulated.

The first steps in achieving insight is to stop using research 'like a drunk uses a lamp post': stop collecting more data than you need, resist the desire to research everyone constantly and ask every possible question. There is also a temptation to jump into research without clarifying objectives, often finding that it has no particular purpose or cannot answer the most important questions. Answers are then often predefined, prejudicing or limiting the responses.

Too much research asks customers to say what they want when they can rarely describe unfulfilled needs. It is also tempting to use the same techniques for everything, because it is the easiest method, or the most preferred by the incumbent research agency. Add to this the bias applied by managers internally – preconceived wisdom, prejudice and laziness often make every mildly insightful research bland and banal by the time it filters through to decision-makers.

Malcolm Gladwell, author of *Blink*, argues that customer research makes more mistakes than any other area of business because it assumes that rational decision-making common within business is also used by customers. Asking a customer how they feel about a new proposition is meaningless, he claims, because they simply don't know until they're in a situation when they need it. He points to cognitive psychology that says that 75–90% of our decisions are snap ones, made using sub-conscious rapid pattern recognition.

He believes that most companies' decision-making is not well-suited to fast-changing markets. They typically gather all the available evidence and then try to make sense of it. They assume that the more you have, the better decisions you will make. Yet too much information is confusing.

Gladwell illustrates his belief using a hospital's emergency ward. Doctors increase their chances of diagnosing heart attacks by cutting down on the number of factors they look for. More information was simply slowing them down, raising other issues and reducing their success rate. Doctors wanted to know more but slowly realized that focusing on less saved more lives. 'Managers need to focus on what matters most, the critical pieces of information, and use their instincts more', he concludes.

Business needs to adopt thoughtful approaches to research, interpretation and decision-making that enable and demand real insight. Research should be defined with the end in mind, focused on learning more about best customers, looking for anomalies and extremes rather than averages. Use a broad range of research techniques, from concept testing and mood boards to neural networking and psychographics. Dig deep into the vast customer databases that most companies sit on but are largely untapped. Find new language to describe insights, metaphors and analogies.

Neuroscience can now offer business an even more scientific approach to understanding human responses, often utilizing brain imaging techniques such as functional magnetic resonance imaging (fMRI), a non-invasive scanning technique, to understand consumer behaviours.

The 'Pepsi Challenge' was conducted whilst scanning the reactions of customer brains. When given Coke and Pepsi separately as unlabelled drinks, the response to Pepsi was five times stronger – most significantly seen in the ventral putamen, one of the brain's reward centres. However, when the brands were revealed, nearly all volunteers preferred Coke. Coke stimulated a different part of the brain – the medial prefrontal cortex, an area more associated with thinking, judging and our 'sense of self'. The brand, or at least some aspect of it, was clearly resonating with people at a much higher level and overriding more functional responses.

There are many different sources of customer information – both quantitative (more statistical) and qualitative (more descriptive). Each one of them is useful in their own way for understand-

The Data Detectives™

The Researcher *for customer surveys*	The Quizmaster *for customer panels*	The Deep Diver *for customer immersion*	The Helpline *for customer complaints*	The Profiler *for internal databases*
The Outsider *for market profiling*	The Facilitator *for focus groups*	The Neurologist *for brain scanning*	The Agony Aunt *for customer feedback*	The Partner *for affinity databases*
The Pollster *for omnibus surveys*	The Cameraman *for customer vox pops*	The Customizer *for previous co-creations*	The Private Eye *for mystery shopping*	The Categorizer *for external profiling*
The Ambassador *for parallel markets*	The Coolhunter *for trend spotting*	The Believer *for personal intuition*	The Front Liners *for staff anecdotes*	The Governor *for census information*

THE DATA DETECTIVES: 20 SOURCES OF CUSTOMER INTELLIGENCE

ing customers better, developing better solutions, delivering more appropriate experiences and finding the best ways to turn anonymous transactions into profitable relationships.

- *Brain scanning* – using neuro-imaging to understand the triggers within the brain for different rational and emotional stimuli. This is particularly relevant to products such as fragrances, or to understand the subconscious appeal of different colours, shapes and styles. Although it is expensive, it can be deeply instructive.

- *Census information* – government-funded research on the lives of every citizen, including much physical, geographical and socio-demographic information. Many research firms will use census data to scale up their sample results and apply them to specific people, names and addresses.

- *Cool hunting* – networks of trendspotters that observe customers and particularly influencers and trendsetters, looking for emerging fashions, behaviours and ideas. These anecdotes are not representative, nor should they be. Remember that 'newness occurs in the margins not the mainstreams', and this is a way to explore the margins.

- *Customer complaints* – learning when things go wrong, about what happened, why it affected the customer the way it did and what would be ways to improve. Being able to discuss a complaint by phone, rather than mail or Web, enables you to probe more deeply and also to turn a disaster into a delight.

- *Customer feedback* – encouraging customers to tell you what they think of their experiences, good and bad, unprompted and in their own words, and how you could do better. Whilst many people will use this only as a way to get satisfaction scores, it is an opportunity for customers to express themselves and can therefore solicit more interesting, diverse comment.

- *Customer immersion* – spending significant time with real customers, talking about their broader needs and ambitions, or even spending time with them to understand how they live and work, what they really think – either about a broad area such as travelling, where you might learn about a new context, or addressing a very specific issue more deeply.

- *Customer panels* – having an ongoing group of customers, physically or remotely, where the changes in their views and opinions can be tracked over time. The panel can become a quick and effective sounding board for new ideas, or for testing initiatives at various points during their development. You may even have a panel for each target segment.

- *Customer surveys* – questions designed to explore specific issues with open or multiple choice answers, typically with large sample audiences. This is perhaps the most common and traditional form of research, leading to statistical analysis, but limited by the questions asked and no ability to probe further.

- *External reports* – expert analysis of your markets or specific opportunities provided by external consulting or research firms, sometimes funded by all the companies in an industry, or more generic to purchase. These tend to be quantitative and insightful, with the analysis already done, but equally available to your competitors too.

- *Focus groups* – inviting small groups of people, customers or non-customers to participate in a discussion-based session, and sometimes observed by staff through a one-way mirror. A better way to discuss and debate an issue, explore new ideas, and engage managers by listening to customers, but can suffer from the 'herd behaviour' of groups.

- *Mystery shopping* – undercover researchers who act as customers of you and your competitors, reporting back on their experiences. The researchers might be specialists or your own managers, but in either case providing real specific insights for improvement and keeping staff on their toes too.

- *Omnibus surveys* – ongoing mass-market surveys about customer lifestyles and shopping behaviours. This tends to be fairly generic information, although it does enable tracking of attitudes and trends. Although the same reports are available to other companies, it is what you do with it that matters.

- *Personal intuition* – we are all human beings, but when working in business we often forget that we are customers too. In fact there is no better activity than being a customer, trusting your own instincts for what you like and dislike about a product, service or environment. Acting on intuition rather than waiting for imperfect information.

- **Previous collaborations** – learning from previous experiences (maybe they ordered a customized product from you in the past) and you still have all of their specific needs. Or maybe it was a conversation whilst delivering a service that can be used by colleagues to personalize their service next time, or even at the next step of the experience.

- **Staff anecdotes** – the customer knowledge inside the heads of customer service staff and sales people is probably greater than any other source, usually captured informally in team meetings and shift reports, or indirectly through suggestion schemes. Better still would be to include such people in project teams for developing new propositions or innovation.

- **Third party databases** – using information collated by another organization – such as a supermarket, a complementary business, a membership organization – to enhance your own data, perhaps by learning more about your existing customers' lifestyles and behaviours, or to find new customers who have similar profiles to your target customers.

- **Transactional databases** – collating and profiling your customer databases, with every customer and address, interaction and transaction, product and service purchased, date and time, location and payment method. This is no shortage of potential analysis; the real trick is to consider what information you really want and then find it.

- **Vox pops** – short video interviews with a range of customers, often edited to capture their key statements, enabling people internally to learn directly from customers. Whilst a small number of 'talking heads' is not necessarily representative of the market, seeing real people and the way they describe issues and ideas can be a very powerful way to engage staff.

When I work with organizations, I typically ask for all their market research reports and analysis completed in the previous three years. The response, after a frantic running around between departments and search in dusty archives, is most often a huge pile of 50–250 documents. Has anybody read them? Can anybody remember the key messages from each? Has anybody tried to combine the messages from each? No.

A 'customer canvas' is one way of trying to capture the key insights from each of these many sources of information in one place – to look for the connections between them, find complementary data that starts to build a more informed picture and identify any gaps in understanding.

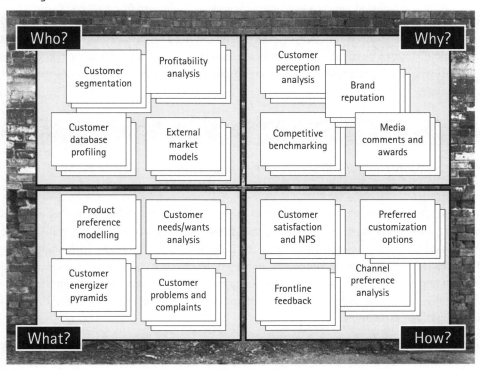

CUSTOMER CANVAS: COLLATING ALL YOU KNOW ABOUT CUSTOMERS

The canvas is typically a huge wall-size piece of paper divided into four quadrants – representing the different types of customer information.

The small team works through the materials to pull out key points and posts them up appropriately. Of course some information will not fit perfectly, but getting it up matters most. Similar information is clustered together, looking for reinforcement or disagreement – and connections by linking information across the canvas.

The customer canvas can become a 'living' representation of the customer world, constantly being updated with latest research, or even driving the need for new research based on gaps or ambiguity. It can be summarized monthly for board meetings, and indeed everyone across the business, and used physically as a starting point for decision-making from a customer perspective.

Insight 18: DOVE

'Flawed or flawless? Wrinkled or wonderful? Dream woman or real woman? What exactly is real beauty?'

That was the provocative, controversial and memorable challenge from Dove, the body and skincare brand. Seeking to re-energize its own fortunes but also to assertively challenge the myths and taboos of the cosmetics world, the Unilever business launched its 'Campaign for Real Beauty'. Rather than the unrealistic images of beauty used by rivals, Dove showed real women and realistic body shapes. It championed mothers, daughters, sisters and girlfriends – real people whom you could read more about and listen to online, all of whom had their own challenges and aspirations.

The critical issue was what made women feel good. Of course, we live in a society where we are surrounded by artificially enhanced images of beauty and a culture where aspiring to these stereotypes is thought to be good. Men don't help, only fuelling the desire. We become obsessed with appearance and the pursuit of perfection. The hours reading the magazines, watching the television shows, standing in front of the mirror, in the changing rooms or at the cosmetics counter.

By showing a wider range of skin types and body shapes, Dove's advertising campaign offered a more democratized view of beauty to which we could all aspire. It also implied a wider ethical challenge, taking on thoughtless consumerism, equal rights and the pressure to conform that can lead to low confidence, eating disorders and much more. From a marketing perspective it is also more memorable because of its distinctive and campaigning approach, rather than offering yet more passive scenes of unnecessary indulgence and unreachable aspiration.

Dove worked with Harvard University and London School of Economics to evaluate the impact of the campaign – on the brand, customers and society.

Their report concluded that we live in a world of stereotypes, judgements and assumptions to which we may not have been party to, but which influence us nonetheless. When these stereotypes are harmful, acknowledging and talking about them is key to changing attitudes and behaviours. This particularly applies to girls and young women.

'There is no denying that influential beauty stereotypes exist – whether focused on a western ideal or a stronger local cultural expectation. They create appearance anxiety for women globally. More than two-thirds of the women interviews said that beauty is often too narrowly defined, which leaves many of these women believing that it is hard to feel beautiful when confronted with these ideals. Almost all women report becoming concerned with their overall physical appearance, body weight and shape at some point in their lives – with concern over appearance, and action to change it, beginning in adolescence ...

'Nine in ten women want to change some aspect of their appearance – with the greatest dissatisfaction found with their body weight and shape. There was also a significant relationship between a woman's satisfaction with her physical appearance and body

> weight and shape, and her sense of self-worth. When women feel good about them-
> selves, it is projected into feeling confident and loved. When women feel badly about
> themselves, it is often expressed in feelings of insecurity and tiredness – which are likely
> to precipitate disengagement and activity avoidance.'

Importantly, the academics concluded, women are passionate about changing this dynamic for future generations, expressing strong desires to create more positive education and discussions for young girls on beauty and body image. Women want to 'actively engage young girls about having a realistic and healthy body image, to eat a healthy diet, and to embrace the idea that 'beautiful women come in different colours'. Dove found the campaign to be commercially its best ever and remains more committed than ever to pursuing the notion of real beauty as much more than an advertising campaign.

3.2 CUSTOMER IMMERSION

The best way to learn about customers ... is to spend time with them.

No surprise there, then. But when was the last time you sat down and had a proper conversation with a customer or, even better, a potential customer? Not just when they have a problem to sort out, or when you asked to as part of training, or asking them what they want from you or think about you – but a real conversation about their world and how you can be a more useful part of it?

Malcolm Gladwell describes the ability of an officer from the NYPD trying to solve a crime to walk into the bedroom of a victim and learn 95% about that person in the first five minutes – the types of books and other possessions lying around the room, the way they decorate their walls and what they choose to emphasize, the pictures on display and why they might have chosen them, the way things are laid out and what that says about their attitudes and style.

He calls it 'thin slicing'.

Similarly, you can learn an enormous amount by spending a short time with real customers. See the world as they see it, try out the alternatives as they see them. Observe how they behave, what is difficult, what frustrates them, how they use and store things, all the irrational things we all do.

Talk to them. Meet them for a coffee, have dinner with them, move in and live with them.

Not 'Hi, I'm from company X, what do you think of my great product?' Instead learn about their broader needs, wants, frustrations and ambitions. Go deeper into areas, which you know from more standard research, matters more to people. Dig for ideas. Listen to the language they use. Capture the quirky findings – don't disregard them as the craze of one person.

Ask your customers about themselves, their lives, their hopes and fears, what they love and what they hate, what they are trying to achieve day by day or in the longer term. Understand what influences them and how they make choices, how the products and services you might provide fit into their lives.

And don't just leave this as a task for your research department. Make it a regular activity of everybody – the CEO, the finance director, the HR manager, the non-executive directors, the data processing team, the customer service team – to help them understand customers more deeply, show customers a human face to the business, rediscover the passion of your people for why they are in business.

There is nothing better than real insights from real people: powerful, emotional and memorable.

A.J. Lafley, the CEO of Proctor & Gamble, encourages every one of his people – including his busiest executives – to spend time every week with families, living in their homes, shopping in the supermarkets. The point is to see, feel and think like a real person – not like a prejudiced, product-centric executive who is conditioned by industry conventions.

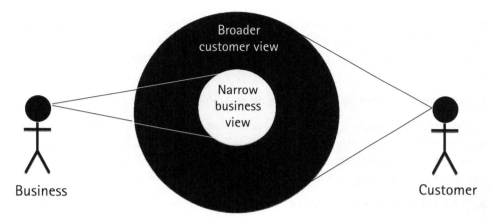

CUSTOMER PERSPECTIVE: SEEING A BIGGER, RICHER PICTURE

When UK retailer Tesco started planning to enter the US market with their Fresh & Easy brand, the project leader Tim Mason and his team went to live with Californian families for months to get a feel for their lifestyles, priorities, influences and motivations – not just what they ate, where they shopped and what they bought, but how it fitted in to their lives.

Such immersions into the customer world are often called 'deep dives' – diving deep to discover new, richer, broader insights. These might be with customers or sometimes yourself as a customer. Another way is to share experiences with a peer in another company in a different sector – for example, if you want to customize your cosmetics, go and learn from the people at Nike ID. Such companies are not competitive, but you may well share the same customer.

Some of the formats of a deep dive include:

- A 30–60 minute one-to-one conversation with a customer.

- Observing a customer task, e.g. watching how a customer shops.

- Doing a customer task yourself, e.g. the weekly shop at the supermarket.

- A 30–60 minute one-to-one with a peer in a company in a different business.

- Being a customer of your own company, e.g. shopping online or by telephone.

- Comparing this with being a customer of a competitor or benchmark company.

It is important to have an 'opening up' conversation – to ask open questions, learn about the broader view and listen openly to what customers say, capturing the unusual or marginal things they mention rather than just the mainstream, predictable things.

Insight 19: H&M

Sixty years after Erling Persson opened the first 'Hennes' shop in Västerås, aimed at offering 'fashion and quality at the best prices', the brand is still contemporary and successful.

The first shop only sold women's clothes ('Hennes' means 'Hers' in Swedish), but when Persson moved to Stockholm he bought a hunting store called Mauritz Widforss, a men's clothing stockist. The shops together became Hennes & Mauritz (H&M) and throughout the 1960s and 1970s expanded across Europe, adding children's clothes and young fashion to the collection.

H&M's 1500 stores can now be found in 28 countries. The H&M proposition is all about fast fashion, making the latest styles available at accessible prices, but also encouraging customers to mix and match their own items across colours and styles, latest fashions and essential basics, vintage and classics. There are now extensive ranges for women, men, teenagers, children and babies, plus cosmetics and shoes too.

The 60,000 staff are encouraged to resist the 'bureaucracy of big business' and stay true to Persson's orginal H&M culture. Margareta van den Bosch has led the 100-strong design team for the last 20 years, for example, retaining a consistency of approach but staying in touch with trends and fashions by recruiting some of the best new designers, and through close relationships with design schools around the world. The approach is incredibly successful, with sales of more than SEK92 billion in 2007 (reflecting 72% sales growth in the last five years, and earnings per share growth of 183%).

Ludovica, an Italian fan, describes why H&M is her 'lovemark':

> 'You can think everything you want but H&M is the solution even if you live in Milan! In Milan, H&M shop is very close to Armani, Valentino, Dolce and Gabbana and others. They are great but they are not the solution ... solution of what? Solution when it is Friday evening, it's 7 p.m. and you just finished work and you look not very fresh and beautiful and your spanking new boyfriend is coming to pick you up at 9 p.m. for a romantic dinner and a big party with all your friends that already know all your clothes and you really need a new great outfit ... Go inside H&M and in 20 minutes you can get your solution without regret for your wallet!'

H&M is a pioneer of design collaborations with celebrity icons such as Stella McCartney, Karl Lagerfeld, Viktor & Rolf, Madonna, and Kylie Minogue that attract enormous media attention, particularly for the huge customer lines that build up outside stores during the night before the range is launched and the fact that they sell out within days. Roberto Cavalli, the Italian designer who dresses stars such as Beyoncé and Charlize Theron, is the latest to design collections for men and women exclusively for H&M.

At a time when transparent supply chains and ethical sourcing has come into focus, particularly for brands that seek to mass-produce clothing at low prices, H&M is very aware of how its clothes are made. It also puts particular focus on organic cotton, initially for babies' and children's clothes, but now also for adults.

The brand's designers recognize that the best source of inspiration and learning from them is not through fashion shows and glossy magazines but by working with the people who walk into their stores every day. The local insights and product mixes are achieved through constant observation, tracking and feedback – and then rapid and flexible logistical responses. It regularly holds competitions, events and even design workshops where it seeks to learn from real people, its customers. Besides offering the right product for each customer, the major purpose of each H&M store as originally defined by Erling Persson back in the 1940s, is 'to create an environment where every customer feels at home'.

3.3 CUSTOMER INSIGHTS

An insight is a new, more profound understanding of a situation.

Customer knowledge in the form of raw data, connected intelligence or deep immersion is the fuel of a customer business – where to focus, what to do, how to be different, what to do better and how well you have done.

There is no shortage of customer information – mountains of market research data, focus groups reports, behaviour tracking analysis and more – but making sense of it is not easy. Much of the information confirms what you already know, or what you believe. Finding something new and important within all of this information is not easy. Needles in haystacks come to mind.

How do you find real insight into what matters to customers that you can act on practically and deliver an impact to customers and commercially?

The Oxford English Dictionary is careful to draw a distinction between insight and insights:

- *'Insight'* is described as 'the ability to perceive clearly and deeply', 'embedded knowledge to structure thinking' and 'the source of more profound decisions'. Others consider it a 'sixth sense' to make sense of complex situations in more useful ways.

- *'Insights'* are described as 'flashes of inspiration', 'penetrating discoveries' and 'specific opportunities'. Elsewhere they are described as brainwaves, realizing what is obvious but never been described, and 'moments of genius'.

Insights are much more than research findings, more profound and with greater implications. They tell you something new and useful, consider aspects that you have not thought about before, which are not described within the conventions of markets or may not even have language sufficient to describe them. They put knowledge into context. They describe why and how, as well as who and what.

Insights come in many different forms, provoking brands to think differently about their customers, to align products and communication around a motivation that challenges conventions but resonates strongly with the target customer.

- Coca-Cola recognized that men wanted to drink Diet Coke but felt alienated by the phrase 'diet' and its female-targeted advertising. It created Coke Zero for men.

- Heinz recognized that children loved its tomato ketchup, not because of its taste but because it was fun to play with, and so created more squeezable bottles in crazy colours.

- Vodafone found that many older customers did not like their phones because they were too complicated, so stripped out all the clever features to create Vodafone Simply.

There are many techniques to generate insights – some of it structured, some of it unstructured. It can come intuitively, by spending time with information or through sheer experience of making sense of customers in lots of different sectors and situations.

More structured insight techniques include hypothesis generation – using your creativity to project an unusual or outrageous insight that can then be proven (or not) by data analysis. Other techniques are to use random connections, putting disparate pieces of information together and trying to make sense of it, or to use pattern recognition, identifying the anomalies, focusing on the bits of information that are normally averaged out.

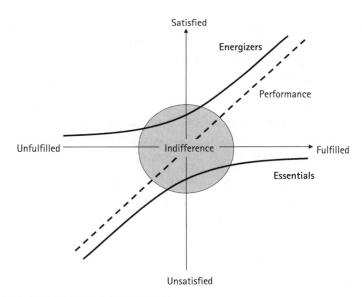

KANO DIAGRAM: WHAT MAKES A DIFFERENCE

The 'Kano diagram' demonstrates how some customer needs will never excite the customer but would hugely dissatisfy them if they were not delivered effectively. These are the basic hygiene factors, such as safety and security. We call them 'essentials'.

However, other customer needs, if not fulfilled, are met with indifference – they are not essential. But when they are delivered effectively, they can provoke extremely positive reactions. Rationally these are the 'enablers', emotionally these are the 'energizers'.

What is also important is Kano's 'zone of indifference', where everything is acceptable but not special. This is where most companies tend to lapse into complacency, doing enough to avoid complaints or trading off performance for efficiency. Indifferent customers will quickly defect as soon as a better offer comes along.

Perhaps the biggest obstacles to being insightful are being blinded by the amount of information and intimidated by the need to respect every aspect of what every customer says. A customer canvas is one way to begin to cut through the information jungle. Another particularly useful way to summarize customer immersions is to use 'energizer pyramids'.

Energizer pyramids are a simple way to reflect what matters most – rationally and emotionally – to real customers. In some ways they are a reinterpretation of Maslow's hierarchy of needs but in a more simple and useful way. For each person you meet, as well as some of the actual facts and stories you learn, seek to identify the following:

- *'Essentials'* that were absolute prerequisites for any brand to deliver in their eyes, both the hygiene factors (such as safety and security) but also basic expectations – even a low-cost flight is expected to serve drinks onboard, although they may come at a price.

- *'Enablers'* that practically helped them to do more, which might be offered by some brands but not others and became part of a rational trade-off against brands and price – faster delivery, 24-hour support, range of colour options.

- *'Energizers'* that might seem small and trivial but can emotionally make a big difference – the biscuit served with your coffee, the free newspapers, the choice of music, the free toy for the kids, the buzz of sales staff.

The pyramid should be completed from the customer perspective – what they need, want and would love to have – in their language rather than business jargon. Language itself can be insightful or can hint at a context that the customer thinks in, that is broader than that to which the company normally responds.

Imagine an internal workshop to develop a new business strategy, creatively explore new innovations or improve productivity in call centres, where each person comes with an energizer pyramid of one customer with whom they have spent 30–60 minutes prior to the meeting, discussing related ideas. Suddenly you have a workshop room where customers are equally represented.

ENERGIZER PYRAMID: WHAT REALLY TURNS YOU ON

The energizer pyramid can also start shaping business responses, define brand communications or specify new products and services – working out what is:

- Essential to provide in terms of information or features.

- Enabling to do what is perhaps also the basis for competitive differentiation.

- Energizing – what gives the communication a buzz that will spread or the service a twist that makes customers smile and tell their friends.

Insight 20: HARRAH'S CASINOS

Harrah's is the slightly run-down-looking hotel and casino on the other side of the road from the MGM Mirage Hotel in Las Vegas. Tourists rush to the erupting volcano outside the $750 million monolith, but few even notice the world's most customized entertainment venue standing opposite.

Yet things are never as they might seem in the world's gambling capital. Harrah's has outperformed all of its competitors over the last decade, delivering at least three times greater profit margins than the Mirage and any other of its competitors. Its secret is not in gimmicks and glitz, or having the biggest game or gamblers. The difference lies in its customer database.

Harrah's built WINet, a winner's information network that provides the chain with a nationwide database of its customers and their gambling preferences, as well as what else they like to spend their money on: their regular pre-play dinner, favourite drink and more. It could estimate each customer's lifetime value – both what their value has been in the past and their projected future worth. This enables them to customize their Total Rewards Program incentives to each individual, as well as being able to anticipate and personalize their every service need.

Call the Harrah's central reservation system and the call centre will identify your number, match it in their database, bring up your profile and be ready to have a fully informed conversation on first name terms even before you speak. Of course, this has to be handled delicately, otherwise it can be a definite turn-off rather than individualized service, but the information is there for the service representative to use as they see appropriate.

The biggest challenge in implementing the approach was not technical but cultural. Previously Harrah's (and indeed the whole industry) assumed that customers generally played only in one location and hoped they would become loyal to it. Because each casino operated largely independently, they had little interest in promoting the brand and other locations in the chain. They were only interested in customers coming back to their casino again.

Local managers therefore initially regarded WINet with scepticism until they started to realize that the benefits of brand rather than location loyalty, of database-enabled personal service and the huge volumes of new customers arriving from other Harrah's locations. Customers could now use the same player card in venues across the country, at home and work, during the evening and on vacation. They recognized that there was far more reason to go to Harrah's wherever they were, rather than try other brands.

From a business perspective, Harrah's recognized that profitability did not come through market share (typically all about driving transactions with promiscuous customers at a high cost of sale) but through customer share – gaining the loyalty of best customers and the resulting higher profit margins, even if the total number of customers was smaller.

The investment coincided with the legalization of gambling on riverboats and Indian reservations, which spurred a rapid growth in customer interest and competition. With its customers demanding a Harrah's wherever they went, the chain grew rapidly during the mid-1990s.

Since WINet and the Total Rewards Program were introduced in 1997, the number of customers playing at multiple Harrah's locations has increased by 72% according to the annual report. Cross-referred revenues have soared from $113 million to $250 million, contributing around 10% to overall profitability. Today, twice as many gamblers carry a Harrah's card compared with any competitor.

As Wharton marketing professor David Bell points out, 'Harrah's can now figure out who is coming into the casino, where they are going once they are inside, how long they sit at different gambling tables and so forth. This allows them to optimize the range and configuration of their gambling games. It also enables them to optimize their network locations, their marketing activities and their overall customer experience'.

Customer propositions

Talk to me on my terms, not yours. Tell me about what your products will do for me, not what they do. Sell me the benefits, not the features. Or better still, talk about what I'm trying to achieve and how you can bring a number of products and services together to achieve that. Don't let me struggle through pages and pages of catalogues and technical specifications. Solve my problems or help create my dreams.

Tell me how you are different. Not with more statistics and gobbledegook – tell me instead what you can do for me or enable me to do what nobody else can.

And do it in a way that is relevant to me. Nobody buys the same product for the same reason, and nobody has quite the same problem or ambition. But we do have similarities – some of us will buy a car more than anything for speed, others will buy it for its design or maybe its storage space. Therefore it might really be about saving time, looking good or going places as a large family. It's not about the car – it's about what I want it for. It's not about the product, it's about me.

4.1   CUSTOMER CONTEXT

Thinking from the 'outside in' means thinking in the customer's world – what they are trying to achieve rather than what you are trying to sell. This is a much greater context for business and a much better starting point to engage the customer.

Imagine that you are a business traveller.

You want to fly to Los Angeles as quickly as possible, with the least hassle, and still feel your best despite an overnight flight. That matters because you really want to clinch this deal, which will require you to give the performance of your life and negotiate incredibly smartly. And if you can do that, you will have a lucrative contract for the next 36 months that will help your business grow, delight your investors and maybe even allow you to buy that second home in the mountains.

The airline, meanwhile, thinks it's all about flight times, seat pitches and loyalty schemes.

You've got much bigger things on your mind. A 36- or 40-inch seat pitch is frankly irrelevant to you, unless they can show you how it might make the difference between winning and losing a deal worth millions of dollars. If they can help you do that, then you definitely want it!

The real context for the customer is not the bigger seat or even the travel. The context is about winning the deal, growing the business or even the home in the mountains.

To engage this customer, we now know much more about their personal and professional ambitions. And whilst the LA trip is important (they might win it, or lose it) we want to work with them over the longer term – and therefore they are most likely to be interested in somebody who can help them grow their business or improve their lifestyle.

If we introduce the option of travelling business class as costing ten times more than economy, then it doesn't seem a very good proposition. But if we introduce the idea of a longer-term partnership where the customer travels business class in return for a faster and more relaxed

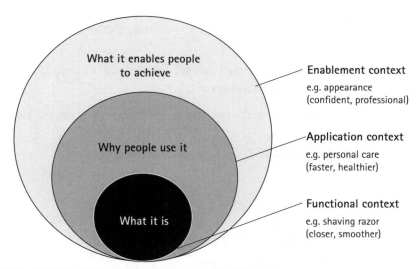

CUSTOMER CONTEXT: WHAT CUSTOMERS ARE TRYING TO DO

travel experience, the opportunity to network with key people in their industry, and the incentive of a vacation in the mountains, then they might be much more interested.

Customers don't start with a need for your product – they start with a problem to solve, a task to accomplish or an ambition to achieve.

Horst Schulze is the founder and president of Ritz-Carlton hotels and frequently tells a story:

A man saw three masons working on a building and asked them what they were doing. 'I'm putting bricks together,' said one. 'I'm building a wall,' said the second. 'I'm building a home,' said the third.

They all do the same thing, but with a different attitude, observes Schulze. Any company can put systems, training and resources in place to pursue great customer service, but without the right attitude you will fail.

'Association trees' are a useful technique for mapping out the 'context' in which customers will or could consider you. It can work in two ways:

- Thinking about the specific need of the customer and continually asking 'Why?' in order to explore the broader drivers of that need.

- It could start with a specific product – you then consider the broader applications of that product.

Or you could do both, combining both perspectives.

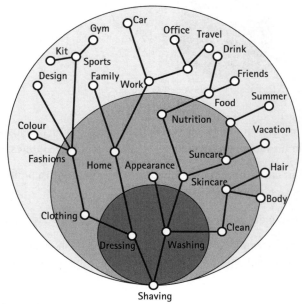

ASSOCIATION TREES: BUILDING THE CUSTOMER CONTEXT

'Perceived value' is therefore a judgement from the customer's perspective based on the price and the benefits derived from it. The customer's perception is conditioned by each person's view of the worth of the relevant benefits.

Companies themselves typically encourage customers to see the value of their offering in a limited way by immediately comparing it with a direct competitor that has similar benefits. In a world where most products are as good as each other and therefore offer the same benefits, forced comparisons are quickly limited to the difference in price.

The only way to avoid this spiral of downwards pricing and ever-squeezing margins is to change the context of your offer so that it is not directly comparable to another similar product. Make it of higher perceived value and easier for the customer to consider more relevant comparables.

 Audi A4

 VW Passat

Design: different
Manufacturing cost: similar

Brand : different
Marketing cost : similar

Performance: similar
Price: 30% more

Target audience : executives
Peers: BMW 3, Mercedes C Class

Design: different
Manufacturing cost : similar

Brand : different
Marketing cost : similar

Performance: similar
Price: 30% less

Target audience: families
Peers: Ford Mondeo, Opel Vectra

PERCEIVED VALUE: A BIGGER, BETTER CONTEXT IS WORTH MORE

In practical terms, changing the context may only be a small twist on the existing perception, so that the customer perceives you to be relative to a more upmarket competitor. Where there is no actual material difference and only the perceived worth increases, any additional price goes straight to the bottom line profitability.

Consider two brands from the same holding company. The Audi A4 and Volkswagen Passat are essentially the same car with the same costs. However, the Audi is marketed in a very different context to the Volkswagen.

The A4 is positioned as a mid-range executive car and is therefore compared by customers and commentators to other mid-range executive cars such as a BMW 3 series or a Mercedes C class.

Meanwhile, the Passat is positioned as a larger family car and compared to the Ford Mondeo or Opel Vectra.

Although the price of the Audi is around 30% more than the Volkswagen, they are seen in different contexts by the customers – and both are seen as good 'value for money' relative to the perceived alternatives.

Insight 21: WHOLE FOODS MARKETS

'Love where you shop!' shouts the banner above the entrance to the huge branch of Whole Foods Market in Austin, Texas, home town of the world's largest natural foods supermarket chain.

A bold and brash statement – but shopping at Whole Foods is a seductive experience. One chef tosses their herb leaf salad, whilst another rolls fresh pasta into shape. Customers sample a new range of organic fruit juices or struggle to choose from the vast array of rustic bread. There are themed restaurants between food counters: a sushi bar, La Trattoria, the Living Foods salad counter. You can stroll down a canyon-styled aisle lined with hundreds of vats of every flour, pulse and bean, and up another that is more like an orchard with enormous displays of the freshest fruits from local farms and around the world, flowers and plants. Then there is the vineyard with fine-tasting organic wines, oils and vinegars. On the shelves you will find books by Al Gore and Mohammed Yunus, and solar-powered radio sets.

In 1978, college dropouts John Mackey and Renee Lawson borrowed $45,000 from family and friends to open the doors of a small natural foods store called Safer Way Natural Foods in Austin. When the couple were evicted from their apartment for storing food products in it, they decided to simply live at the store.

Two years later, the couple partnered with Craig Weller and Mark Skiles to merge Safer Way with Clarksville Natural Grocery, resulting in the opening of the first Whole Foods Market. At 12,500 square feet and with a staff of 19, the store was quite large in comparison with the standard health food store of the time.

Then the natural foods market began to take off. Speciality health foods evolved into natural foods and Whole Foods Market led the way.

Today, with 270 locations in the US, Canada and the UK, Whole Foods is a $5.6 billion business, all about 'whole foods, whole people, whole planet'. The Whole Foods team is committed to selling the highest-quality natural and organic products, looking after its customers and employees, and also making the world a better place.

Part of Whole Foods' success and style is constantly to raise the bar in terms of the kinds of foods it offers, how it presents that food and what it tells you about how the food got to the store.

It has an intricate internal concept called 'Whole Trade', inspired by the fair trade movement, to certify that products it sells from developing nations are produced in economically and environmentally sustainable ways. In 2008, it introduced an animal welfare rating system: every animal product for sale is rated from 1 to 5, based on how the animals were raised. All plastic bags and non-essential packaging have been eliminated.

It is proactive too, recently launching a loan programme for its food suppliers, creating a pool of $10 million per year to provide low-interest loans to small food producers to encourage the local agricultural movement.

Mackey, now chairman and CEO, is famously messianic in his quotes. This is a company 'based on love, not on fear'. 'We believe in a virtuous circle embracing the food chain, human beings and Mother Earth', proclaims another sign at the store's entrance.

The 54,000 employees are 'passionate, attentive team members', according to the website. In 2007, the business was voted by *Fortune* magazine as one of the '100 best places to work' for the tenth year in a row. Whole Foods people are incredibly knowledgeable, attentive and charming. You are their 'guest', not a customer, and this really is a mouth-watering adventure – not a store.

One customer described her experience:

> 'From my first visit I was enchanted. Whole Foods is a temple worshipping all things gourmet … Each location I have visited has left an indelible mark within my stomach and soul. The Massachusetts location is where I lost my organic virginity, changing forever the way I selected what I ate. When in Portland I never pass an opportunity to head downtown to gaze at the colourful varieties of the heirloom tomatoes. In Louisville, I introduced my father to the wonders of the pastry case – together we bonded over fresh macaroons and cheesecake. I look forward to visiting the new store in downtown Seattle during my upcoming travels and am debating securing a hotel room with a stove just for the occasion.'

4.2 CUSTOMER PROPOSITIONS

Defining what you do from the 'outside in' means thinking customers not products, benefits not features, perceived value and then price.

'Customer value propositions' are perhaps the most important tool in business today, yet are too commonly misunderstood and used without sufficient definition or thought.

They offer a lens through which customers see your products and services in a more relevant and valuable way. They are themes that enable conversations, collaboration and customization:

- They focus on the issues or aspirations of specific audiences and are therefore only relevant to certain people. Different segments, by definition, require different propositions.

- The same product can be sold to different audiences in different ways much more successfully than trying to sell the same product to everyone in the same way.

- They will sometimes require entirely new products and services to fulfil their promises, or iconic components that bring existing products together as integrated solutions.

Propositions into themes based on the critical issues for the target customer. They pull customers towards you. In the business world, 'how can you make more sales' attracts companies with that ambition, whilst in the teenager market 'getting your band online' attracts every wannabe young musician and 'securing the future of your new family' is important to any parent of a newly born child.

This way, you provoke the audience's interest in something important and relevant to them, cutting through the noise and price obsession of your competitors, and are in a position to shape a better, more personal and valuable solution. They are much more interested when the discussion is about them rather than you.

The theme sets a context beyond the product. More significant themes have more perceived value, which enables you to price more profitably too. It might even be a more enduring theme that can stretch over time, enabling a richer relationship to develop. Cross-selling becomes easy, not at a discount, but at a price premium because of the perceived additional value of the theme. It will also attract more similar customers, potentially forming communities around the issue too.

Propositions typically work alongside products in a matrix structure.

Imagine a financial services company with typical products such as current accounts, investments, credit cards, loans, mortgages, car insurance, home insurance, etc. Imagine also the customers, with typical motivations such as buying a new home, having a baby, starting a business, travelling the world or preparing for retirement.

If you sell mortgages as distinctive products, you will attract customers only interested in them. The conversation immediately degenerates into discount rates and the complex options within mortgages. The customer is forced to go through this when they are more interested in attaining the home of their dreams.

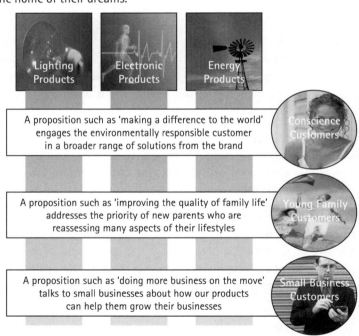

PROPOSITIONS AS THEMES: A CUSTOMER VIEW ACROSS PRODUCTS

Instead of selling mortgages and competing purely on price, you offer a 'home buyer' proposition. You become their trusted adviser through a complex and intimidating task, helping them to build a personal jigsaw of everything they need – ultimately selling more products, often at a higher price, and with the prospect of a longer-term relationship too.

Propositions are about being relevant to specific customers – at an individual, segment or market level – interpreting the brand in a more relevant way, articulating products and services in a more relevant way, setting a more relevant context, and enabling a more profitable relationship.

The proposition captures the benefits and therefore superior value to the customer. The conceptual value of a proposition is illustrated below. The basic and distinctive value, less the price and alternatives, results in a net value to the customer – hopefully superior to that offered by alternatives:

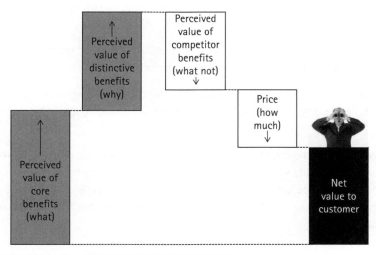

PROPOSITIONS AS VALUE: THE NET VALUE TO CUSTOMERS

Although this sounds obvious, the key is to focus on the benefits, not the features. Benefits create value for customers; features don't. Products describe features; propositions describe benefits. 'Twenty-four hour home maintenance' is a feature and 'Peace of mind at home' is a benefit of it. 'Wireless emails on your phone' is interesting, but 'stay in touch with clients anywhere' is more valuable.

A value proposition therefore starts as an internal document, now the required starting point for any customer-related activity. The key parts are:

- **Who?** The target audience, their issues and motivations, and the key insight into the world of these customers that we are addressing.

- **What?** The primary benefits that we offer, supported by the key features of some of the products and services that can deliver these benefits.

- **Why?** The competitive difference in what we offer, how it is better or different from what others offer, and why it is difference.

- **How much?** The price position relative to alternatives, given the superior benefits offered and compared with other ways of achieving the benefits.

- **What not?** The trade-offs that the customer makes in choosing you compared with someone else, i.e. the differentiators of your competitors (although you wouldn't communicate this!).

Collectively, these dimensions articulate the superior value that we offer customers (usually not expressed numerically, although it could be). This is, of course, an internal document, that can then be rearticulated externally for the customer in a compelling way. Key to marketing propositions is to link them to the target customers for which the issue-driven themes are most relevant.

Who ... Profile the target customer physically and emotionally

What... Describe their context, what they seek to achieve

Why... Identify the distinctive customer benefits that you offer

How ... Describe the specific features that deliver these benefits

What not ... Internally, note the benefits offered by competitors

How much... Position the price as % relative to competitors

CUSTOMER VALUE PROPOSITION

Although it might not be possible (or desirable) to 'push' the propositions through direct marketing to specific names and addresses, such people will be attracted to certain special events (conferences, exhibitions), membership networks (associations, hobbies), television programmes (specialist interests) and press (specific sections, special features). Self-selecting, the customer is 'pulled' towards you, coming out of the woodwork.

The propositions might be communicated through conventional advertising or working with partners relevant to the particular theme. For example, the 'home buyer' proposition might be offered through estate agents to engage customers before they start approaching other financial service companies.

Propositions are then fulfilled through dialogue, by bringing combinations of standard products together under the umbrella of the theme, or sometimes by also adding specific 'iconic' ingredients – for example, a special guidebook or dedicated adviser for the home buyer, or unique diagnostic tools and industry forums for the high-growth manufacturers. These icons add value and differentiation, and provide a 'glue' to bring together more comprehensive and profitable solutions.

Slightly better perception of comparative benefits, expressed through a value proposition, therefore enables you to increase price, maintain the same value for money and directly improve profitability.

Insight 22: OXFAM UNWRAPPED

Ever been stuck for that perfect gift for your father, that deep and meaningful surprise for your girlfriend, or the obligatory thank you to your corporate clients? Do you find yourself searching the shops and websites for something just right, a bit more fun, maybe a bit more thoughful and a little bit different?

Oxfam, the international charity that focuses on relieving poverty and supporting self-development across Africa, has the perfect solution for you.

Give him a cow or a donkey, give her some chickens, or maybe a sheep or goat, maybe even a hive of bees. Of course there might not be room in his garden for the cow or in her apartment to keep the chickens. But Oxfam have thought of that too. Give them to somebody whose life it really could change, save them from starvation, get them back on the road to looking after themselves or even starting their own little business.

Oxfam has been hugely successful as a charity, raising money in times of crisis, famine and other natural disasters. It also has a chain of branded shops selling second-hand goods and some Third World items. Although these retain visibility of the brand, they exist in a highly competitive charitable market and struggle to survive amidst high retail rents.

'Oxfam Unwrapped' was a great way to retain people's interest and introduce significant new income streams throughout the year. A website and funky mail order catalogue demonstrate the diversity of gifts on offer. After a few clicks of the mouse or a phone call, and a credit card number, your perfect gift is on its way to those in need. Of course, the recipient is not forgotten, because they can receive a gift card or email to to tell them about their gift.

The gifts are described by Oxfam as 'positive pressies', helping those in need and bringing a smile to the faces of a loved one. The catalogue is updated regularly so that the gifts won't become repetitive. And there's much more than animals – the ultimate gift of water, seeds to grow a new life, equipment to help people help themselves or contributing to their broader education with a new school. Or you can opt to allocate the gift directly to an emergency fund.

Whilst the customer proposition focuses on the gift, Oxfam recognizes that it requires much more than an animal to get people in desperate situations back on track. The price of gift also includes everything that is needed to ensure that the gift has the most positive impact:

- Equipment, for example the cost of the beehive in which to keep the bees.

- Sourcing the bees, typically from local places, to support others and reduce costs.

- Delivery – transporting the bees and hives to the places that really matter.

- Training in how to use the beehive and produce the best quality, nutritious honey.

- Engaging and encouraging local people to take up beekeeping.

- Retailing – educating the new beekeepers in how to package and sell their honey.

- Enabling this to happen, with essential Oxfam staff locally and centrally.

- Marketing the programme through websites and catalogues to create demand.

- Supporting broader initiatives by Oxfam in the region.

Everybody wants to do some good, but sometimes pledging more money can seem a little impersonal and repetitive. Oxfam succeeds by reframing giving as gifting, and changing the customer 'context' for gifting too. It comes with real benefits – not just to those around the world less fortunate than ourselves, but also in solving that problem of buying something for someone who has everything.

4.3 CUSTOMER CONVERSATIONS

Imagine that you are about to go to meet your customer – the perfect opportunity to get your new proposition across and engage them in a more compelling and relevant way. But it all tends to come out the wrong way. We start talking about our world: who we are, what we do, the products we offer, how we think we are better.

Yet people are much more engaged when you talk about *them*: 'I understand that your strategic priorities for this year are ...', then get them excited about how they can achieve their targets faster and better, and work backwards to describe how you can help make this happen.

'Customer narratives' are structured ways to introduce ideas to customer, a script for a conversation about them, for introducing the proposition in a relevant and engaging way.

The customer narrative starts with the customer, their issues and opportunities, and takes them through a logic that stimulates dialogue, moves the conversation from commoditized products to individual problem-solving and hopefully inspires them to take the actions you seek.

Customer ... Initiate a dialogue with a target customer

Context... Confirm what they are seeking to achieve

Complexity ... Establish an issue, why they need support

Challenge ... Articulate the key problem that needs addressing

Core message... Propose the solution the customer needs

Conversation... Discuss the steps in making this happen

CUSTOMER NARRATIVES: TALKING ON CUSTOMER TERMS

There are four stages to the narrative structure:

- *Context*: The customer's situation, the issues and opportunities they face, showing a good understanding of their world and their challenges, aiming to achieve agreement in the importance of the subject, and interest to discuss it further.

- *Complexity*: The customer's problem, why their current solution is not enough, using some new research or real experiences to demonstrate where things go wrong, to 'throw a spanner in the works' and prompt a question from the customer.

- *Challenge*: The customer's question – how can you address the context better, overcoming this new complexity? The question can be posed rhetorically and therefore planned in order to lead the conversation towards a new idea, theme, or solution.

- **_Core message_**: The customer proposition, the big idea that you would like to introduce to the customer, establishing the theme that you'd like to discuss in more detail with the customer or the solution you'd like to propose.

The core message would typically incorporate the proposition that you want to deliver – the big idea that you want to stick in your audience's mind. This establishes a new context for dialogue and from which to form a solution that is more relevant to the customer and more profitable to the business.

The narrative might then go on to explain 'why' the conclusion is appropriate, or 'how' it can be achieved in a sub-structure of messages, potentially replicating the narrative in a series of more specific ways to support the argument, or more detailed description as to how it will be achieved.

The structure can be applied to anything from a script for a TV commercial to the copy for the brochure or the slides to support a sales pitch. It might run to many pages, but it should also be possible to capture the essential narrative on one page.

At the same time, we want to find a narrative that is emotionally engaging and memorable.

Nike's Phil Knight once explained his passion for sporting icons' endorsement by arguing 'You can't explain much in 60 seconds, but when you show Michael Jordan, you don't have to. It's that simple'. Some words, symbols or icons can capture a thousand words, and be far more memorable.

Richard Dawkins coined the phrase 'meme' to describe 'a unit of cultural evolution analogous to the gene', arguing that replication and mutation happens within our culture – in the language we use, symbols we use and behaviours we adopt – in a similar way to way to genetic evolution. He considers memes as the units of information that reside in the brain and we see memetic structures in everything from catchy pop songs to new fashion designs.

Memes help turn brands and propositions into stories, symbols and slogans. They catch people's attention, stick in their minds and quickly spread virally, by observation or experience, word of mouth, email, or text. In order to reach out to target audiences, leverage the power of virtual or physical networks, and be there in people's minds at the point of purchase, value propositions and communications needs to embrace memetics.

A meme should be catchy, memorable, easy to say and recall. It should imply a key benefit, something to describe it by. It should be different, original and easy to distinguish, with emotional impact, imparting positive feelings. It might have shape, perhaps in terms of rhythm or rhyme. Above all, memes should be simple, short and easy to understand, and can therefore spread easily.

Memes stick in your mind and can be quickly accessed. They are constructs of memory that are more memorable, recognizable and contagious:

- Slogans, such as Nike's 'Just do it'.

- Colours, such as the *Financial Times*' pink paper.

- Music, such as Intel's five-note jingle or the 'Nokia tune' as played by every Nokia phone.

- Designs, such as Apple's translucent white computers.

- Numbers, as illustrated by Peugeot's trademarked central '0'.

- Smells, such as that bottled by Singapore Airlines.

- Typography, such as the script of Coca-Cola.

Insight 23: JIMMY CHOO

'It doesn't matter what you are wearing – if you have good shoes and a good bag, you'll look right' says Tamara Mellon, founder of Jimmy Choo.

This philosophy runs through the elegant, beautiful, sexy and adventurous ranges of shoes and accessories that are luxurious and practical for all occasions, whilst also creating a look that is instantly recognized as 'Jimmy Choo'. Exclusiveness is assured through limited collections, carefully managed distribution and expensive prices.

Jimmy Choo is Malaysian, born in Penang. He grew up in London, where he made his first shoe when he was only 11 years old. He learnt his trade at Cordwainer's Technical College, now part of the London College of Fashion, supporting his education with part-time work as a cleaner in a shoe factory. On graduating in 1983, he set up a workshop in an old hospital in Hackney, East London. He soon became noticed for his distinctive styles and craftsmanship, and was featured across eight pages of *Vogue* magazine in 1988.

Tamara Mellon, meanwhile, had grown up in a wealthy and fashion-conscious world, her mother a Chanel model and father an entrepreneur. Following schooling in Beverly Hills and Switzerland, she returned to London in 1990 to become accessories editor of British *Vogue*. Looking back through recent editions, her eye was quickly captured by the Choo feature. She became excited by the potential of the luxury accessories market, which was dominated by the larger fashion houses rather than by dedicated accessories brands. She felt there was a lack of attention on accessories, with limited styles and variety.

In 1996, Choo and Mellon got together to form a ready-to-wear shoe company. They brought together investors, suppliers and manufacturers; with Mellon at the helm and Choo's designs, they opened their first boutique in Motcomb Street, London in 1997.

There was clearly a market for their shoes and they quickly climbed to the top of London's rich and fashionable women's shopping list. Next they took their concept to LA. Oscar nominees just had to be seen on the red carpet in a pair of Jimmy Choos; singer Beyoncé went further, singing about her shoes in a global hit.

They continued to build their reputation and range, bringing in Choo's apprentice Sandra Choi as creative director, and together they travelled the world looking for new inspirations for new collections. Inspired by the ancient, intricate designs of Italian wedding dresses, the intricacy of Belgian lace, the art of Pablo Picasso and the architecture of Jeff Koons, they continued to produce the most eye-catching, desirable shoes.

The luxury brand has continued to prosper under the leadership of Mellon, although Choo himself sold his 50% stake in the business for £10 million in 2001. He continues to work on his Jimmy Choo Couture line under licence and has also set up a shoemaking institute in Malaysia.

Mellon recognized that for the business to grow, she needed to create a global chain of stores. This required investment. The business has since featured a succession of investment partners, although Mellon still retains a small share. In 2001, Equinox provided the capital to open 26 new stores around the world, and extend the range into handbags and other small accessories. In 2004, Lion Capital acquired the majority shareholding, valuing the business at £101 million. When TowerBrook Capital succeeded them in 2007, the valuation rose to £185 million.

The company, still under the creative direction of Mellon and Choi, now has 60 branded stores in the world's leading cities, as well as many other franchised locations. The shoes and accessories are still sexy and desired, at the cutting edge of fashion, and ensuring that whatever you wear, 'if you have good shoes and a good bag, you'll look right'.

Customer solutions

Together we can do so much more and so much better.

In the past, you made the products and put them on the shelves, then I came along and decided whether to buy them or not. Today I want to be much more involved. Because I typically know what I want better than you, I want it designed exactly to my requirements, and it's more fun to be involved. Try buying running shoes from Nike ID, a computer from Dell, or jeans from Zafa. I design them, you make them, I buy them and they're perfect. Why can't everything be so good?

More than just the product – shoes in the colours I love, a computer to my personal specification – I'm searching for a bigger solution. This might mean bringing together a number of products – shoes and clothing in my favourite colours, software to do my specific job. Some of this you can provide, others from different places and maybe some expert advice or service to help get the most of them. These are solutions. They solve problems. And that is worth much more to me than products.

5.1 CUSTOMER COLLABORATION

Companies sell things: what they think people want or what they have always made, standard and anonymous.

The focus is on the sale. In most cases, the company cares little what the customer does with the product. They just hope never to see it again.

How can you help customers to do, use, apply and achieve what they want?

Creating solutions from the 'outside in' is about focusing on customer goals rather than bundling products together. Customers want to be part of the solution – they understand their problems and can often describe their desired solutions in some detail. Most typically they lack the skills, materials, resources or time to do it themselves. That's why they turn to you.

Their role could be incredibly useful. Rather than seeing customers as an inconvenience during the design or production process, consider how they could add value by participating in the creative process of problem-solving, selecting the best options for development, testing ideas at each different stage to save time and improve quality, adding their own experiences in how the product is used or the service received.

Not only is this engaging for the customer – 'this is the product that I designed' – but also for other customers too. Of course, when Boeing told the world that its awesome new Dreamliner aircraft was designed by the customer, we hoped they were referring to the interiors rather than the aeronautics. Whilst you can imagine customers usefully describing new designs for interior decor, better seats or preferred food and drink, they might also be able to give insight into cabin pressure noise and air pressure, or more generally their future travel patterns.

Customer co-creation has four important phases:

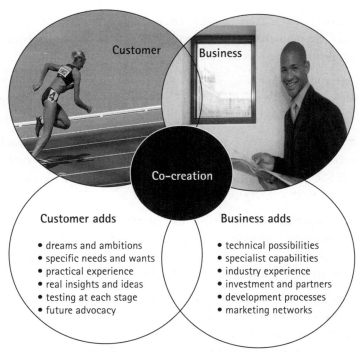

CUSTOMER CO-CREATION: WORKING WITH CUSTOMERS

- **Co-defining**: Inviting and encouraging customers to participate in the design and development of their products and services, either as part of an innovation programme or a more everyday aspect of their purchase.

- **Co-designing**: Understanding the priorities and preferences of the customer, giving them simple language or tools for expressing what matters most and listening to the more subtle aspects of their desires, which could however make a big difference emotionally.

- *Co-developing*: Enabling them to make choices, helping them to understand trade-offs and assemble the appropriate solution in terms of product features, service levels, payment terms, delivery times, support options and much more.

- *Co-delivering*: Installing and applying the solution when 'where' and 'how' is most appropriate. Helping to get the maximum benefits out of the solution, for example through integration with other activities, training and support.

Whether you are co-creating a new car (a BMW car is said to typically offer more than 12000 combinations of customer options) or a birthday cake (the most popular customized item of food at Marks & Spencer), the customer will be more engaged, more willing to pay a small premium and definitely more likely to tell their friends.

Consider the world of professional services – a management consulting firm, for example. Such companies have knowledge and expertise to sell, but it is only valuable when it is relevant to the customer. Therefore the whole way of working, of consulting, is in collaboration with the customer, bringing together the specialist knowledge of both sides.

Management consultants are essentially problem-solvers – they don't come with a specific solution, but work with customers to shape the right solution. They use a series of collaborative steps in order to engage a customer, understand their issues, solve their problem and make it happen so that the customer achieves the results they seek. This process has seven steps:

- *Identify* the key issues, objectives, challenges and opportunities.

- *Analyse* the current situation, identifying areas for improvement.

- *Explore* the possible options, creatively stretching and connecting them.

- *Design* the right solution for the customer and define it in detail.

- *Agree* the proposed actions, the financial case and implementation plan.

- **_Implement_** the agreed solution, working collaboratively with customer.

- **_Review_** at regular intervals to evaluate success and further improve it.

The first collaborative step would be to understand the problem, identifying all the issues and their likely causes and possible impact. Although it might seem like a problem of staff motivation in the customer service function, the real issue might lie in the low quality of after-sales support and subsequent complaints back to customer service people. The process helps the customer and consultant to get a feel for the scale and importance of the project in terms of its implications on customers and commercially, and together to shape a sensible approach.

This usually happens pre-sale: it is free advice for the customer and an investment for the consultant. However, the collaboration, by having access to the internal information and people, helps the consultant to scope out a potential solution that might be much more significant that at first sight and to access internal commercial data from which they can estimate a financial value at risk, and to be gained if successful. This can then lead to a much more appropriate customer solution, as well as a bigger and more profitable consulting project.

Insight 24: HEINZ TOMATO KETCHUP

One hundred and twenty-six grams of ripe, fresh tomatoes go into every 100g of the world's favourite tomato ketchup. In fact, enough tomatoes to fill an Olympic-size swimming pool are used every day by Heinz in making the famous red sauce.

Henry Heinz launched the iconic glass-bottled ketchup seven years after founding his company, describing it as a tasty convenience food and 'a blessed relief for mother and other women in the household'. It was certainly a lot quicker and less messy than making ketchup at home, and made any meal appealing to children.

Of course, the ketchup is healthy as well as convenient, made without artificial colours, flavours, preservatives or GM ingredients. In recent health-conscious times, Heinz has made much of tomatoes as a source of the antioxidant lycopene.

After a century of ketchup, Heinz dared to tinker with the product – not the recipe, but the packaging. It introduced a more convenient plastic bottle that was lighter and easier to squeeze. By 2003, 80% of the bottles were plastic, whilst the glass bottle was retained for traditionalists. The squeezable bottle was a hit, but then Heinz started to innovate too far. Seeking to entertain the kids who loved it, it tried launching ketchup in multiple colours, easy to squeeze on your food as multicoloured ketchup art. Although certainly distinctive, it was seen as a novelty, and started to make people question the natural ingredients of the product.

Heinz wanted to know what to do. In its biggest ever research project, it used a database of customers built up through competitions and customer feedback to ask 'What makes you mad, sad and glad about Heinz Tomato Ketchup?'

The answers were clear and consistent, saying that the traditional ketchup recipe was perfect but more work was required on the packaging. 'The ketchup sometimes makes a mess around the cap' said one. 'You have to turn the bottle upside down when they're nearly empty' revealed another. 'It is difficult and takes time to get the last of the ketchup out of the bottle.'

The innovation, obvious after listening to customers, was to retain the plastic bottle but to turn it upside down. A broad cap created a stable base for the upside-down bottle and the sauce was always packed near the cap, ready to be squeezed out. Turning the bottle on its head resulted in around 60% cannibalization of existing bottle volumes, but that also meant that it was attracting significant numbers of new customers to Heinz.

The 'top-down' plastic bottle retained all the iconic values of the traditional ketchup but was now even more convenient and fun for customers.

5.2   CUSTOMER INNOVATION

Innovation lies at the heart of every customer interaction.

Innovation is problem-solving, whether applying a standard problem to a customer's issue in some innovative way or bringing a number of products together to form an innovative solution. Serving the customer in a slightly different way or in different place is service innovation, as are changing the pricing structure or designing a new product or service together uniquely for that one customer.

These are all forms of customer innovation.

And if we define 'innovation' as the creative development and commercial implementation of ideas, then they are as worthy examples of innovation as the Apple iPod, the Dyson bagless vacuum cleaner, or the Virgin Galactic spaceship.

In fact most of the significant innovations we see today have their origins in small-scale problem solving with customers that was then taken, adapted, improved and scaled up into new products or services for everyone.

Consider the Nike ID customized shoes business, which occupies an entire floor of Niketown in New York City and London. Not only is it attractive to the individual who wants a unique pair of Nike Free 5.0 shoes in lime green, raspberry and tangerine orange with their name on the back – designed by them from an extensive palette, all for a 30% price premium, and delivered from factory to their home a few days later – but it is also the best source of new insights and innovation for Nike. By tracking these premium customizations, Nike is able to spot trends in real time and fast track the most popular emerging designs into stores around the world within weeks.

Whilst it is natural to think of products, customer innovation is even more common with the non-product aspects of a proposition or experience – sales materials, marketing activities, retail environment, opening hours, specialist advice, complementary products, payment terms, service style, installation process, customer education, delivery times, packaging formats, ongoing support, returns policy, complaint handling, loyalty incentives and a relationship programme.

However, employees need the flexibility and desire to do things differently for customers, spend a few seconds extra listening to the real needs, be aware of what and how they can make things better for each customer, and be able and allowed to do it.

They also need to learn from these many customer innovations, which act as millions of small-scale experiments and prototyping for the future of the business. In small companies it is easier to track these small innovations – they come naturally and become part of a more flexible experience. In larger companies, there might need to be more structured learning so that it feeds into an overall innovation strategy.

The customer innovation process – whether it happens at an individual level or a large scale – is identical to any other innovation process other than it is collaborative with customers at every point. Indeed, you might argue that any innovation should happen this way, even with the most complex new technologies.

The starting point is to be clear on the customer issue to be addressed, engaging the customer in the importance of this and the benefits that could be attained by doing so. In a large-scale innovation project, this should be supported by immersion into the issue – what research already exists, talking to more customers about their needs and wants, frustrations and aspirations, and more broadly about how they live or work. It might also involve talking to companies in other markets who have addressed and overcome similar issues.

Innovation is then an 'opening up' and 'closing' down process.

1   *Discovery*: Creativity enables us to stretch our domain of thinking, consider what's possible (even if it doesn't yet seem practical or profitable) and generate many diverse ideas. Using customer insight or even through joint workshops with customers, we generate a

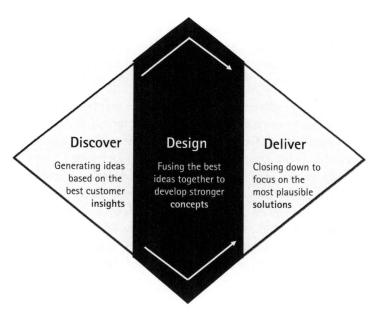

Discover

Generating ideas
based on the
best customer
insights

Design

Fusing the best
ideas together to
develop stronger
concepts

Deliver

Closing down to
focus on the
most plausible
solutions

CUSTOMER INNOVATION: DEVELOPING SOLUTIONS TOGETHER

diverse range of possibilities – many different ways of solving the problem, including the obvious and outrageous – to combine and select the best ideas. Imagine how Richard Branson would solve the problem, or if you were on a desert island with only natural resources, or look to extreme users such as NASA and how they would do it. Anything is possible – don't judge or filter at this stage. You should use a wide range of creative techniques, not just limited by the inadequacies of linear 'brainstorming'!

2   ***Design***: Clustering, connecting and combining different ideas drives the formation of distinctive new concepts – still a creative approach. Combining ideas that might previously have seemed inconsistent, unconventional or unrealistic is how we start to drive more significant solutions. Customers might start to volunteer more significant solutions that

address other issues at the same time. Explore how you could use existing products and services, capabilities and partners in new ways to help deliver these solutions. Still don't judge or filter them. Shape the strongest concepts, perhaps 8–12 of them, giving them names and bringing them to life through illustrations or models.

3   ***Development***: The concepts are then filtered to ensure that they are strategically, practically and commercially sound both in terms of solving the customer's problems and being commercially viable. Maybe this would include the customer selecting the best options so that they understand that they may need to pay significantly more for the best solutions. For larger-scale innovations it would also require considering strategic fit, competitive differentiation, development and operating costs, time to market and risks involved. The solution must then be implemented in order to address the customer issue. Further shaping might be required at this time to ensure integration with the customer's other activities so that they can use it easily, perhaps by transferring specialist skills or knowledge and then ensuring that they begin to realize the full benefits as a result.

When British Airways sought to think how it could regain a competitive advantage in its premium cabins – where the seats of each competitor just seemed to get incrementally bigger, and the meal services ever more extravagant – it brought 100 of its customers together for a 'big talk'. They met for a series of weekend workshops, working together with the top 100 managers, to explore their frustrations and aspirations, ideas and dreams for air travel. They were then consulted regularly through the development process, acting as the evaluation filters and enhancers at every stage of the innovation process.

The managers added their own experiences as managers and travellers, and learnt directly from customers. This is not only useful in terms of capturing new ideas but also in emotionally engaging sponsors rather than waiting to persuade them through easily manipulated business cases. Using a carefully facilitated process, customers and managers designed a better customer experience.

The idea of a 'fast track' for premium customers through security and immigration came from the express check-out in a supermarket. The idea of dining in the lounge before boarding came from a search for creative ways to maximize the in-flight sleeping time. The concept of flat beds came from a customer who was a passionate yachtsman and suggested that the airline talked to yacht designers rather than its conventional seat manufacturers. The inspiration for hot chocolate and cookies before going to sleep in first class came from customers describing their perfect night's sleep in their own home.

Innovation is a creative and commercial activity, only successful when they deliver significantly better results for both the customer and the business.

The launch of a significant customer innovation is often just the beginning of a successful development. The 'early adopters' of a new solution are invariably the most challenging to satisfy, and can often provide lessons for improvement but may require quite different solutions to the mainstream. The solutions may require flexibility and adaptation for each customer, therefore requiring specific development. More strategically, markets must be developed to cope with the new ways of working – in their knowledge and capabilities, distribution and support structures, with related products and service – if the innovation is to be successful.

Innovation should live in the organization as a fundamental practice and a constant source of energy and opportunity for finding better, more engaging and more energizing ways of working with customers.

Insight 25: SMART USA

The Smart car emerged out of unlikely collaboration in the early 1990s between watchmaker Swatch and car designer Mercedes Benz.

Nicolas Hayek, the Swiss Swatch inventor, had an idea for an urban car that he set about designing and then approached the Stuttgart-based car company for help with its engineering. The resulting 'Smart Fortwo' was unveiled at the 1997 Frankfurt Motor Show to excited reviews. It was small, cute, strong and efficient. You could park it sideways in the street and fit three of them in front of your house. It was like no other.

The 'Smart' went into full production the following year and was an international hit. Its removable plastic scratch-proof panels were easy to switch following an accident, or if you wanted to change colour. It used exclusive partnerships in each country to give it exclusive and dedicated distribution, and kept independent from the Mercedes brand. Around 900,000 customers in 36 countries loved Hayek's 'micro car' and it became a feature in the cities of Europe.

In 2008, the Smart was ready to enter the increasingly environmentally conscious US market. In fact, the only place you could find one prior to that was in New York's Museum of Modern Art.

However, first it needed some alteration to meet US standards and the needs of its slightly larger customers. Still smaller than its competitor, the Mini Cooper, the car was constructed with the highest standards of safety (a wrap-around steel frame creates a protected cocoon) and improved fuel consumption (33 mpg in cities, 41 mpg on the open road). Inside it didn't seem small with the help of staggered seating, compact dashboard, large windscreen and transparent roof.

Retailing at less than $12,000, customers could also upgrade to a panorama-roofed Passion Coupé or a fully convertible Passion Cabriolet. Smart USA was established as an exclusive dealership network, actually a franchised partnership with the large Penske Automotive Group. Customers could go to any Smart location and test drive or simply marvel at the little car. However, to buy one they needed to go online and make a $99 deposit. This reservation concept was innovative and risky; however, it was part of a strategy to maximize viral marketing and desirability. More than 30,000 customers paid the deposit in the first year and the car already has a waiting list stretching six to nine months. In fact, the demand is so popular that Smart cars have been a big hit on eBay, selling at up to 50% more than the normal retail price.

5.3 CUSTOMER SOLUTIONS

Customer solutions are like Lego.

The Danish 'toy of the century' comes in packs of many pieces, including different colours and sizes, square and rectangular, doors and windows, flower pots and flags – sometimes even a motorized engine or a software programme.

Similarly, business comes in packs of many products and services or advice and customization. Just as you can build an infinite number of Lego models – from cars and houses to flowers and monsters – you can create an infinite number of customer solutions.

The solutions take on a molecular-like structure.

At their core is a number of the most common items, just like carbon atoms, but from this an infinite variety of different atoms are attached in different ways. The molecules are far more distinctive than simple atoms, difficult to imitate by competitors and much more valuable to customers. The molecules might be unique – a one-off for a customer – or replicated many times because they prove appropriate for a whole workforce or all customers with similar characteristics.

The molecules might be entirely home-grown in that they are made of all the company's own products and services. Or they might include components provided by a wide range of different suppliers, complementary brands and even the customer's own resources. The more diversely sourced the molecule, particularly through exclusive networks of partners, the more difficult it is to copy and the more valuable it is to the customer.

If they love it, there will be only one place to come back to for more.

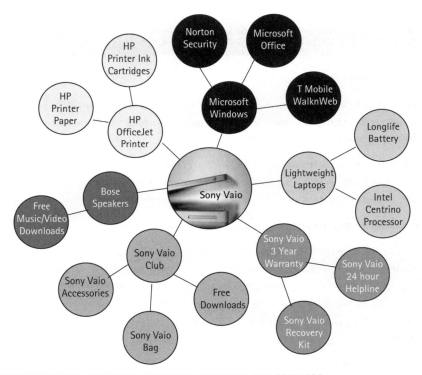

CUSTOMER SOLUTIONS: BRINGING TOGETHER PRODUCTS AND SERVICES

Molecular solutions can be named and packaged in the same way as products and services, although by definition they represent a bigger concept, a bigger idea that creates a total experience for the customer, enabling them to work better and achieve more.

They can be scaled up into mass production if appropriate or they might simply form an ongoing template from which further customized molecules are then evolved. Over time, the business develops a great many customer solutions in this form. If effectively codified and managed, these can then make future customized solutions fast and efficient.

Insight 26: BOEING 787 DREAMLINER

Aircraft manufacturing is essentially a two-horse race between the US giant Boeing and Europe's Airbus. Boeing had been the pioneer for decades, delivering the first aircraft with a pressurized cabin (the 307), the first commercial jet (the 707), the biggest selling jet in history (the 737) and the aircraft that revolutionized non-stop global travel (the 747). However, in recent years it had lost its momentum.

That was until July 2007, when Boeing opened the gigantic doors of its Washington assembly plant to reveal its most important and impressive jet of all – the 787 Dreamliner.

It is one of the most adaptable, quietest, fuel-efficient planes in history. Half of the fuselage is built of lightweight material, helping to improve fuel consumption by 20%, whilst it is 60% quieter than similar planes and with lower carbon emissions. It is by no means perfect, but in an environmentally sensitive world it is better than anything else.

The technical innovation continues inside, where higher cabin pressure and humidity seek to imitate life on the ground. Lighting adjusts with shifting time zones, seeking to reduce the headaches, aching limbs and dry-mouth feelings of long-haul travel. There is more legroom and larger overhead bins, self-dimming windows, and a wireless Internet and entertainment system. And in some versions, there are personal cabins, stand-up bars and meeting spaces, and an onboard gym. In the cockpit there is a new in-flight self-diagnostic maintenance system and many other technical improvements to improve safety and reduce delays on departure.

Uniquely, Boeing has achieved all of this in partnership with suppliers, airlines and passengers. Japan's Mitsubishi created the wings, whilst Italy's Alenia Aeronautica produced the rear fuselage and the horizontal stabilizer (the small wing on the plane's tail). Internally, Boeing struggled with the perceived loss of control, but this was counterbalanced with joint consulting teams and shared best practices. The collaborative approach has paid off, with development time reduced by about a year. The approach has kept costs down both for Boeing, which will spend an estimated $6–8 billion on the plane, and its airline customers, who will pay about $130 million per aircraft.

Other airlines were fully involved in the design and development at every stage, working individually with Boeing and collaborating in cross-industry forums. With sufficient opportunity to influence the future aircraft, or at least the opportunity to build in flexibility for future customization that will enable airlines to create their own points of difference, such co-creation has evolved naturally into sales.

Potential passengers from around the world could contribute to and review the progress of development through regular surveys, shared technical specifications, discussion forums, blogs and videos on the website. They even named the plane, with 'Dreamliner' emerging from some 500,000 votes cast in more than 160 countries. The collaboration is ongoing and more than 120,000 people have now joined Boeing's Web-based World Design Team.

By the beginning of 2008, 55 airlines had ordered more than 800 Dreamliners – the biggest and fastest-selling passenger aircraft in history, co-created with customers.

Customer connections

> *The pile of unsolicited mail on my doormat, the telesales call when I'm sitting down to my dinner, the deluge of spam clogging up my inbox ... there is no shortage of companies trying to sell me stuff. But I just don't want it! And the more you mail me, call me or spam me, the more I don't want it. Can't you get it, that I'm not just going to buy something because you decide to have a marketing campaign about what you want to sell and at the time of your choosing?*
>
> *You seem to do everything for your benefit, not mine.*
>
> *I have to buy your products and services from places that are convenient for you rather than me. Why should I get in my car and go to you when you could come to me? And why aren't you open at a time that suits me rather than when I'm doing other things? Then when I call you with a problem, I get passed from one person to the next person, giving them my same details time and time again. Worst of all is when you give me different answers to the same question. Do you really want to serve me? Are you really on my side?*

customer
genius

6.1   CUSTOMER COMMUNICATION

Customers want to do business when, how and where they want.

Yet companies still choose to push things at them on their terms. We still think of 'campaigns' in order to get 'our' message 'across' – push, push, push. Customers are deafened by marketing messages, estimated at around 1500 messages per day – from cereal boxes to coffee cups, television and newspapers, billboards and shop windows, T-shirts and sandwich boards, inflatable balloons and pop-up shops – only around 300 of which our brains are actually able to cope with, even subconsciously.

One advertisement looks like another. Sometimes they are great to watch, but even with those we rarely remember what brand they actually seek to promote. One message sounds like another – words that float straight over your head with ever more abstract and meaningless taglines.

The more messages we receive, the less we are likely to take in. Today's trusted brands communicate from the 'outside in', on customers' terms:

- Pull not push.

- Stories not slogans.

- Advocacy not awareness.

- Permission not interruption.

- Relationships not transactions.

- Conversations not campaigns.

Customers have too little time, energy or trust for traditional forms of communication. Once, TV advertising relied upon us all switching onto the same channel, the same programme, at the same time. It assumed that we were predictable in our reading behaviours, the music we liked, the events we attended, the people we respected and the brands we trusted.

We know that this is no longer true – television has fragmented into hundreds of digital channels, whilst baby boomers love rock music and young people reject anything mainstream.

We also value our privacy much more, no longer tolerating unsolicited mail or phone calls, no longer prepared to give unknown companies time. We are sceptical about advertising claims and sales techniques, and there are few brands that we actually trust. We reject interruptive communication – commercial breaks or sponsor messages that interrupt our entertainment.

About the only people we do trust are people like us – our friends and colleagues, other people with similar interests or ambitions.

In searching for a hotel, we don't read what the hotels or their agents say about themselves – we go to TripAdvisor to read what people who have stayed there say about the hotel, how they ranked it compared with others and where to go for the best deal. If we are considering buying a book, we read the reviews on Amazon.

Not only this, but we don't select the hotel or book from the bottom up. We select a genre – business hotels in Paris, for instance, or books about scuba diving – and then search the most popularly ranked examples for more detail. Customer opinion therefore shapes our searches and selections – the hotel or publishing house has very little influence in traditional ways.

The notion of 'campaigns' still dominates the marketing department. Advertising as one of many possible media for conveying messages still dominates the campaign, and marketers over-rely on their agencies far more than financers do on accountants or company secretaries on lawyers.

Campaigns don't work because they expect customers to conform to their terms – 'You will watch this ad, at this time, on this channel and you will consider buying this car' – even if you aren't looking for a new car. Advertising still dominates the media mix because we feel good about big messages with emotive visuals: our bosses expect it, it's great fun to make and a

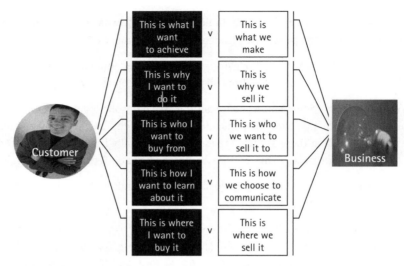

CUSTOMERS IN CONTROL: WHAT, WHEN AND HOW I WANT

tangible outcome line for the CV, and it is still seen as a brave step to take. Agencies are too often used as the surrogate brains for marketers who, once they've written their short brief (the shorter the better to maximize creative interpretation, goes the argument), surrender the consequences to agency planners and creatives.

We need to think, work and communicate in very different ways: emails and text messages, blogs and video logs, customer rankings and reviews. Communication is driven by the experience of one customer and their recommendation to others.

A business can still influence this, even if it's not possible to control: facilitating peer-to-peer interactions and encouraging word-of-mouth recommendations through forums and events, online structures and virtual communities. Some of what people say will be good, some of it will be bad; if we want it to be trusted and to spread, we have to live with both.

Affinity marketing becomes crucial in connecting our brand with specific issues, ideas or communities. This might be about working in partnership with a particular membership organization to be more relevant to certain people, or linking up with a charity to align us with particular issues and concerns.

Whilst much advertising expenditure migrates online, PR and sponsorship also become more important in creating the context in which people see our brand, be it in terms of the values and lifestyles by linking to the latest fashions, celebrities or music, or the alternatives we want them to position our products alongside (as with Audi seeking to be in the BMW league rather than a peer of Ford).

Red Bull, the energy drink company from Austria whose main product was derived from an exotic Thai tonic supposedly containing ground bulls' testicles, focuses on communication that is based on viral impact within target communities:

- 'Student brand managers' are volunteer students who act as brand ambassadors, for example organizing parties and other events in return for free cases of Red Bull. They spread positive word-of-mouth quickly and cheaply within their target communities. Students clamour to be the cool Red Bull guy on campus, credibility within the most cynical of audiences.

- Red Bull drives a fleet of shiny silver trucks and jeeps, with huge scaled-up versions of the distinctive red and blue Red Bull attached to the back. The drivers jump out at regular points to distribute free drinks. These educators tangibly add to the brand's hip image and the sampling sprees add further word-of-mouth.

- Extreme sponsorships are another reason to talk about the brand, adding to its 'liquid adrenalin' image. Sports such as BMXing, hang-gliding, skateboarding and cliff-diving are typical sponsored sports. The Red Bull Air Race is a phenomenal exhibition of aircraft acrobatics in spectacular venues and the Red Bull Music Academy promotes everything from podium dancing to turntable skills.

'AIDA' (awareness, interest, desire, action) was often used to describe the phases of communication that led to a sale. Today, these initial phases are largely in the hands of customers. It is only towards the final stage that the customer may seek to talk to the company – on their terms, when they want, using the medium they prefer.

Yet too many companies still measure their communication effectiveness based on the 'weight' of their advertising – the budget, minutes of airtime and number of prompted recalls. In today's world, a $10 million ad campaign that lacks a distinctive proposition and relies upon unutilized channels gets lost in the morass.

If spread across the right customer network, a passionate recommendation (maybe influenced by a real experience) can be far more effective – and not only that, it's free.

When Volkswagen's US business reached a low point in the early 1990s, it turned to customers rather than its German head office for help.

Sales had dropped below 50,000 per annum – less than 10% of the brand's scale in the late 1960s when models such as the Beetle and the camper van captured the hippy spirit of the times. Product and service quality had plummeted, there was little innovation, and advertising lines such as 'German engineering the Volkswagen way' and 'Fahrvergnugen' were unloved or incomprehensible to the American audience. *Car & Driver* magazine called the brand 'more conservative than Ronald Reagan'.

Volkswagen decided to rethink its entire brand and marketing strategy in the USA. Its starting point would not be the product, corporate values or adapting German successes, but a better understanding of its local audience. Volkswagen worked with customers and dealers to redefine its target customers – 'fun-loving, 21- to 45-year-old drivers who like to drive a little faster, a little longer, and enjoy driving a little more than other car owners'.

This better definition of the local, target audience led to a new brand positioning for the market. Ad agency Arnold Communications developed the line 'On the road of life, there are passengers and drivers. Drivers Wanted'. Most famously the new brand positioning was captured by its 1997 'Sunday afternoon' television ad. It features two young, chilled-out guys 'just driving around' in a VW Golf listening to The Police singing 'Do Do Do, Da Da Da' on the radio. It wasn't about speed or comfort, like most other car ads – it was about people, an alternative mindset and the love of driving.

'Drivers Wanted' has proved to be an enduring platform for Volkswagen USA in rebuilding customer preference and loyalty, introducing many new models such as the New Beetle and its SUV, and revitalizing older ones. By 2002, the brand's market share had quadrupled and sales had grown rapidly to 350,000 per annum. The US market remains key to Volkswagen, where the brand continues to be about freedom, youth and driving.

Insight 27: WUMART, CHINA

It is sometimes called a Chinese version of Wal-Mart, but it is threatening to become much larger, more profitable and much more loved by its surrounding population than the US retail giant.

With the rush of western retailers now entering China, it is easy to forget that China is rapidly developing a strong local challenge. Chinese retailers such as GOME and Orient Home have made life difficult for the likes of Best Buy and B&Q, who perhaps thought they could just ride straight in. Similarly, in the grocery sector, the likes of Tesco and Carrefour have come up against Wumart.

> 'Wumart is a dream we share, a dream of establishing an everlasting retail chain that Chinese people love patronizing and that mingles with their daily lives. We are committed to cater for, with ever-improving standard, quality product and unconditional service. Serving the People, for invention of benefit to all mankind, we wish to sow the seed of our pursuit and our ideal. Our team is dedicated, wholeheartedly, to strive for

exemplifying at its best what is unique about retail chain business and its success in China.'

WuMart was founded by Dr. Zhang Wenzhong in 1994. At the time, chains had only 0.5% of retail sales in the Chinese market, which preferred local businesses or unbranded stores. It grew rapidly from a local suburban store to become China's largest supermarket chain. It now has more than 600 stores and in 2008 generated $7.9 billion revenue and $503 million profit. It plans to increase space by around 20% each year.

It has done this by focusing on one of China's wealthiest regions – Beijing, Tianjin and Hangzhou in Zhejian province and Yinchian in the Ningxia Hui region – using low-cost expansion strategies including franchising and restructuring state-owned businesses. It has also embraced technologies such as scanners and barcodes before most of its competitors, and operating systems that centralize procurement, logistics and inventory control.

Wumart's chairman Wu Jiangzhong believes that his success is due to 'a regional focus [that] has helped us to concentrate our efforts, and for people to know us. It has also given us stronger bargaining power over suppliers. The multi-format strategy has also been important. With a customer-oriented merchandise mix, effective promotions and better customer service than previously seen, Wumart has been able to achieve superior brand recognition in Beijing and across China'.

He sees a rapid change in the buying patterns and behaviours of Chinese shoppers:

'A rapidly rising middle class means that China is one of the largest and fastest-growing domestic markets in luxury goods. People are becoming more concerned about quality and food safety issues. Increasing bank card use is reshaping shopping habits, although cash is still the main form of payment. Chinese customers want to drive to do shopping, they want to buy more but less frequently.'

6.2   CUSTOMER NETWORKS

It is said that everyone on the planet is separated by six other people. This is the power of networks.

YouTube, Facebook, Wikipedia are often described as second-generation websites (or Web 2.0): they enable collaboration and content is largely generated and shared by users.

They represent online communities that some regard as social networks but also form the basis of collaborative production. Millions of people worldwide can participate in this economy like never before: selling antiques through eBay, uploading home-made documentaries to Current TV, remixing their favourite music for iTunes, designing new software, editing school home-work, inventing new cosmetics, finding cures for diseases or sequencing the human genome.

The value of these networks is in the content.

The scale is awesome. In 2007, a staggering seven billion user-generated videos were streamed each month; 120,000 new blogs were created every day, adding to more than 70 million world-wide; in the US, 30% of all Web users accessed YouTube, iTunes and Wikipedia each month. Meanwhile, Google paid $900 million to provide advertising on MySpace, but also got sued $1 billion by Viacom for alleged copyright infringement on its $1.65 billion acquisition, YouTube.

Customers have many different reasons for connecting, their motivations driving the networks they use and the applications most attractive to them. Before embracing networks as part of your communications or relationship programmes, you should consider why and how your target audiences might want to participate collectively:

What kind of networkers?	Why do they use the network?	How do they network?	How many are there?
Creators	Express views Promote themselves Upload and publish	Blogs Websites Videos and podcasts	10%
Collectors	Search for collections Buy and sell Rank preferences	RSS Tags Ratings	10%
Connectors	Profile themselves Connect with others Chat to friends	Social networks Applications Messaging	12%
Commentators	Post comments Contribute to others Rank preferences	Forums Wikis Ratings	20%
Curious	Read content Watch videos Explore websites	Search engines Blogs Videos and podcasts	37%
Non-participants			53%

(Sources: Harvard Business School, Groundswell)

As broadband penetration soars and connection speeds accelerate, people are drawn to the rich and interactive, personalized and on-demand content of 'social' (or network) media.

The impact is not only digital and youthful. In 1995, there were 225 terrestrial channel TV shows across the UK that were watched by audiences of more than 15 million. Now there are none. Viewers have migrated to other channels as their choice has mushroomed from 5 to 500. Similarly, advertising revenues have fallen dramatically as advertisers lose faith with traditional broadcast media and seek out more focused, interactive ways to engage potential customers.

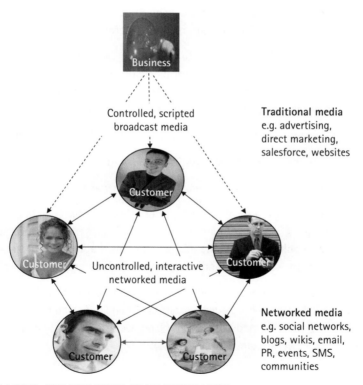

NETWORKED MEDIA: THE NEW RULES OF COMMUNICATION

The difference between traditional and networked media is profound:

- **Traditional media**: Access is controlled by location and time; content is produced, edited and distributed for a fee; the experience is professional and standardized, transactional and predictable. The audience is a passive consumer.

- **Networked media**: Access is open to anyone, anywhere, anytime; content is self-generated and shared freely; the experience is collaborative and multi-format, based on users' interests and relationships. The audience is an active creator.

As a business or brand, you inevitably want to tap into part of these networks – particularly the ones that have the closest profile to your target customers. You'd like to create your own, based around your brand, but customers just wouldn't want this. Brands don't do enough for these people, certainly compared with what they can do for each other.

- You can't own customer networks, but you can influence and support them.

- You can't push messages at them, but you can listen and learn from them.

- You can't control them, but you can encourage them to want you.

Chris Anderson describes the reality of network power in his book *The Long Tail*, where he asks what happens when there is almost unlimited choice – when everything becomes available to everyone and the combined value of the millions of items that only sell in small quantities equals or even exceeds the value of a handful of bestsellers. He argues:

'The future of business does not lie in hits – the high volume end of a traditional demand curve – but in what used to be regarded as misses – the endlessly long tail of that same curve ... Wherever you look, modest sellers, niche products and quirky titles are becoming an immensely powerful cumulative force.'

Look at the music charts, no longer governed by the bestselling albums within the confines of a music store but driven more by the individual and eclectic choices of online downloads. Elvis Presley and The Beatles have both returned to the charts, not because they have a new release but because there are enough people somewhere in the world who still want their music.

The story is the same in every sector: the mainstream, based on volume production that meets the average needs of customers, no longer drives success. Success lies in the margins, niches, eccentrics and old favourites – as long as they're available and that people can find them. Networks, particularly digital networks, make this possible.

Insight 28: ZOPA

Zopa is an online money exchange, enabling people to lend money to and borrow money from others around the world. If you think about it, we only have banks because people did not have the access and networks to achieve this themselves. Technology has changed that.

Zopa is a London-based company, founded in 2005 by the same people who had previously created the Internet bank Egg. With investment from Benchmark Capital and Wellington Partners, it has already succeeded in attracting around 250,000 members and now operates in the UK, US, Italy and Japan. It uses a slightly different model in each market due to financial regulations. The name stands for 'zone of possible agreement', a financial negotiating term identifying the limits within which agreement can be reached between two parties.

The business model was based on extensive research, which identified a customer group known as 'freeformers': people who display different attitudes towards many aspects of life, including money. They have strong interests in how things work and are guided by their own beliefs and judgements rather than following the mainstream.

The process, sometimes called peer-to-peer or social lending, means that the customer can be the lender or borrower, and opt to use a 'market' or 'listing' model:

- In the markets model, the potential borrower is graded by risk from their credit report. Full underwriting checks are also likely at this point, with many applications being rejected. There are two loan periods – 36 months and 60 months. The system then searches for compatible lenders who are willing to offer their money to potential borrowers at the defined risk and period, hence the 'zone'. Offers are matched on a many-to-one basis so that each lender's loan is spread across many borrowers.

- In the listings model, the potential borrower is able to state their reasons for wanting to borrow money and their preferred interest rate. They choose over a broader range of time periods. Lenders are then able to offer funds to the potential borrower in a reverse auction where the lowest interest rate wins. The borrower is then able to accept or reject the loan, but with less stringent underwriting checks.

For 'borrower' customers, the loans are very flexible, allowing flexible monthly payments and early repayment without penalty. For 'lender' customers, the money is committed for the period of the loan but with better returns than from most banking schemes.

Applicants to Zopa tend to have a slightly worse credit rating than average, but the strict checking and awareness that it is a real person's money that they need to pay back have led to very low default rates. The risk of bad debt is taken by the lender, priced into the borrowing rate, and debts are normally sold to a debt-collecting agency from which lenders receive a proportion of any money recovered.

Zopa acts as a facilitator in this process, its fees varying by market. In the UK, it has moved to a fixed fee to borrowers, whilst lenders are charged 0.5% per annum on all money that has been lent deducted from their account.

6.3   CUSTOMER GATEWAYS

Channels have conventionally been about 'pushing' products and services to customers. Direct channels such as your own retail stores, websites, call centres and physical sales teams are used to sell to customers and service their orders. Indirect channels such as third party retailers, aggregator websites and sales agents are used to broaden the reach further, pushing your products to even more customers that you cannot reach or it is inefficient to do so.

Conventional distribution thinking has been about reach and efficiency in order to maximize sales transactions. Channel management is about making these channels work together so that the customer's experience is consistent across them, they all deliver appropriate levels of service and support, information is shared across them, and customers (for example) can buy an item from one channel and return it to another, if required.

It has also been about doing business on terms that are efficient for the business rather than the customer. Located stores that are efficient to operate and supply, and have opening hours to fit the social lives of employees rather than the non-working hours of customers, service styles to improve efficiency such as limiting call times to maximize call volumes and fewer check-outs to reduce the number of staff required.

It has been about 'you come to us' rather than 'we will come to you', about serving customers when and how it suits the business rather than what is best for each customer. This has started to change – out-of-town shopping malls in more convenient locations, 24-hour opening of convenience stores, banking online or by telephone, and ordering a sandwich online and have it delivered to your desk. Customers expect you to do business when, where and how it suits them, not you.

'Customer gateways' are no ordinary distribution channels.

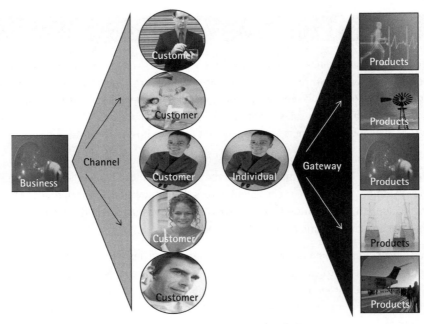

CUSTOMER GATEWAYS: THE FUTURE OF DISTRIBUTION CHANNELS

They are your trusted partner who will always find exactly what you want, your personal assist-ant in the outside world, your corner shop that stocks everything, your best friend who knows you best and your loyal servant who will do everything for you. Conveniently accessible, when and where you want, or even anticipating or reminding you what you need.

They don't have any products, but they do have deep customer insight, understanding your needs, issues, aspirations, nuances and foibles, then going out to find the right ingredients to build the ultimate solution for you. They will work across suppliers rather than being tied to anyone, negotiating the best deals with ingredient suppliers and bringing them together on your terms. In many ways this is Amazon, but with significantly more customization and personal service.

'Gateway' brands are on your side. In fact, you typically pay them a management fee rather than them needing to secure commissions like other channels might, and therefore not necessarily being impartial to find the best solution for you. Their values reflect yours; they are a lifestyle brand.

Their processes start and finish with you the customer. And they are the first port of call when a customer is ready to buy, rather than waiting to be bombarded with irrelevant promotions. They may seem a little like intermediaries, but gateways are the principals: they are the brand the customer forms a relationship with, cares about and trusts.

'Ingredient' brands will be the product and service suppliers to gateways, the vast majority of brands we know of today. Today they try half-heartedly to build relationships with customers, but there just isn't time in our lives for relationships with ketchup, tissue or even electronics brands. The best will be like Intel, which we all know make the best microprocessors; the less good will be like Mitsubushi, who make just as many chips but we don't know or care that they are inside our computers or phones.

Gateway brands will be those of strongest affinity with customers. Whilst their role for many of us is currently occupied by the likes of Tesco and Wal-Mart, these are unlikely to be the gateways of the future. More likely they will be the football clubs who engage passionate supporters, membership brands with a paid-up following or fashion brands that define lifestyles.

Gateway brands will be the ultimate in individualized, interactive communication and distribution. They will be information-rich and have customer service to their core. Their expertise is in problem-solving and relationship-building. They will be the power hubs of the intelligent markets, redefining the power bases, market structures and sources of value.

Insight 29: QUINTESSENTIALLY

Imagine a private members' club with a 24-hour global concierge – it can get anything you want, anywhere, anytime.

Whether you need a private jet now to Beijing, the perfect gift for your mother's birthday, a rare Aston Martin or tickets to see The Police play in Rio, Quintessentially will get them for you or knows somebody who can. Some of the more memorable requests have included finding two white peacocks for a party and arranging for a pair of false eyelashes to be flown by helicopter to the South of France.

Quintessentially is firstly a club for people who believe life is too short to waste time on search-ing around for what they want or compromising with second best. It isn't cheap, with fees ranging from around $1500 to $30,000 or more. Members receive a membership card and a dedicated line, and the club learns about every members' nuances and preferences. Some use the concierge as a shopping portal or for advice on all matters professional and personal; others see it as their personal assistant.

However, this is not about database marketing or customized solutions – it is about individual-ity. For some people it is the antithesis of one-to-one marketing, shielding from the deluge of offers and incentives of eager brands; for others it is a perk of the job, increasingly offered to time-starved executives as part of their remuneration package. Many see it a status symbol, more exclusive and more useful than an American Express Platinum card.

Aaron Simpson and Ben Elliot founded the luxury lifestyle brand in 2000. Today, it employs 800 people in 37 offices around the world and serves many a household name. It aims to be in 80 countries by 2010.

The concierge will arrange anything that's moral and legal. 'We won't lay on young ladies to visit hotels, but we're often asked to get tables at The Ivy at short notice, for instance, and can help because of the relationships that we have built up over the years, both business and personal.' If restaurants have a last-minute cancellation, they are the first people they'll tell. If there are tickets going for a sell-out show, they'll know which members could be interested.

It has also spawned several spin-off businesses:

- **Quintessentially Events**: the Serpentine Summer Party is one of its many hot ticket events, where members get exclusive access alongside stars.

- **Quintessentially Publishing**: including the most enticing coffee-table travel guides to the world's most exclusive spas and hotels.

- **Quintessentially Estates**: a specialist property search service for those who feel they don't have time to deal with the average estate agent.

- **Quintessentially Escape**: with extreme experiences such as private guided tour of the Pyramids and spy training by former MI5 agents.

As students, Simpson and Elliot staged drama festivals using undergraduate actors, persuading Oxbridge colleges to let them use their lawns and then making a beeline for rich and naive American tourists who thought they were getting a once-in-a-lifetime experience.

And the most requested services of members? Birthday gifts, theatre tickets ... and plumbers.

Customer experiences

You work for a great company, don't you? Your vans always look cleaner than others, your buildings always smell a little fresher, you always offer that little extra advice and support, your packaging always looks good and is recyclable too. I love that music you play and your people always seem to smile a little more. There are so many great things about what you do and I haven't even mentioned the product itself.

But there is still much more you could do. From the moment I first realize I need you, to helping me get the most out of the products I buy, I expect the same great experience. The shop is great, the parking is terrible. The cake tastes fantastic but the coffee is average. The product works superbly but if something goes wrong, you haven't a clue. I expect the same greatness from you in everything you do.

I want you to be consistent, reliable and easy. I want you to sort out my problem, not pass me from one person to another. I want you to do business when, where and how I want. In fact, it's not just about satisfying me – or even delighting me, as I think you like to say. Sometimes I want you to surprise me, educate me, entertain me or even thrill me. Give me something to really tell my friends about.

7.1   CUSTOMER JOURNEY

Harley-Davidson's CEO eloquently describes the experience by which he seeks to bring his brand to life:

> 'It's one thing to have people buy your products, it's another for them to tattoo your name on their bodies ... What we sell is the ability for a 43-year-old accountant to dress in black leather, ride through small towns and have people be afraid of him.'

Brands and propositions are delivered through every possible medium that the organization can utilize – from names and logos to leaders and buildings, products and services to advertising and brochures, colours and packaging to uniforms and interiors, culture and behaviours to training and rewards.

People in the organization need to rethink what they do from the 'outside in'.

Jan Carlson, the former CEO of Scandinavian Airlines gave each of his employees a little black book called *Moments of Truth*, where the few words inside spelt out incredibly simply how every interaction is an opportunity to make or break a lifetime relationship with that customer.

However, customer 'experiences' are much more than just consistent delivery across all the different touchpoints – they're about ensuring that the journey (not just the flight, in the airline's case, but from the first moment of need until the mission is accomplished) is connected and coherent, consistent and complete. On top of this it's about bringing it to life, making it distinctive and relevant, and ultimately adding value at every point along the way.

Meaningful experiences are about relevant and distinctive interactions rather than irrelevant and undifferentiated transactions. Instead of customers searching, selecting and buying, they are about helping customers to explore, play and learn.

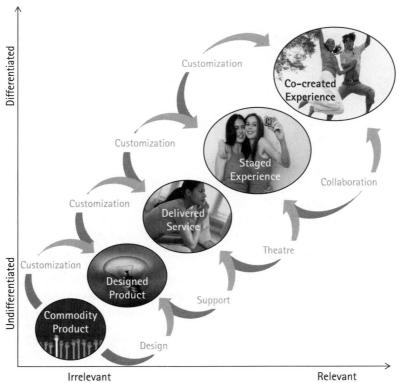

CUSTOMER EXPERIENCES: FROM COMMODITIES TO CO-CREATION

Customer experience design requires the same amount of dedicated investment, process and evaluation as product design or service definition. TGI Friday's, the restaurant chain with the red-and-white-striped waiting staff, for example, applies a 'Three-Ring Service Model' to all its franchises to ensure that there is a consistency of brand experience anywhere in the world. The inner ring defines what is core and must be delivered always, everywhere. The middle

217

ring defines local enhancements depending on the location or customer type. The outer ring describes ways to make the experience personal, spontaneous and memorable for every customer.

A typical air traveller will have around 45 real or perceived interactions with an airline, from the time they decide to travel to the moment they arrive at their destination.

The starting point in designing a great customer experience is to understand what happens now, either by design or default, or because the customer and other partners compensate for what you don't do.

Every customer 'touchpoint' is mapped for different types of customers: in a business-to-business environment this might be for every key account, in mass markets you might start by considering specific types of customer, such as a first-class business traveller or a random selection of types. This doesn't need to involve extensive research; it might be done in collaboration with customers describing the experience – or even by staff thinking through what happens.

You might for example do this in a workshop, writing each different touchpoint as a separate Post-it note and then mapping them out on a large piece of paper – sometimes a linear sequence, sometimes with various diversions and loops. Important things to remember include the following:

- Think as a customer, writing each different stage in the customer language – buy not sell, pay not charge. Include interactions beyond your own influence – what they do, potentially with other companies too.

- Consider the whole customer context, from the initial moment of need through to realization of benefits – don't just focus on the purchase transaction. For example, how does the customer get to your shop? Where do they park?

- Describe each touchpoint separately, considering both tangible and intangible moments – everything from the design of your stores to ease of payment and the aesthetic importance of the packaging back in their home through to how it is disposed.

The customer journey can now be evaluated in more detail – from the customer's perspective. You might use qualitative feedback or more quantitative research to understand how much importance the customer places on each step of their journey, and how good they feel about it.

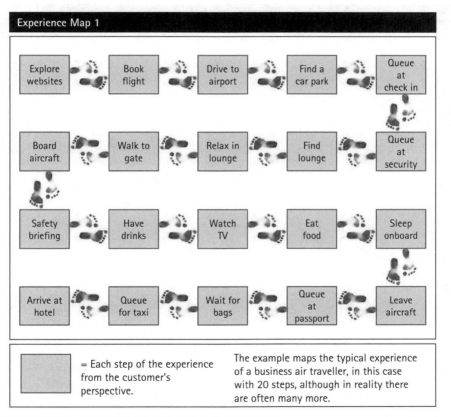

Experience Map 1

☐ = Each step of the experience from the customer's perspective.	The example maps the typical experience of a business air traveller, in this case with 20 steps, although in reality there are often many more.

EXPERIENCE MAP 1: MAPPING THE EXISTING TOUCHPOINTS

219

'Customer heartbeat' is one technique for understanding the customer's emotional roller-coaster through their journey. Which are the moments are pleasure, enjoyment and achievement? Where are the points of anger, frustration and stress?

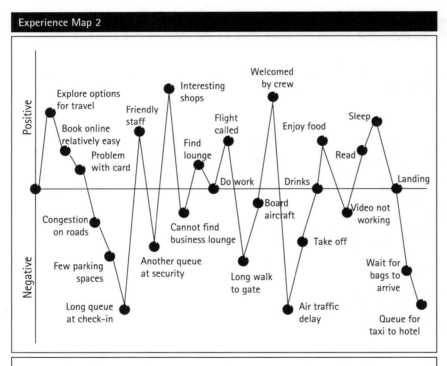

Experience Map 2

● = reflects each of the customer's real or perceived interactions, and their positive or negative emotional response.

The example illustrates a typical emotional 'rollercoaster' for the customer, with some good moments but ending on a low.

EXPERIENCE MAP 2: EVALUATING THE EXISTING TOUCHPOINTS

You might even 'tell the story' of a number of individual customer's experiences by mapping their pulse through each interaction, labelling what happens at each point across what looks a little like the map of their heartbeat. This can be very powerful in communicating internally how different people collectively deliver one experience, where are the good bits and where is improvement needed.

Insight 30: NINTENDO WII

It's high-tech and friendly, Japanese and sociable, and lots of fun.

The Nintendo Wii was launched in late 2006, seeking to reach a broader family audience than rival games consoles such as the Sony PlayStation 3 and the Microsoft Xbox 360. It trades off some of the sophisticated graphics for a much more physical, connected experience with motion-sensitive controllers: a whole body experience.

As Nintendo designer Shigeru Miyamoto put it at the launch: 'We're not really thinking about Sony, but about how we can get more people playing games. We're not thinking about consoles, but about making games richer, more personal experiences.'

With the Wii you can play tennis against Rafael Nadal from your living room or take part in an aerobics workshop without anybody watching. You can watch yourself on television as you do it, get advice and encouragement from your virtual coach, and even compare your performance with your friends down the roads in their own homes, or on the other side of the world.

With a retail price of around $250 (more than a portable PlayStation PSP or Nintendo DS, but much less than a PlayStation 3 or Xbox 360), the system arrives well-equipped – other games consoles are bought separately and require many other accessories to make them work. As well as your controller, the Wii remote ('Wiimote'), you also get a *Wii Sports* game that offers a rich compilation of tennis, golf and boxing games. The game helps you to get accustomed to the system and its controls, as well as getting you hooked and wanting more.

Your Wii can also be personalized with names and avatars, allowing you to create your own digital image to appear in games on the 'Wii Channel'. Because the system is WiFi-enabled, you can use the console to shop online for new games and connect with other players in different locations in real time. The Wii is small and compact, so can be left out in the room for easy start-up, and can even play games from the older Nintendo GameCube, so your previous investments are not redundant.

Wii Fit was launched a year later with a special balance board, so that you can really work your whole body rather than just your fingers. Marketed as a fitness game, it has four training categories aimed at improving a player's muscle condition, balance, flexibility and aerobic capability. For adults, particularly women, it has a sparked a fast-growing online workout community, comparing routines and even bringing their avatars together on screen to imitate a group session. For children, it is fun and healthy, a breath of fresh air after hours of satellite TV or video games – although maybe not quite *Swallows and Amazons*.

And the name? The distinctively spelt brand name is supposed to reflect the collective 'we' and the thrilling 'wee', as well as being available as a trademark worldwide.

7.2 CUSTOMER THEATRE

Now consider how you might create a more positive customer experience.

As an exercise, remove all the value 'destroyers' – the negative moments, irrelevant points and activities that do nothing for customers but are perhaps only there for the business's convenience or efficiency. Consider whether, practically and commercially, it might be possible to still deliver this experience – now entirely consisting of positive value 'creators' – without the eliminated activities.

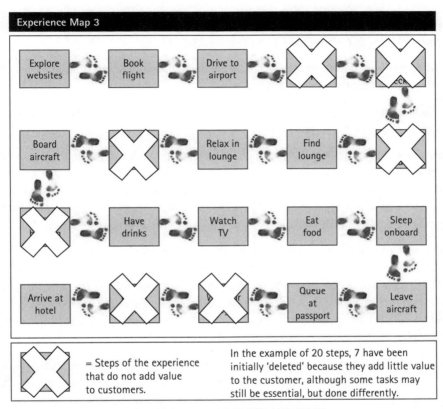

EXPERIENCE MAP 3: DELETE EVERYTHING THAT DOESN'T ADD VALUE

Of course, you may now have eliminated negative steps that are still important for the business, such as receiving the bill, making the payment, making the furniture or disposing of the waste. Now consider replacing such essential steps with a different way of achieving them that fulfils the business need but in a more positive way for customers.

Another way to consider improving the basic experience of customers is to consider each of the essential steps in terms of how it can be enhanced:

- *Streamlining*: making interactions that are unimportant, uninteresting or irrelevant to the customer shorter, simpler and faster.

- *Elaborating*: making interactions that are important, enjoyable and desirable to the customer longer, enhanced and memorable.

American Express recognized that its main communication with customers – the monthly statement of payments – was not an entirely positive one for its cardholders. Instead, it sought to make it more positive by tying individual rewards and incentives to the transactions – for example, 'We hope you had a good meal at your local restaurant, so we've arranged with them for you to have a free bottle of champagne on your next visit with our compliments'.

Hotels have eventually recognized that checking out on the morning of departure causes delay and frustration to the customer, meaning they leave with a negative feeling. Since credit card details are always recorded at the time of check-in and all transactions are recorded automatically during the stay, a summary of payments can be posted under the bedroom door on the evening before departure, only requiring customers to interact if they are not happy with the details.

Airlines recognized that the time that frequent travellers spend in their executive lounges could be more positively used by customers rather than just for food and drink. Virgin's Clubhouse is a treasure chest of treats: playing on a Nintendo Wii or with an old-fashioned train set, a complemintary haircut or revitalizing massage, business facilities or a sleep – Virgin has created an antidote to the stresses of airports and air travel.

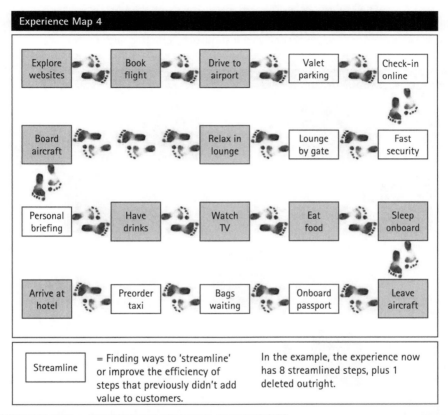

EXPERIENCE MAP 4: IMPROVE THE ESSENTIAL TOUCHPOINTS

Another approach to innovating the experience is to consider how you can add more significant value to customers by adopting an enhanced role rather than just being a supplier of products and services – how can you enable them to do more. Imagine you are a performer and the dif-

ferent ways in which you could interact with your audience: following a script or improving, allowing the audience to passively enjoy your show or interacting with them.

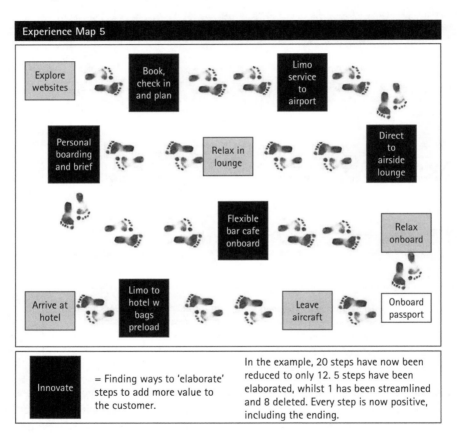

Experience Map 5

Explore websites	Book, check in and plan	Limo service to airport
Personal boarding and brief	Relax in lounge	Direct to airside lounge
	Flexible bar cafe onboard	Relax onboard
Arrive at hotel	Limo to hotel w bags preload	Leave aircraft / Onboard passport

Innovate = Finding ways to 'elaborate' steps to add more value to the customer.

In the example, 20 steps have now been reduced to only 12. 5 steps have been elaborated, whilst 1 has been streamlined and 8 deleted. Every step is now positive, including the ending.

EXPERIENCE MAP 5: ADD NEW INNOVATIVE TOUCHPOINTS

In a similar manner, you can consider the types of performance (and therefore types of experience) that you seek to create for your customers at each interaction: will it be passive and scripted, or spontaneous and responsive to each different customer? This leads to a number of different roles and potential new ways of enhancing the value you create for your customers:

- *Entertaining* experiences, from sporting events to rock concerts, far more dramatic than when edited and viewed remotely. Example: Red Bull Air Races absorb you in the adrenalin rush of a canned drink.

- *Educational* experiences, from historic monuments brought to life through re-enactments to training courses based on role-play and interaction. Example: Schwab Learning Centers demystify the investment world.

- *Guiding* experiences, from art galleries that embrace all the senses to health spas that stimulate and pamper them. Example: Michelin Restaurant Guides take a lowly tyre manufacturer into a different context.

- *Coaching* experiences, from adventure sports to videogames that take participants into extreme or imaginary worlds. Example: Subaru Driving Experiences teach drivers how to handle the toughest terrains.

Any business can embrace any of these types of experiences to enhance their proposition or exploit adjacent revenue streams, and simply to engage customer like never before.

Insight 31: VOM FASS

'Look, taste, enjoy.'

Johannes Kiderlen inherited his wine-importing business from his father and set up a chain of specialist stores, 'Weinkauf Getraenkemarkt', selling wines and other drinks across Germany's Baden Wuerttemberg.

In 1994 he launched a new concept. Inspired by the customer trend for more authentic and local experiences, he started selling wine from the cask. This gave him a much more intimate experience with each customer as they discussed the wines before asking him to pour their chosen one into a bottle. They started to take a real interest in the grapes and their origins, and the processes used in making the wines.

Recognizing that a supermarket format didn't support this more traditional, personal experience, he set up a new type of store called 'Vom Fass', translated as 'from the tap'. The first store opened in Regensburg and was quickly followed by others across Germany. The distinctive experience was an immediate hit and he started to extend his range to include a broad range of exclusive spirits, exquisite oils and fruit vinegars.

The liquids were introduced in person, or with detailed and evocative descriptions. Even more engaging were the bottles customers could choose from. He built up a range of almost 100 bottle designs, turning the liquids into unusual gifts and talking points. There were stacking towers, ladies' stilettos – even an Adam and Eve two-piece set. Each bottle came inscribed with the details of its contents and a personal message too, if requested. He also recognized that many people wanted to try different items, so small bottles enabled them to sample more.

Kiderlen has now taken his unique brand of retailing across the world, largely through franchising the concept to carefully chosen partners who continue to deliver a knowledgeable and personal Vom Fass experience.

7.3   EXTRAORDINARY EXPERIENCES

Customer experiences are most memorable when they are like nothing else and enable you to do things that you might never have imagined.

Having eliminated the negative moments and found ways to create a more positive emotional journey, through streamlining and elaborating, and maybe even a touch of theatre, the designed experience can be delivered uniquely for each customer.

This is not one person or department's challenge – it is a whole business challenge, perhaps even requiring the cooperation of suppliers, distributors and partners. It is not just about putting in place the tangible activities, products and processes; it is about attitude and behaviours, service and style, and being seamless and consistent – acting as one.

However, experiences are emotional.

To adopt the title of the excellent book by Andy Milligan and Shaun Smith, it is about what customers 'see, feel, think and do'. They encourage managers to use their intuition, based on all their senses, to make better decisions, and enable customers to be multi-sensory too. We are familiar with the far greater impact of our non-aural senses – what we see, feel or touch – yet it is easy to dismiss these in the rush to maximize transactions.

Singapore Airlines will leave you with a lasting smile, but will also sell you a bottle of its air. The fragrance as you board its aircraft is perhaps subtle, but it grows on you and relaxes you as you settle into your flight. Its experienced design team spend many hours working perfecting it. Similarly, as you test-drive a new Lexus car, you are seduced as much by the scent and softness of the leather as by the acceleration and fuel efficiency of its hybrid engine.

In finalizing the design of your customer experience, consider how you can bring it to life – make it a multi-sensory experience rather than a sterile one. Add to your touchpoint map what you want customers to see, how you want them to feel and what you want them to think, as well as what they do at each different interaction.

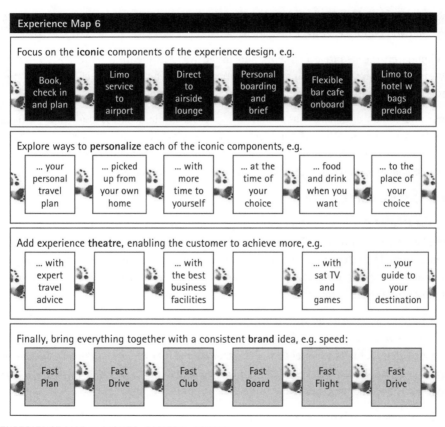

Experience Map 6

Focus on the **iconic** components of the experience design, e.g.

| Book, check in and plan | Limo service to airport | Direct to airside lounge | Personal boarding and brief | Flexible bar cafe onboard | Limo to hotel w bags preload |

Explore ways to **personalize** each of the iconic components, e.g.

| ... your personal travel plan | ... picked up from your own home | ... with more time to yourself | ... at the time of your choice | ... food and drink when you want | ... to the place of your choice |

Add experience **theatre**, enabling the customer to achieve more, e.g.

| ... with expert travel advice | | ... with the best business facilities | | ... with sat TV and games | ... your guide to your destination |

Finally, bring everything together with a consistent **brand** idea, e.g. speed:

| Fast Plan | Fast Drive | Fast Club | Fast Board | Fast Flight | Fast Drive |

EXPERIENCE MAP 6: LIGHTS, CAMERA, ACTION

230

This might be achieved through a more personalized style of service: being more responsive to each customer, finding ways to connect with them, or learning from information in databases more about them and previously expressed preferences, rather than following a standard list of procedures.

The Ritz-Carlton taxi driver will alert the hotel doorman and receptionist of the imminent arrival of a new guest, so that they can be waiting and greet the guest by name when they arrive. As soon as a regular customer calls First Direct, the telephone bank, the incoming number will prompt a personal profile to pop up in front of the person answering the call, summarizing the customer's details, preferences and financial background, and enabling a more informed and relevant experience.

The information and experiences of each interaction with each person can be useful in anticipating, improving or personalizing future interactions, whether moments or months later, by the same person or by different people across the organization.

Brands are not names or logos. They are distinctive concepts that become personal experiences.

'Bringing your brand to life' is all about finding ways to make the brand come alive in relevant and personal ways at every interaction. This might be through a recognized visual identity, distinctive language and exclusive features, or service delivered with a trademark attitude and style.

Don't forget the big idea of your brand (for example, enabling people to run faster, make new friends or cook better food) and what makes you different from the others who also seek to do this – the most environmental, caring or refreshing. Then develop ways in which you can symbolize this at points throughout your experience – the 'brand gestures' that tangibly and emotionally bring the brand to life.

As you enter Disneyland, brand gestures are all around you – the music playing as you walk through the gates, Mickey Mouse waiting to greet you within the next few steps, the smell of fresh bread as you walk down Main Street, the flash of magic dust as Tinkerbell flutters by, the big ears on top of the water tower, the smile and banter from the street cleaners, the surprise and delight as Pluto waits around the corner, Cinderella bursts into song or Winnie the Pooh invites you to try his honey.

Through research into people's experiences in all walks of life, Nobel prize-winning psychologist Daniel Kahneman has found that the quality of an experience is almost entirely determined by two events: how the experience felt at its peak (the best or worst moment), and how it ended. It suggests that the memorable experiences end on a high: spending as much time advising customers after their purchase as you do when helping them to buy, or celebrating when a customer moves into their new home rather than just selling the house to them.

Make it special, make it magical, make it extraordinary.

Insight 32: BUILD A BEAR WORKSHOP

'Bearemy' was born on 21 August 1998 in St Louis, Missouri, stands 6 foot 4 inch (nine and a half paws) tall, and is very shy about his weight.

He is the huggable mascot of retail sensation Build a Bear Workshop and travels the world meeting children at store openings, special events and in hospitals. His name was chosen by one of his many fans.

Build a Bear Workshop is the ultimate retail experience for anybody who loves teddy bears or knows somebody who does. Located in more than 400 shopping malls around the world, often with queues of eager children waiting to get in, one exhausted but happy parent reflected 'I can't believe I just waited an hour for a stuffed animal'.

You start by selecting your 'pawfect' bear or a wide range of other animals too. Many of them are linked to charities – the WWF Panda supports endangered animals, the Boxer Dog supports local animal shelters and Nikki's Bear supports specific children's hospitals or causes. You can help stuff your bear with filling, and you may even want to record a personal message that's put inside, to be activated whenever you squeeze it. Before sewing it up, choose a heart, give it a kiss and he comes to life.

Now you can really start spending money. First it will need some clothes – underwear and a selection of jeans, T-shirts, dresses and much more – and shoes, including some specially designed by Sketchers for really cool bears. And how could you resist the other accessories as you approach the checkout – sunglasses, mobile phone, beach bag? Finally you need a birth certificate, recording the time and location of birth, and giving it a name (or you can have a think about that and add it later).

Build a Bear Workshop's mission is 'to bring the teddy bear to life':

> 'An American icon, the teddy bear brings to mind warm thoughts about our childhood, about friendship, about trust and comfort, and also about love. Build a Bear Workshop embodies those thoughts in how we run our business every day.'

The recently retired 47-year-old Maxine Clark pitched her idea round every venture capitalist she could find – but in a world of high technology start-ups, she found no interest in a teddy bear shop. She had 30 years' experience in retail, most recently being the president of Payless shoe stores, and was convinced the idea would work. She eventually decided to invest $750,000 of her own cash.

She says the idea came to her when a friend was struggling to find a particular Beanie Baby during the height of the craze.

Shortly after opening her first store in 1997, a local investor read about the story in a local paper and offered her $4.3 million in capital to grow the business. Within six months the bear shop was doing so well that she was getting more offers of investment than she could reply to. She expanded rapidly and within eight years had created a business with annual sales of $302 million.

Little touches made a difference, like the barcode on the bear that meant that Build a Bear could track down the owner of a lost bear and return it to its home, or the database of bear birth dates from which the company can send birthday cards every year to the owner, suggesting that their bear might be interested in some new clothes or accessories for their birthday.

Clark talks about delivering a great customer experience as 'managing to the emotional' and the challenge of involving the customer in every aspect of the business. In fact, she calls her customers 'guests' (although most parents would argue that the kids don't pay for it anyway). Her mantra is:

- Stay focused on the guest experience.

- Ensure that it is integrated into every aspect of business.

- Deliver great service and great results.

Ongoing customer research – through guest satisfaction surveys, focus groups, online surveys, 7500 letters every month, trend tracking and a customer advisory board – is crucial to the business. As Clark says, 'even the most emotional customer-centric experiences can be quantified … measure it, report it, talk about it and reward it'. Indeed, employee rewards are linked directly to guest satisfaction and loyalty, and as she frequently reminds them: 'when a customer has fun, they spend more money'.

Many companies have tried to imitate her concept, to which she replies 'anybody can copy a product, but not an experience. Anybody can copy a bear, but they will struggle to copy the thrill and excitement of allowing children to create their very own bear.'

As you head out of the store with your very newborn bear complete in its favourite football strip or new season dress, Bearemy will be at the door to give you one of the best hugs you have ever had – because a bear hug is understood in any language.

Customer service

> *Good morning, sir/madam. Yes, sir. No, sir. Have a nice day, sir ...*
>
> *I know that you're just trying to be pleasant, but it does get a bit repetitive and irritating. I don't want the standard service patter. That's nearly as bad as those interactive voice systems that I get when I call you. The options they give me never seem to match what I need. They are the most non-intuitive, inhuman, frustrating experience. When I do get to talk to you, you always have more reasons I cannot do things – your rules and policies are all about you rather serving me.*
>
> *Great service is about listening to what I want and then finding a way to help me achieve it. Great service is really a lot of common sense – delivering what you promise and, if you fall short, saying sorry. Great service is about finding ways to solve my problem, even if it means doing things differently and sometimes even breaking your own rules. Great service is about being human, you and me as real people. Great service is about remembering me, what I want and how I like it. In fact service is probably what I remember most and the reason I choose you. So don't make it an afterthought – make it the most important thing you do.*

8.1 CUSTOMER DELIVERY

Service can be your biggest differentiator. Indeed, it is reasonable to suggest that every business today is a service business. Consumer goods businesses and heavy engineering businesses must deliver just as good service – advice, delivery, support – as more conventional services such as an airline or a hotel.

Yet most customer service is standard, routine and boring, typically limited by unnecessary rules, inflexible policies, conventional practices, and demotivated people. Even worse is automated, non-intuitive service such as the automated voice response systems that cannot accommodate anything but the most common of problems, leaving the customer frustrated and unserved.

How can you deliver service that is more responsive and engaging?

'Outside in' service doesn't start with what you do, but what the customer seeks from you. A Starbucks barista spends weeks learning how to serve a great coffee and about the philosophy of the brand: significant investment in an industry with short tenures, although not necessarily in the case of this coffee shop. Learning to make a great coffee matters because it lies at the heart of the proposition: if you want to be a great athlete, you have to learn to run efficiently before learning to run fast.

More important still is the philosophy of the brand. If Starbucks is to be 'the third place' between home and work for customers, it matters that they feel comfortable there, there is space to meet people, it feels like home and they can stay as long as they want. This doesn't come in a training manual – there is no right or wrong. It comes through Starbucks people understanding what it really means to be 'the third place', making the right judgements for every customer on every occasion.

The acronym 'CARER' represents the key factors driving effective service delivery, whether delivered by a person or automated:

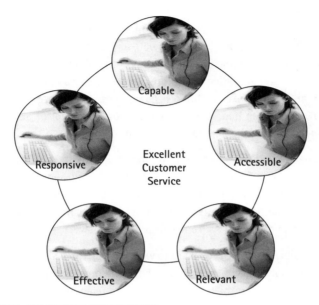

CUSTOMER SERVICE: DELIVERING THE PROMISE

- **Capable** – has the knowledge and skills to deliver the right service.

- **Accessible** – fast and easy to find, ready and willing to serve.

- **Relevant –** understands me, engages me, and feels like is on my side.

- **Effective** – delivers the service as promised, quickly and efficiently.

- **Responsive** – anticipates and responds to my specific needs.

Customer service should not be made complicated. At its heart should be simplicity and common sense – the ability to solve a customer's problem in a fast and effective way. Of course, systems and databases can help, but they can equally hinder.

The corner shopkeeper did not need customer profiles, product databases and customer handling systems in order to treat each customer well, and personally. He was a character who people enjoyed talking to and doing business with because of who he was. As he got to know each customer, he was able to anticipate and remember their names and needs too. He was also his own boss, and could make and break his own rules. If he wanted to give a young child a lollipop, nobody would stop him; if he wanted to close his shop for 30 minutes to help a customer carry their shopping home, that was his choosing.

Technology has enabled customer service to be more intelligent and virtual, but this is not always to everyone's benefit. Service can be delivered online at any hour, through kiosks within large supermarkets for more convenience or by mobile wherever you might be. It can be voice-activated so that you can be hands-free as you drive, using biometrics to enhance personal security and intuitive so that it learns from your previous answers.

This all sounds incredibly good until you want to work outside the system. Try making an online complaint to Expedia that doesn't fit within one of its predefined categories, or communicating with Sony's helpdesk by email rather than their preferred telephone approach, which requires you to enter your 16-digit serial number before speaking to someone.

Although customer service typically involves many people, doing operational roles on relatively low salaries, it should never be a process – particularly one where standardization and efficiency are the measures of success. Customer service is not the result of a training course, rule book or process diagram. In a world of automation, it is important that people add even more value than before.

People create personal, emotional, memorable experiences – through the attitudes and behaviour of both employees and customers – that turn products into experiences, a transaction into a relationship, and a person into a friend. Indeed; service across the customer experience can take many forms:

- Advising potential customers on what might be most appropriate to solve their problem or meet their need. Finding the right components to achieve a DIY challenge, or ingredients for a great meal.

- Guiding them to put together the right solution, addressing technical requirements such as the most appropriate spec for a new computer, and helping them make informed choices across a bewildering range of brands.

- Selling in terms of taking the money and making available what they want when they need it, from the locations of stores and opening times to knowing what is in stock and how to get there.

- Delivering the solution, which might include installation or set-up – of a home entertainment system or wireless LAN, for example, and making sure all the software works.

- Supporting the customer in making the most of it – for example, to enjoy their in-flight experience with their favourite magazine or cater for their special needs and requests.

- Maintaining it as good as new, keeping things going and continuing to deliver the promise day after day – sustaining the positive experience of the car showroom, for instance, into the workshop.

- Solving the specific problems that inevitably arise, dealing with complaints in a way that shows your true colours and making the most of the opportunity to really 'show what you can do'.

- Building relationships person-to-person, remembering customers and seeking to enable people to build one-to-one relationships rather than anonymously with the brand.

Stephen Covey developed the idea of service as an emotional bank account. Humanicity, a specialist customer service training company focused on engaging frontline service people, has developed the concept as a practical tool for everyday service.

The 'Bank Account' is akin to the strength of relationship between customer and organization. You can pay deposits in or make withdrawals. The balance in your account needs to be in credit to the customer in order to ensure a good strong relationship – one that is likely to yield additional business or greater loyalty. Every person in the business can pay into the customer's account:

- Delivering on the proposition as promised.

- Showing genuine interest in the person.

- Listening and understanding their broader issues.

- Going the extra mile to meet their specific requests.

- Empathizing and treating them as an individual.

- Acting with integrity, standing by commitments.

- Apologizing and fixing things when they go wrong.

Another powerful Humanicity tool, again incredibly simple but effective, is called 'The Spiral of Positivity'. Most people know how to greet people, make eye contact, ask questions, listen and show interest. The problem is that they just don't do it.

The spiral illustrates to people that they have a choice about how they respond to the daily grind of working life: difficult customers, staff not turning up, systems not working, losing a sale, disagreement with someone or a gloomy economic outlook. They can choose to respond like a victim or a winner, positively and proactively. It reminds them that they choose this attitude, which takes them up or down the spiral.

Choose to be at the top and they will have a better, more enjoyable, more productive day at work. Choose to be at the bottom and they won't feel like giving great service and so don't. The choice of whether to enjoy their job, engage with customers and deliver great service is theirs alone.

Insight 33: DISNEYLAND

'What youngster has not dreamed of flying with Peter Pan over moonlit London or tumbling into Alice's nonsensical Wonderland? At Disneyland, these classic stories of everyone's youth have become realities for youngsters of all ages to participate in.'

Walt Disney had a vision of a place where children and parents could have fun together. The more he dreamed of a 'magical park', the more imaginative and elaborate it became.

His original concept was based on eight acres of land next to his film studio where employees and their families could relax together. Over time, he realized that he needed more space. He wanted to build 'rivers and waterfalls, mountains and jungles, flying elephants and giant tea-cups, railways and fun fairs, a fairytale castle and moon rockets'.

He eventually found 160 acres of land in Anaheim, California. The orange groves provided cheap land not too far from Los Angeles and close to the fast developing road networks. He struggled to find anybody willing to finance his venture, finding that dreams were not sufficient collateral for investors at the time. He therefore funded the development by launching a television series called *Walt Disney's Disneyland*, which offered a glimpse of the project and built much anticipation among the 1950s American youth.

People remained sceptical. How do you build a castle in the middle of Orange County? How will the huge Mississippi paddle ship get there? Will people believe that the animals are real?

Walt was passionate about making his dream a reality and gave himself a year to create it. He took a personal interest in every detail, often rejecting the ideas of his designers and redefining them himself. His Disneyland blueprint was precise and is still followed to the letter in Disneyland parks around the world today.

Main Street USA was where he would welcome people, engage their emotions and take them back to the free and happy memories of turn-of-the-century USA. He called the street a 'weenie' along which people would be drawn to the magic of Sleeping Beauty's castle in the distance. This was Fantasyland, bringing the classic fairy tales to life.

Next there was Frontierland, 'celebrating the wild and wonderful history of our forefathers'. Adventureland would be an exotic and tropical place, conjuring up 'the deserts and jungles of Africa and Asia'. And then there came Tomorrowland, 'opening the doors of the space age that will benefit generations to come' – although he also recognized that he would have to work hard to keep this zone up to date.

The park was stunning in its concept and equally difficult to build. They struggled, for example, to keep water in the 'Rivers of America' because it constantly drained away through the sandy citrus grove soil, eventually managing to find clay that formed a cement-like river bed. On opening day the 6000 invited guests were swamped by another 20,000 with counterfeit tickets, and a heatwave meant that much of the asphalt road surfaces became hot and sticky. But Walt kept smiling.

Eventually the $17 million 'Magic Kingdom' became a phenomenal success, with 50 million visitors coming through its gates in the first ten years. The park continued to grow as the Disney empire itself developed and diversified. A new movie produced new characters, which inspired new attractions. And the parks spread across the globe, initially to Florida, and then to Paris and Tokyo.

Today, there are few customer experiences better than a day at Disneyland – particularly for children, but also their parents once they let their child-like imaginations take over. From the magical music that plays as you walk to the entrance gates to the regular character parades and seasonal themes, it remains an incredible experience. The hotels and restaurants that surround the park are equally designed to thrill a child – attention to detail is everywhere, including the back of the road signs.

As Walt Disney said on opening day, this is a place where dreams really can come true.

8.2   INDIVIDUALIZED SERVICE

Customer service is a personal experience. But how can you possibly judge how to treat a customer in exactly the right way?

Nobody is predictable – everybody wants something slightly different both from the product they are buying and the wider experience they seek. How do you do the right thing?

INDIVIDUALIZED SERVICE: PERSONAL, RELEVANT AND INTUITIVE

There are three dimensions, used here with the example of a coffee shop:

- **Doing** the right thing for customers. The standard procedures: what the book says, delivering the basic promise, the minimum service level. The right way to grind coffee, the right temperature of the water, the right frothiness of the milk.

- **Knowing** why you are doing it. This is more tailored to the customer's stated or perceived needs and preferences. It might be a regular that you know has the same thing every morning, a special topping or doing a little more than is actually required.

- **Being** emotionally with customers. This is the hard one, unpredictable day by day. It could mean sensing when to chat and when not, getting inside the customer's head. An extra shot of espresso to cheer someone up could make their day – or backfire.

However, the most significant aspect of all is the person delivering the customer service. If they don't have the right attitudes and behaviours, and are not treated in an individualized way, they are unlikely to do as such for customers.

The first step is therefore to 'de-programme' people from the ingrained standardizations of service delivery: the enforced smile, the sir/madam routine and the prejudiced assumptions of how people want to be treated and what they want.

Getting people to be themselves is not easy, but it allows people to rediscover their own personalities, bringing out the best in themselves naturally and engaging with customers in a more natural way too. And because every employee has differences in their personality and natural behaviours, each interaction will be somewhat different: some will be formal, some will be fast, for example.

First Direct, the award-winning telephone and Internet bank that is part of the HSBC but with a completely separate brand and culture, focuses on the following factors to ensure that it delivers individualized service:

- Recruit people who speak their mind. Don't recruit people for technical or functional skills – recruit them for their willingness to speak their minds, project their personality and resilience in getting things done.

- Make decisions like a customer. Decision-making starts by thinking what would customers want us to do, what meets their needs better, and then considering how this can be aligned with operational and financial success.

- Define your customer equation. At First Direct, Service + Price = Value, Culture + People = Values, Value + Values = Brand. Keeping these three equations aligned becomes the challenge of management.

- It's not all about teamwork. If you want to treat your customer as an individual, you need to treat your people as individuals too. This in particular is different from the received wisdom of so many organizations.

- Throw away the script. There is no scripting at First Direct, except for a brief security question. Otherwise it's a conversation between real people – a spontaneous dialogue that is more relevant, personal and enjoyable too.

- Keep talking. Most call centres race to answer a call and then finish it as quickly as possible so that they can get the next. This is no way to build a relationship. The person who answers the call handles it and can chat away for as long as they like.

Insight 34: SINGAPORE AIRLINES

The beautiful orchids in the cabin, the fragrance in the air, the rich fabrics on the seats, the innovative personal cabins, the wonderful and diverse food, the punctual arrival, and the smile on the face.

It's hard to beat Singapore Airlines and its customer service.

The airline's history goes back to 1947 when Malayan Airways launched its first flight linking Singapore with Kuala Lumpur, Ipoh and Penang. It eventually split in 1972 into Malaysia Airlines and Singapore Airlines. Since that day, the latter has earned a reputation for innovation and service, and has – almost uniquely for the industry – delivered a profit every year.

Serving 100 destinations in 41 countries from Singapore's Changi airport, it connects Asia Pacific with Europe and America. The airline is 55%-owned by Singapore's government and has set the standard in long-haul travel: the first to offer complimentary food and drink in economy cabins in the 1970s, the first to offer in-flight email access to all passengers in 2001. In 2007 its 14,000 employees flew 19 million people around the world, generating SGD11.3 billion and picking up *Traveller* magazine's 'Best International Airline' award for 19 of the last 20 years.

The 'Singapore Girl' is more than the beautiful and attentive cabin crew who greet you as you walk on board, she is an icon of the airline. Every advertisement, brochure, poster, video features the legendary girl as a symbol of the service that sits at the heart of Singapore Airlines.

Business priorities and issues are always considered first from the perspective of providing world-class customer service. Training is continuous, not a one-off, and is inspirational as well as educational. As customer expectations continue to rise, so must the service delivered by its crew. This is achieved in classrooms, on the job and through full-scale flight simulation.

In particular, the airline seizes on moments of economic downturn to invest in its people when other airlines seek to cut costs, reduce training and freeze salaries. These are opportunities to leap ahead and get an extra edge on the competition. It intensifies its training at such times and encourages staff to see the bigger picture: the concerns and dreams of its customers, and the long-term benefits of working for a successful business.

High-potential employees are identified early and given additional opportunities to learn and develop. Senior managers are rotated across key positions to increase their understanding of business functions and appreciate the full impact of each activity on others. It ultimately enables them to see across the whole business, championing the totality of the customer's experience, rather just being blinkered by the goals or activities of one touchpoint or department.

Singapore Airlines is constantly listening to both staff and customers. Staff suggestion schemes, discussion forums and team meetings bring together issues and ideas. Customer panels are supplemented by ongoing in-flight surveys, focus groups and a careful ear for both compliments and complaints. These factors are consolidated into a monthly 'Service Performance Index' that is as important as seat factor, revenue and profitability.

From the earliest days, Singapore Airlines has taken a lead in doing things differently from others, including free drinks and headsets, onboard fax machines, individual video screens and telephones in every seat, leading edge gaming and in-flight entertainment, 'book the cook' service for special meals in first and business classes, online check-in, and innovative cargo facilities. The culture is to try things, evolve things, and keep going until they work – and then to do them better.

'The Deputy Chairman's Award' goes to the team or individual who responds to unique customer situations with exceptionally positive, innovative or selfless acts of service. Winners and their families are flown to Singapore for a special celebration, the story of their unique efforts is published in the monthly magazine, and their status as a DCA winner remains a badge of distinction for life.

There is an incredible pride in working for Singapore Airlines and a culture that is human, passionate and incredibly profitable. As the CEO frequently reminds his people, 'profits are the applause we receive for providing consistent quality and service to our customers'.

8.3 SERVICE RECOVERY

Complaints are not good, are they?

That is still the attitude in many companies, where they see a customer letter, phone call or email as failure. They even measure complaints as a KPI, addressing a rising number as aggressively as a falling revenue.

But complaints are good. What better way is there to learn from customers? What better opportunity do you have to show them how good you really are? And surely it's better for them to tell you when things are wrong rather than just walk away silently?

Imagine the millions of customers who shop in your stores and use your products or services but never say a word to you. You might even claim to have a relationship with them, but have never had the chance to speak.

When things go wrong, customers want an answer, their problem fixing or even compensation – but more likely they just want you to say sorry. They also want you to improve so that it doesn't happen again. However, an obscure address to write to is unlikely to do this in time. It is better if every one of your people are ready and willing to solve a problem, or to introduce a hotline that waits for the unhappy customer to call.

Then you have an opportunity: a chance to solve the problem quickly, make amends before it becomes a bigger issue, correct the failure so that it doesn't happen again or even use the insight as the basis for improvement or innovation.

Service recovery is the best opportunity to build a relationship – to treat the customer as an individual and maybe do something that they go away telling their friends about in a positive rather than negative way. However, there are a number of steps before a disaster can become a delight:

1   **Recognize** that the situation has occurred, listen to the problem, understand the impact from the customer's perspective, and empathize with how they are feeling. Of course, there might be a good reason why the situation has occurred, but at this point they're not interested in your logic or excuses.

2   **Apologize** to them for what happened and the inconvenience and stress that it might have caused.

3   **Fix** the problem quickly and efficiently. Firstly this means finding out what an appropriate solution might be. It might be as simple as an apology, or might require more. 'An exchange? No problem! A repair? No problem! A refund? No problem! No receipt? No problem'. Break the rules if you need to – go the extra mile.

4   **Compensate** them in some relevant way. This might be anything from a simple gesture to a significant sum. You need to judge what would make them smile or even 'wow' them. Take it to their home, send them flowers, don't charge them or give them a voucher for next time.

5   **Improve** the product or service, using the specific anecdote but also collating all of the different complaints to drive service improvement and find the insights that will really create a better product. Also, use the personal contact to build an ongoing relationship too.

Service recovery is often seen as a paradox: something bad has to happen in order to do some real good. But nobody is perfect; things will always go wrong and you will certainly sometimes fall short of customers' ever increasing expectations. Therefore, service recovery is a fundamental part of customer service, and indeed of customer research and relationship-building too.

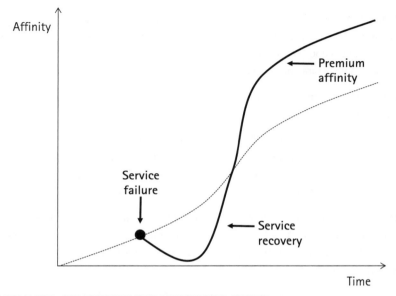

SERVICE RECOVERY: OPPORTUNITY TO DO SOMETHING SPECIAL

The emotional curve that the customer goes through demonstrates the positive impact you can make on customer loyalty.

However, this requires a fundamental attitude shift in a business – one that is ready to act when things go wrong. It means educating people of the importance in addressing complaints quickly and effectively, and equipping them to be able to act. Any employee of Ritz-Carlton hotels can spend up to $1000 without authorization in such circumstances. Or it might be as simple as having $20 gift vouchers available to give to people at an employee's discretion.

Addressing a problem before a customer even complains is even better. For example, airlines will often know that a passenger's bags have not been loaded well before arrival, giving it the opportunity to get the bag sent by alternative means immediately. The passenger can then be informed with an apology and with a reassurance that it will be delivered directly to their home or hotel a few hours later.

Many companies now recognize that customers want to complain online. One company that specializes in such areas is Tagish, which deals with companies large and small. The Web provides an opportunity for instant dialogue, anywhere and anytime, but also for support services such as tracking and updating how a problem is being solved. Tagish uses a simple three-phase 'TAG' process to develop appropriate Web-based service recovery solutions:

- *Talk*: engage the customer quickly in a dialogue, listening and understanding their issues, dissatisfaction and preferred solution.

- *Act*: respond quickly and effectively to the complaint, apologizing to the customer and fixing the problem appropriately.

- *Grow*: use the interaction to learn how to improve, to build a better relationship, and in both ways drive growth.

In the book *Nuts!*, Kevin and Jackie Freiberg tell the story of Southwest Airlines, the US carrier that for many years won the leading awards for its customer service and went about business in a customer-centred but also slightly crazy way.

They write about a woman who frequently flew on Southwest but was disappointed with every aspect of the company's operation. In fact, she became known as the 'Pen Pal', because after every flight she wrote in with a complaint. She didn't like the fact that the company didn't assign seats, the absence of a first-class section, not having an in-flight meal, the boarding procedure, the flight attendants' sporty uniforms and the casual atmosphere. And she hated peanuts.

Her last letter, reciting a litany of complaints, initially stumped Southwest's customer relations team. The airline prided itself on answering every letter that came in, patiently explaining why we do things the way we do them. In this case the response was quickly becoming huge until they showed her letter to CEO Herb Kelleher, wondering what to do.

The Harley-riding, leather-jacket-wearing customer champion didn't hesitate, quickly writing a note back saying 'Dear Mrs. Crabapple, We will miss you. Love, Herb.'

Insight 35: RITZ-CARLTON

The Ritz-Carlton Hotel Company was founded in 1983 with the purchase of the Ritz-Carlton of Boston and the rights to its brand name. It is now a division of Marriott but continues to operate independently, managing 45 hotels in the world's leading cities.

It describes itself as 'ladies and gentlemen serving ladies and gentlemen'. And 85% of these ladies and gentlemen – the ones who work there, also known as associates – work in direct customer service roles, applying the brand's simple but prize-winning concept of service:

- A warm and sincere greeting.
- Using the customer's name if possible.
- A constant anticipation of the customer's needs.
- A warm goodbye, again using the customer's name when possible.

Every associate carries their 'credo' in their pocket, purse or wallet at all times. It captures everything about what they do, and why they do it:

'The Ritz-Carlton Hotel is a place where the genuine care and comfort of our guests is our highest mission. We pledge to provide the finest personal service and facilities for our guests who will always enjoy a warm, relaxed, yet refined ambience. The Ritz-Carlton experience enlivens the senses, instils well-being and fulfils even the unexpressed wishes and needs of our guests.'

The company also believes it has broken the old vicious circle of the hospitality sector – low salary and high turnover – by redesigning all its business processes, including recruitment and remuneration, around the customer. Associates are recruited for their customer attitude more than their specialist skills and are rewarded based on customer satisfaction more than sales and occupancy rates.

Managers in hotels are not seen as the bosses sitting in their offices holding meetings of their leadership teams and keeping head office happy. They define their role as the first line of support to the customer service team. Similarly, head office describes itself as the service centre, even drawing its organization as an upside-down pyramid to symbolize the inversion of traditional hierarchy.

Working at Ritz-Carlton is also all about excellence. Job profiles are defined by the performance of the best people – hotel managers, dishwashers, housekeepers. They profile their best people and then use that as a template for recruiting others like them. These best performers in each role are also responsible for writing the training manuals for others who do the same role.

Companies across the world in different sectors see the Ritz-Carlton training school as the ultimate place to learn about customer service excellence: banks, retailers, airlines and IT companies are all disciples of the credo.

They learn about relationship maturity, emotional engagement, creating mystique and specifi-cally of course about 'The Ritz-Carlton Mystique'. They explore the importance of first impres-sions and grooming, phraseology, and being a positive ambassador for the brand. They under-stand the 12 reasons why associates really do feel special when they work for the brand:

- I build strong relationships and create Ritz-Carlton guests for life.

- I am always responsive to the expressed and unexpressed wishes and needs of our guests.

- I am empowered to create unique, memorable and personal experiences for our guests.

- I understand my role in achieving the Key Success Factors and creating The Ritz-Carlton Mystique.

- I continuously seek opportunities to innovate and improve The Ritz-Carlton experience.

- I own and immediately resolve guest problems.

- I create a work environment of teamwork and lateral service so that the needs of our guests and each other are met.

- I have the opportunity to continuously learn and grow.

- I am involved in the planning of the work that affects me.

- I am proud of my professional appearance, language and behaviour.

- I protect the privacy and security of our guests, my fellow employees and the company's confidential information and assets.

- I am responsible for uncompromising levels of cleanliness and creating a safe and acci-dent-free environment.

They sound like good words, and there are many companies who could write similar mantras. But few companies have a culture where it runs deep – where people don't just know the words but embrace them.

As a senior executive of the chain's Ritz-Carlton Istanbul recently said to me, 'I am truly proud to be Ritz-Carlton. I know it is a great place to stay, but it is also an amazing place to work.'

Customer relationships

Do you trust me? Do you want me? Do you love me?

You want all these things from me but do you give the same in return? If you want me to do more for you, come back and buy more, tell my friends about you or even be loyal to you, maybe it will take more than a few points and a plastic card. Have you seen how many loyalty cards I have in my wallet? Loyalty is more than a small discount, a monthly magazine or a dedicated service desk. It requires passion and commitment too.

Relationships are never easy and having a relationship with a company - even a brand - is not easy either. To be honest, I'm much more interested in getting to know other people like myself rather than spending time with a company. Why don't you bring your like-minded customers together? We all buy the same things from you and probably share the same broader interests. I'd love you more for bringing people together with a shared passion rather than using relationships as a cover for trying to get me to buy more and buy more often!

9.1 CUSTOMER PARTNERSHIPS

Customers are much more interested in what they do with their products and services than the companies they buy them from. Similarly, customers are much more interested in building relationships with other people like them, who share their problems or passions, than with a company who is only interested in selling more to them.

Yet companies invest millions (sometimes billions) in the technologies, customer relationship management (CRM) programmes and incentives that they hope will build customer relationships and potentially customer loyalty.

An 'outside in' approach to relationships seeks to facilitate people coming together with a common purpose rather demanding a direct attraction. So how do you become the facilitator of relationships between people and retain some part in those relationships?

Start by considering what makes a good relationship. Beyond the business world there are many theories, from transactional analysis to personal relationship counselling and experts geopolitical cooperation, although a number of themes come through. Relationships require:

- Common purpose.

- A sense of equality and humility.

- Mutual attraction.

- Tolerance.

- Something special.

- Mutual benefits.

Another way to summarize these factors is to consider the three dimensions of committing (a deepening commitment to each other), contributing (both sides giving and taking), and

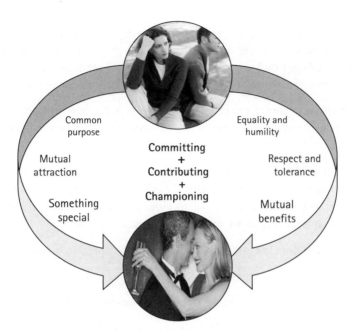

Common
purpose

Equality and
humility

Mutual
attraction

**Committing
+
Contributing
+
Championing**

Respect and
tolerance

Something
special

Mutual
benefits

CUSTOMER RELATIONSHIPS: DOING MORE FOR EACH OTHER

championing (supporting and encouraging each other). The dimensions illustrate the interdependence of these factors – you need to be good at all aspects, not just some of them.

Combining these factors and sustaining them over time is never easy, as we all know. The three most practical and important aspects to customer relationships today are partnering, connecting and advocating.

Partnerships are best illustrated in the business-to-business world, from which consumer markets can learn much. Connecting is most significant in developing communities and advocacy is recognized as the most important driver of future purchase intensions and building reputation.

Customer partnering is fundamentally about working together for mutual success. Of course the nature of that success might be more than just financial; a partnership is typically based on a collective vision of what each is trying to achieve, a mutual dependence in doing so and then sharing of resources, knowledge, investment and time in order to create a better solution.

Business-to-business organizations often feel like the poor relation compared with the glamour and focus on business-to-customer. Yet in many ways they are way ahead in thinking, not least in how to build and manage relationships.

Clearly, it is easier to build stronger relationships if there are far fewer customers. Intel's primary customers, electronics manufacturers, can be listed on one page, as could the major retailers targeted by P&G. Indeed, some might argue that this is organizationally the domain of the sales team. It is still key to the marketing process.

There are a number of principles that we can learn from business-to-business relationships:

- Focus on a few key accounts rather than many.

- Seek to build relationships over time rather than one-off sales.

- Build a team of people dedicated to supporting the client.

- Understand the client's business, strategy and priorities intimately.

- Map the key activities, people and opportunities.

- Allocate specific people to build relationships with their opposite numbers.

- Engage senior management on both sides to collaborate strategically.

- Develop a relationship plan identifying key projects and ways of working.

- Coordinated and managed by an overall relationship manager.

This becomes more than a customer-supplier relationship; it becomes a business partnership. This must become a win–win relationship if both sides are to commit to it and can only be achieved by openness, patience and commitment on both sides. Examples of the level of commitment might include the following:

- The supplier having an office and staff full-time within the client building.

- The relationship is mentioned in the annual report as a strategic 'asset'.

- Regular meetings of CEOs on both sides on wider business opportunities.

- Secondment of staff on either side, for personal and business learning.

- Rewards based on sharing in the success, for example as a percentage of profits or shares.

- Talent is attracted to the supplier, specifically because of the relationship.

Look at many ad agencies and their large clients. St Lukes' office in London is a series of client rooms, where you step into a client experience and meet the agency's dedicated account team, often complemented by client people too. Conversely, the agency's team often also has a desk in the client's office so that they become part of the extended team.

'Key account management' typically takes four different forms, reflecting the evolution of a partnership and the deepening of integration between the partners – in this case two companies:

- Buyer and seller, or more typically purchasing manager and key account manager, coming together on a regular basis.

- Buyer and seller working as a dedicated team, almost like colleagues, developing plans and operationally delivering them on both sides.

- Buyer and seller teams – including strategic, operational and financial representatives – working together with coordinated processes and systems.

- Buyer and seller businesses become integrated, with a seller team integrated within the buyer business – mutually dependent, deeply connected.

Key account management is a more thoughtful model for CRM in consumer markets. It recognizes what a partnership requires and is more than a database and torrents of mail, or a loyalty card and an abundance of points and prizes.

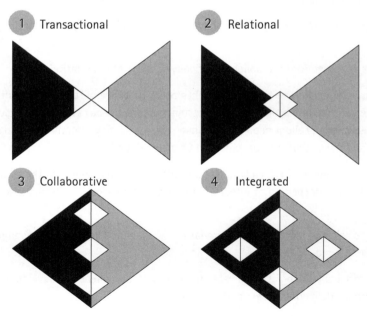

CUSTOMER PARTNERING: LEARNING FROM KEY ACCOUNT MANAGEMENT

Insight 36: HARLEY-DAVIDSON

'What we sell is the ability for a 43-year-old accountant to dress in black leather, ride through small towns and have people be afraid of him' declared CEO James Ziemer as he sought to capture the Harley-Davidson experience in words.

He went further in his 2008 annual report to shareholders, saying:

> 'Throughout the world, Harley-Davidson unites people deeply, passionately and authentically, and in this unity there is a rich and unending variety of personal experiences. From town to town and country to country, Harley-Davidson transcends cultures in ways that resonate locally. With both global significance and local relevance, it's no surprise that Harley-Davidson ranks as one of the strongest brands in the world. But igniting the fire within people all over the world is much more important.'

William Harley and Arthur Davidson would be amazed by what their brand has achieved. The school friends always shared a passion for all things mechanical and started working together in a Milwaukee factory. Together they studied the mechanics of engines and in 1901 designed four engines and fitted them to bicycle frames. In 1903 they built their first Harley-Davidson 'motorcycle' and quickly built an order book that stretched years ahead.

In 1913 they started their first racing team with star rider Joe Petreli publicly declaring that Harley's were far better than its two competitors at the time, Indian and Excelsior. Motorbikes really took off during the First World War, when Harley-Davidsons were adopted by the US Army. Twenty thousand bikes were used during the conflict, spurring mass production and an enduring love of the tough, reliable brand.

In the 1920s a team of pig farmers known as the 'Hog Boys' become the best motorbike racing team across America. They carried a pig, or hog, as their mascot, and following their frequent wins would put the pig on the back of their bike for the victory lap. The team loved their Harleys and their name would be remembered years later, redefined as the Harley Owners Group (HOG).

The 1960s was the era of sex, drugs and rock 'n' roll. Harley owners reflected the times by modifying their bikes to create extended front handlebars and adding as much chrome as possible. The 'chopper' said everything about what a man wanted to be.

However, the company wasn't keen on promoting such customizations at the time and opted to focus on lighter, faster bikes as were now being produced by the Japanese, and targeting a younger audience. But the strategy didn't succeed and in 1967, the company was sold to AMF (American Machinery and Foundry). It tried to reduce costs and increase productions, but falling quality started to damage the brand and sales fell further.

In 1981 the old executive team was able to buy back the brand at a low price and started to reclaim its good name. Customers still loved the heritage brand but their loyalty had been stretched in recent years. The company refocused on its origins, making classic American bikes and positively encouraged customizations and extra chrome.

The HOG was launched in 1983 as the official riders' club, quickly establishing a six-figure membership with chapters across the world. *Hog Tales* was launched as a bimonthly newsletter, with articles about the bikes and the people who rode them. It also featured the many biker rallies – events such as Daytona Bike Week and the Sturgis Rally in South Dakota became dominated by Harley enthusiasts. Local chapters organized group events, known as Hog Rides, and if you fancied a vacation you could go on a Hog Holiday, with Hog Hires providing the bikes on location.

As Harley-Davidson re-established itself, its typical customer changed too. Over the last two decades, the average Harley rider has gone from a 35-year-old to a 47-year-old, with an average income of $83,000 rather than $38,000. In some ways this reflects the loyalty of its customers and the desirability of its brand. Today, the HOG is international, with over one million members and 1400 chapters. In a recent poll by Millward Brown, Harley-Davidson was found to be the world's most popular branded tattoo.

9.2   CUSTOMER COMMUNITIES

People come together with a common purpose and passion. Online and offline, customers are increasingly finding each other in local and global networks. Web 2.0, the more connected applications of the Internet that encourage user-generated content and interaction between people rather than just with locations, is driving this into the mainstream.

Emerging communities such as Facebook, MySpace, Xing and LinkedIn are reshaping markets in more connected ways. No longer do they have physical barriers, and no longer are customers alien to each other, walking down the shopping aisles in mutual ignorance. Now they can start to connect, act collectively and assert their power.

This will increase as the networks become more focused. At present they are poorly defined in their purpose. People join Facebook to connect with new and existing friends but struggle to do much else. As sub-communities emerge with common passions, then they will become more active, with more reasons to connect. In the business world, for example, Fohboh is a specialist community connecting everybody who works in the catering world. Unlike the general sites, the topics of debate suddenly become much more specific, collaborative and heated.

The role of companies and more specifically their brands in these networks is still unclear. Some brands have tried to form networks based on the common interests of their customers – Huggies bringing together new mothers, Tesco bringing together people who love wine. Other networks have established themselves as brands, such as supporters' clubs and professional associations, and then brands have sought to sponsor them or explicitly promote themselves to the members.

The question is whether an established brand can really attract a network of customers with a common passion not necessarily for the product but for its application – the DIY store bringing people together with a passion for DIY, perhaps. Alternatively, potential customers form groups themselves, enabled by the social networks, and then brands will have to find a way of adding value to those existing structures if they want to be let in.

The implications are enormous if a brand really can connect with a community of customers, rather than just customers as individuals:

- Brands can connect with large groups of relevant customers quickly, through collective and viral-based communications.

- Customers can assert more power than before, shaping the reputation of a brand over-night either positively or negatively.

- Brands can transact directly with larger groups, for example by facilitating the connections within the community or using its hub as a network distributor.

- Customers can leverage collective negotiation and bargaining power to secure better prices or influence how the brand behaves.

- Brands can align themselves to communities and grow quickly, becoming an exclusive supplier or through co-branding and licensing.

- Customers can collaborative directly to drive new product developments and secure more relevant and customized solutions.

The 'third place' is a construct created by the sociologist Ray Oldbenburg. He describes humans as requiring a third place away from home and work, where a person can interact with others that they have come to know as members of the same community.

A customer community has the potential to be 'third place', where a group of like-minded individuals who enjoy interacting under a common umbrella can come together. This umbrella

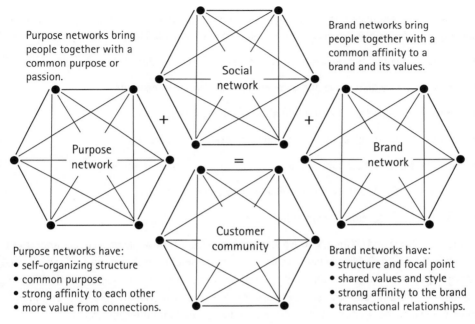

Purpose networks bring people together with a common purpose or passion.

Brand networks bring people together with a common affinity to a brand and its values.

Purpose networks have:
• self-organizing structure
• common purpose
• strong affinity to each other
• more value from connections.

Brand networks have:
• structure and focal point
• shared values and style
• strong affinity to the brand
• transactional relationships.

Customer communities have:
• self-organizing structure
• shared purpose and values
• strong affinity to each other
• desire brands with their purpose.

CUSTOMER COMMUNITIES: NETWORKS OF PEOPLE WITH PURPOSE

might be a brand –indeed, Starbucks has gone so far as to define itself as 'the third place' – or the umbrella might be a broader concept such as an aspect of gardening, a genre of rock music or a sports team.

There are six essential characteristics of any community, real or virtual. Think of a small village coming together or a group of people setting up a reading club. The community must:

- Primarily serve the interests of the members of the community.

- Be sufficiently distinctive and compelling to attract new members.

- Have a collective identity but still allows individual expression.

- Facilitate communication and interaction between its members.

- Create, share and consume value – such as content – between themselves.

- Allow the members to shape the development and its agenda.

- Have time to develop its own culture and rules.

Academics Muniz and O'Guinn wrote a seminal article about the application of communities to brands in the *Journal of Consumer Research*. They describe a brand community as 'a specialized, non-geographically-bound community, based on a structured set of social relations among admirers of a brand' and say such networks exhibit three traditional markers of community: shared consciousness, rituals and traditions, and a sense of moral responsibility.

Shared consciousness is illustrated by Apple users, who will always vigorously defend and promote the virtues of the Mac, for example, with total passion. Rituals and traditions are illustrated by drivers of Morris Minor cars, for example, who flash their headlights at each other.

Another academic, Robert Kozinets has sought to define the types of participants in such communities, considering the different level of commitment they have to the community and how they see themselves within it. Imagine yourself in a local village with different characters emerging, each seeking to participate in different ways. He identifies:

- ***Devotees*** – weak affiliation, strong personality.

- ***Tourists*** – weak affiliation, weak personality.

- ***Insiders*** – strong affiliation, strong personality.

- ***Minglers*** – strong affiliation, weak personality.

Any community will have a diverse mix of these types. In the physical world, some people will want to be the activists – on committees, wearing badges of office, shaping the agenda. In the online world, they will be writing blogs, driving discussion forums and shaping opinion. However, both communities need the quiet masses too, some of whom will care deeply about why they are there, others who will be 'cruising for novelty'.

Another way of considering the players in a community is to take Malcolm Gladwell's concept of 'mavens' and 'connectors', as described in *The Tipping Point*. Mavens aggregate significant amounts of content, knowledge or expertise. Connectors have diverse networks of friends and associates. In order to spread an idea, you need to convince the mavens that it is right, then engage the connectors to spread the idea to as many people as possible. If you can effectively do this, you achieve a 'tipping point'.

In the business world, therefore, we need to understand which communities we should align ourselves to and who are the most important members within that community both to influence and incentivize. We need to align our purpose to theirs and then dig deep into the collectiveness for real insights. We need to engage them in new ways and align our experiences to their networks as well as to the individuals within it. And we need to recognize that whilst direct relationships are important, it is the relationships between people the communities that matter more to them.

Probably the best example of a brand community is the Harley-Davidson community. HOG members love the brand, although their greatest loyalty is to each other. The brand brings them together, but their passion is for the open road. They tattoo themselves with the Harley-Davidson logo, but it is real people who they ride with, drink with and do anything for.

Insight 37: THE CO-OPERATIVE GROUP

The Co-operative Group is the UK's largest cooperative, democratically run by members to meet their common needs and aspirations.

Just £1 enables anyone to be part of The Co-op and each member has an equal right to say how the business should be run and achieve its social goals. Every member receives a dividend, a share in the profits that they help to create.

Although the organization has wider goals than just making money – in particular, making a positive contribution towards the communities it operates in – it does so in a way that still has all the financial disciplines of a commercial business. It still has suppliers and employees to pay, and a business and new products and services to invest in. However, it goes about this in a more balanced way, thinking more about customers, broader society and the environment, always trying to do 'the right thing'.

Ethics sit at the heart of the business, with its ethical policies developed in partnership with its members, its customers. Or as it says, 'we work with members to make changes for the better'.

What this means in practice is that the aisles of its food stores are packed with locally sourced or Fairtrade-certified organic products at reasonable prices. Booking a flight with its travel business includes an option to offset the carbon emissions or ideally, encouraging people to travel less distance and still have a good time. Money you save in the Co-operative Bank won't be used to support corrupt regimes or unethical activities, which is surprisingly common with other banks.

In recent years the group has worked hard to find a contemporary way of delivering the values that were originally developed with the mill workers of Rochdale, Lancashire in mind. In those days, local communities were tightly knit, money was scarce and ambitions limited. Today, there are still many with limited resources, but communities are more diverse, life more complicated and aspirations are greater.

In 2007, the group sought to bring together many of the fragmented cooperative societies around the country and relaunch the concept of membership, and the benefits it delivered to the business and its members. This meant considering new ways in which it could deliver its principles that would be simply understood and valued by local people.

Cooperative values such as 'self-help', 'equality' and 'solidarity' needed to be rethreaded through its activities. How do you help people to manage their money better? How do you seek to listen at meet the needs of every member? How do you speak up for members on social or even political issues in a world of instant communication and packaged media?

Ethical values such as 'openness' and 'social responsibility' were equally important to re-establish and articulate. Should we even have a travel business in a world of unsustainable climate change? How do we explain ethics to people in a relevant and interesting way? What does the bank do about customers who get into debt? Should we have credit cards that encourage people to spend beyond their means?

The group agonized over these dilemmas but also saw them as opportunities. It gave them the chance to do business in a different way. Who else had such deep community roots? As environmental concerns rose up the customers' agenda, wasn't this now the time to make the most of what it does? How can it use their nationwide store footprint to support its other businesses, in particular financial services?

That same year, the group introduced a new identity. Becoming known as 'The Co-operative' rather than the 'The Co-op' reminded people of its difference, and the name was consistently used as a common prefix to each of its business brands. Colour, style and language were added to its brand communications, particularly in retailing, and membership was positioned at the heart of everything it did. This has taken some time to implement, partly because of the separate nature of some of its businesses and internal processes that in some cases stem from its founding days.

Members began to see a difference. The local store became the centre of the community again rather than an uncompetitive discounter. The bank began to reassert its difference by targeting customers with a conscience and developing propositions uniquely for them. As well as sharing in annual profits, members could access exclusive offers and benefits that other customers could not. Members could get involved, attending events and online discussions with other members, supporting community initiatives, and electing representatives to local, regional and national member forums – or even putting themselves forward.

The business began to thrive again too. In 2007 it delivered a turnover of £9.4 billion, achieved with 87,000 employees serving around ten million customers a week buying their organic bread and locally farmed vegetables in local shops, and saving their money and insuring their homes in a way that also contributes to social and environmental projects.

In a fast and transient world, it was great to have a brand that cared, that was local and listened to real people – a brand to hang onto.

9.3 CUSTOMER ADVOCATES

Customer loyalty is rare and difficult to achieve. Choice, convenience and cheap prices mean that it is now incredibly easy not to be loyal. Indeed, the initiatives that were supposed to drive loyalty – loyalty cards and their points schemes – have deeply marginalized the pursuit from business mainstream to marketing gimmick.

Customer loyalty has become associated with cards, points and rewards. 'Loyalty cards' came to our attention initially through the frequent flyer schemes of airlines. More recently, everything from luxury goods to bagel stores offer loyalty cards too.

Whilst there are many useful aspects to the best programmes, the basic principle of collecting points buying more is tired. The monetary value of such programmes is usually 1–2% and although it might seem like you are getting something for nothing, there are far easier and quicker ways to save more money.

Customer loyalty, if anything, is typically centred on a brand rather a business. There is little to engage with emotionally within a business overall, particularly when staff are rotated and you are rarely able to build personal connections; brands can have more depth and personality, reflecting customer aspirations and defining the kind of person they are or want to be. Kevin Roberts, Worldwide CEO of Saatchi & Saatchi, calls such brands 'lovemarks' and describes them as being rooted in a combination of intimacy, sensuality and spirituality.

Martin Lindstrom, author of *BrandSense*, took this idea and considered how to measure the amount of 'love' for a brand. Inspired by Christof Koch, one of the world's leading neuroscientists, who is also the owner of an Apple tattoo, he researched which brands people would be most willing to have tattooed on their bodies. He found that the world's leading 'tattoo brands' were as follows:

1   Harley-Davidson – 18.9%

2   Disney – 14.8%

3   Coca-Cola – 7.7%

4   Google – 6.6%

5   Pepsi – 6.1%

6   Rolex – 5.6%

7   Nike – 4.6%

8   Adidas – 3.1%

But gaining a person's genuine loyalty – so that they will drive an extra ten minutes to their preferred supermarket, pay a premium for their preferred brand, dress themselves from top to toe in the same label or forgive a company when something goes wrong – is a much more involved and long-term challenge.

The economics are important too. Fred Reicheld in *The Loyalty Effect* defined the financial logic for building customer loyalty, arguing that loyal customers will:

- **Stay longer** – renew their purchases over time.

- **Buy more** – add other products or services.

- **Pay more** – prepared to tolerate a premium or no discount.

- **Cost less** – cheaper to serve, requiring less selling and support.

- **Tell others** – become advocates, telling their best friends too.

'Would you recommend us to your friends?' Reicheld proposes that as the 'ultimate question' to ask customers. He argues that in today's markets, where word of mouth has replaced all other media as the most powerful and trusted method of influencing customers, advocacy is the most potent outcome of a relationship. It is the best measure of customer engagement and the most significant driver of future profitability.

'Net Promoter Score' (NPS) is the proprietary term developed with Bain & Co. to reflect the net number of positive recommendations by customers to their peers. It recognizes that there is likely to be a combination of positive and negative recommendations from different people and indeed many others who are not likely to recommend in either sense.

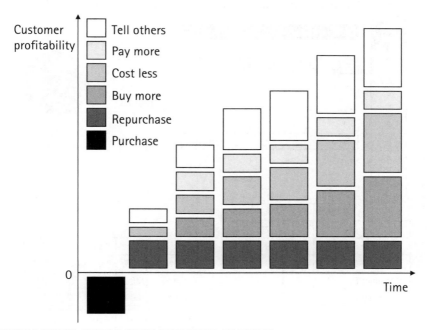

CUSTOMER LOYALTY: IMPACT OF RELATIONSHIPS ON PROFIT

"On a scale of 0 to 10 how likely are you to recommend us to a colleague?"

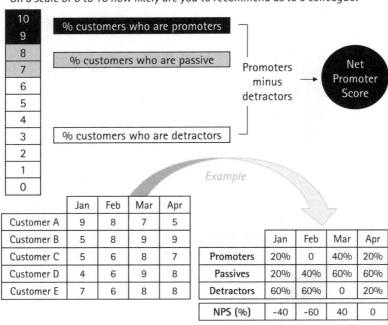

MEASURING ADVOCACY: YOUR 'NET PROMOTER SCORE'

NPS has been adopted by organizations large and small with the same enthusiasm with which they previously embraced customer satisfaction measurement, the latter recognized more as a hygiene factor than an indicator of customer attitudes and behaviours. At GE, for example, from CEO Jeff Immelt through to local branches of subsidiary businesses, everyone awaits the monthly NPS score alongside revenues and profits.

Some of warned of companies becoming over-reliant on the term, adopting it as a single metric that will secure their future, or developing NPS strategies to improve the score. This, of course, is nonsense. It is simply an important measure of effectiveness in engaging customers and a useful forward-looking indicator of financial performance. It should not be looked at in isolation, separately from the overall customer strategy, or used as a singular driver of evaluation and rewards.

Insight 38: NEW BALANCE

'Achieve new balance.'

That was the simple but distinctive advertising line that captured the New Balance difference. It was about finding a physical and mental balance in life through the natural pursuit of running for pleasure or performance. It also recognized that running is about feet, comfort and support. Everybody's feet come in different widths as well as lengths, yet there was only brand that did likewise.

New Balance was founded in Boston in 1906 by William Riley, a 33-year-old Briton who made foot arch supports and prescription footwear. He designed his first running shoe for the Boston Brown Bag Harriers, of which he was a member. The business remained small and local until 1961 with the development of The Trackster, the world's first performance running shoe made with a ripple sole and available in multiple widths.

During the 1960s, New Balance's reputation for running shoes in multiple widths grew through word of mouth. When Jim Davis bought the brand on the day of the Boston Marathon in 1972, he was spurred by his own experience: 'I got a pair of the shoes, started running in them, and people would come up to me and comment that I must be a good runner.'

At the time, New Balance was primarily a mail-order business. Davis set about building a presence within retailers and tripled revenues within two years to around $300,000. The business grew rapidly as running took off as a mass participation sport, retaining its commitment to width fittings, unlike any of its competitors.

In 1978 New Balance reached Europe. With revenues now at $60 million, the company launched its iconic NB 320 shoes, which were my own first experience of the specialist brand. These were followed by the highly successful NB 990s, the first athletic shoe priced at $100. New Balance was recognized as a shoe for serious runners. It was an antidote to the mainstream brands that appealed as much as street wear as for track and road running.

'We do not endorse athletes. We focus on high performance rather than fashion. We sell every shoe that we make in multiple widths, because we believe that fit is a critical performance characteristic. We maintain a high level of stock so that dealers can always offer a full range of sizes and widths,' explained Davis in a rare interview with the *Boston Globe*.

Because the company remained private, Davis felt that he could take a longer-term perspective, being more socially responsible than the high volume, high fashion, publicly quoted brands such as Adidas and Nike. 'If we were a public company, I am sure the shareholders would suggest we close local factories and manufacture in Asia because of the lower manufacturing costs.'

New Balance continues to make its own shoes. With marketing spend a fraction of competitors, it relies upon word of mouth – people talking about the high performance of its shoes. In the first ever London Marathon it was a New Balance branded vest, shorts and shoes that crossed the line equal first, worn by the runners' runner Dick Beardsley. By the following year, it was the most popular shoe crossing the finish line. Every runner wanted to wear the winning shoe.

Today New Balance has worldwide sales approaching $2 billion, having brought its customized philosophy to other sports such as hiking, tennis, boxing and basketball. It has also become an anti-fashion statement, its grey and brown trainers becoming the desired footwear of the no logo generation – because they feel so good and look so different.

Customer performance

I want you to succeed, be profitable and work as a high-performing company – because then you can invest in me. You can invest in developing even better products and services, recruiting great people who will serve me well, making my life even easier and more enjoyable, and knowing that you will always be there.

But I don't want you to get greedy. I see all the business reports, the rocketing profits and incredible bonuses to a few executives. I don't begrudge you a fair reward for making my life better, but I do want you to share it with those great people who work for you and buy from you.

It's my money that creates your profits. If you do the right thing I'm happy to spend a lot more with you at no extra cost to you. Indeed, the more profitable our relationship becomes, the more successful you will be in the future. And imagine if I can persuade lots of my friends and colleagues to do likewise? Have you ever considered your customers as your most valuable asset? Together we can help you drive incredible, profitable growth – and I guess your investors would be interested in that!

10.1 VALUE DRIVERS

Customers are the most important drivers of business performance, yet one of the most perverse aspects of board meetings is that they typically spend less than 10% of their time focusing on where 90% of their success comes from. Little time is spent on discussing where the revenues come from and how they could be improved, before the conversation quickly progresses to operational performance and cost management.

Measuring the effectiveness with which we manage customers should therefore be the most important aspect in measuring and managing business:

- **Value**: Customers are the scarcest resource in business today. The way we manage them has a direct impact on the value of the business and its market capitalization.

- **Drivers**: Customers are the best indicators of future performance. How we manage them and what actions and investments we make drives the profitability of future years.

- **Customers**: The notion of customer-based performance is a much more engaging way to drive results – it is more relevant and worthwhile, encouraging collaboration and interest.

Too much time is spent counting the cash and not enough on where it comes from.

An 'outside in' approach to performance management requires us to connect the conventional measures of customer activities, with the typical measures of financial performance. This is entirely possible (the specific correlations being different for every business) and essential if managers and investors are to take customer retention or advocacy as seriously as revenue and profitability.

Customer-related performance metrics are typically more informative about the future health of the business, whilst most financial metrics look backwards.

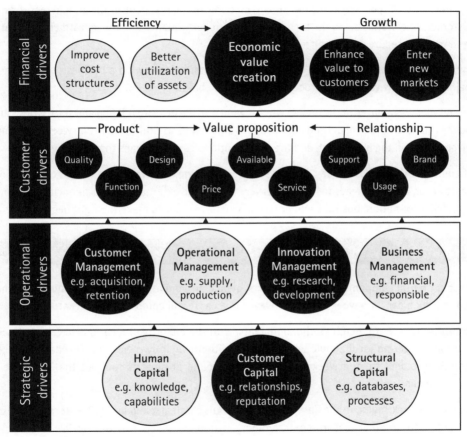

VALUE DRIVERS: CONNECTING CUSTOMERS WITH BUSINESS PERFORMANCE

285

Imagine the CEO speaking at the next board meeting, or the first page of the annual report, and customers and brands being the focus: their current performance and the investments that are been made to secure and enhance future results.

This might seem an obvious and engaging place to start in reviewing a business, yet the vast majority will start with costs, processes and supply chains.

One retailer was amazed at the impact when it went into the investor briefing and started describing the financial impact of getting new fashion from catwalk to clothes rail in two weeks less than anybody else on the high street, and the incremental sales and margins that this drives.

Of course, at the end of the day, business is not a machine; performance does not come out of a calculator. Business needs to bring together internal and external insights, financial and non-financial information, business and personal beliefs, in order to make the right decisions.

Insight 39: ENTERPRISE CAR RENTAL

Most car rental companies focus on airports, people arriving at destinations away from home and renting a car for a week or two. However, one car rental company is different.

Enterprise focuses on neighbourhood markets, with the majority of locations in central town locations targeting local people who might be without their own car for a few days or need something bigger for the weekend. They can be found at airports too, but that's not their primary focus.

Founded by Jack Taylor, in the basement of a St Louis car dealership in 1957, Enterprise is also distinctive for another reason – extraordinary customer service. It is the world's largest car rental company, operating from 7000 locations around the world, with 720,000 vehicles and 120 different makes and models of car. Most important are the 65,000 'extended family' of employees who are passionate about the service they deliver and incentivized so that a great customer service record can turn a branch manager into a millionaire. In fact, Taylor is as proud of the number of self-made millionaires he has created as the company itself.

The company's mission might seem a little awkward and uninspiring – 'To fulfil the automotive and commercial truck rental, leasing, car sales and related needs of our customers and, in doing so, exceed their expectations for service, quality and value' – but at least it's about the customer.

It goes on – 'We will strive to earn our customers' long-term loyalty by working to deliver more than promised, being honest and fair, and going the extra mile to provide exceptional personalized service that creates a pleasing business experience' – capturing all the important concepts in a sentence.

Most employees would struggle to recite this, but they would know in their heads and their hearts that Enterprise is all about customer service.

Despite these service mantras, Enterprise genuinely focuses on its customers through a business model that encourages attitudes and behaviours to do the right thing intuitively. Whilst many companies articulate their business models in complex structural and financial terms, Enterprise focuses on the power of people:

- We hire smart, motivated people.

- We deliver exceptional customer service.

- Completely satisfied customers come back and tell others.

- Profitable growth enables personal growth.

- Growth drives financial rewards and attracts more great people.

The service culture is underpinned by a single-minded, company-wide measurement system. The Enterprise Service Quality Index measures the number of customers on each day, in each location, for every employee that says they are 'completely satisfied'. Hundreds of thousands of customers are surveyed daily by telephone and online in order to provide fast and direct results.

Good service is not enough. Only exceptional service counts.

10.2 CUSTOMER METRICS

The old adage that 'what gets measured gets done' is still true, and even more so 'what gets rewarded gets done'.

Targets, metrics and rewards should therefore be considered the starting point of a customer business.

The wrong performance indicators, an unreasonable performance target or a badly balanced 'balanced scorecard' (measuring people, customer, financial and improvement factors) will drive business in the wrong direction. Strategic decisions will be based on false criteria, investments will not deliver optimal returns, people will become demotivated by their inability to hit targets and investors will lose confidence.

Get the right measures and then you can make the right decisions; people and resources are focused in the best places for high returns, and everyone can share in the rewards.

Market share, for example, is an increasingly meaningless, depending entirely on how you define your boundaries: you could have a 100% share of one market and 0.1% of another. As customer needs change and market profitability varies, markets are unequal. P&G and Unilever might be big competitors in some sectors or segments, but are irrelevant to each other in others.

This gives the big picture and unifying goal, but is less practical in enabling day-to-day decision-making. Developing a business scorecard, the right portfolio of metrics, should be based firstly on the 'value drivers' of the business. These will differ by company, but in simple terms there are:

- **Inputs** such as operating costs, headcount, and time to market – factors that can be managed directly because they relate to decisions and actions.

- **Throughputs** such as productivity, sales growth, customer retention – factors that are direct consequences of operations and can quickly be influenced.

- **Outputs** such as profitability, return on investment and share price – factors that are more complex to influence but are clearly driven by the previous ones.

Within most organizations, customer-related metrics are fragmented and unconnected from each other, as well as from their financial impact. Marketing people are obsessed with the customer awareness and engagement achieved through their actions. Sales people are concerned about their reach, and ability to retain the best customers. Operational people are focused on customer satisfaction. Yet there is little point in engaging people in great promises if they are impossible to deliver. There is little value in satisfaction if the customer doesn't come back again.

Customer-related metrics enable us to see the bigger picture of business and the collective actions that drive value creation. As a result, we can prioritize the value drivers that are most important to the business. This enables better investment and decision-making, as well as better measurement and management of performance.

Within this system of value creation are the implications of short- and long-term actions and effects in the organization: a sales promotion will give an immediate return, building a new brand will take longer for its impact to be seen, investing in new product developments will take even longer.

Short- and long-term both matter, particularly when most of the value is in intangible assets that typically deliver long-term returns. This comparing this year's costs and revenues is a rather simplistic way of looking at business.

'Value' provides the answer, calculating the sum of likely future cash flows and embracing both the short and long term. Value-based decision-making therefore becomes crucial to deciding strategically – which are the right businesses and brands, markets, products and customers to focus on for the longer term? Out of the business portfolio, which businesses 'create value' and which 'destroy value'?

One business might have strong sales and market share, and even operating profits look good – yet because the cost of capital is greater, every additional sale will destroy value. In terms of operational value, what is the most effective allocation of budgets of people and resources in the short term? Whilst long-term performance matters, the markets might still be immature – and the business needs to generate cash flow in the meantime to survive and fund the longer-term investments.

Ultimately we must combine the drivers of value to the customer and business – the inputs and outputs, the short and long term, the strategy and operational implications – and ensure that the metrics we choose are 'smart' (specific, measurable, achievable, realistic and timely).

Don Peppers and Martha Rogers, who work with many companies on customer programmes and introducing a 'one-to-one' approach, sought to define the Holy Grail in terms of customer-to-shareholder connection in their book *Return on Customer,* which proposed that ROC should become a critical metrics for any business:

> 'Repeat after us: the only value your company will ever create is the value that comes from customers – the ones you have now and the ones you will have in the future. Businesses succeed by getting, keeping and growing customers … Without customers, you don't have a business.'

Customer Reach We currently reach 90% of the UK population. This is more than our nearest competitor at 79% **Customer Preference** 45% of our customers say they prefer us. 60% of existing customers intend to use us next time **Customer Satisfaction** 27% of our customers say that they are very satisfied. 45% say they are satisfied to some extent.	**Customer Contracts** 40% of customers are on long-term contracts of > 2 years **Customer Retention** 67% of our customers have stayed for over one year We seek to increase this retention rate to 80% in the next 3 years **Customer Loyalty** 60% of existing customers intend to use us next time 12% of customers say they would recommend us
Customer Volume We currently have 12.2m customers. This has grown by 12% over the last year. **Customer Share** We currently have 33% of the UK market. **Customer Yield** We generate £365 per customers This is 45% higher than the market average	**Customer Growth** We expect to grow customer numbers by 15% for next 3 years. The UK market will grow at 7% for next 3 years **Customer Innovation** 26% of our revenues come for services released in last year. We expect 12% of next years revenues to come from new products
Tactical marketing costs We spent £120m on sales promotions and discounts **Revenues** We generated £2.1b in revenues This is 12% increase on the previous year **Operating Profit** We generated £254m operating profit This is 45% increase on the previous year.	**Strategic marketing investments** We spent £180m on marketing costs relating to brand and relationships **Intangible Assets** We calculate that its brand, consumer and distributive relationships are worth £4.2bn **Business Value** We project that profits will grow at 12-15% each year over the next five years (producing an intrinsic value of £xbn)

CUSTOMER METRICS: EXAMPLE OF A BUSINESS PERFORMANCE SCORECARD

But that's not how many companies behave, is it? The demand to satisfy Wall Street on a quarterly basis drives executives to pursue contradictory business goals. Most believe, intellectually, that customers represent the surest route to long-term growth and value – yet in practice, they're quick to compromise that belief in the rush to generate current revenue.

Insight 40: FIRST DIRECT

'We treat our customers like lemons.'

The bold, monochrome press ad certainly caught the eye as First Direct, the pioneer of direct banking in the UK, described how the first challenge for a new recruit to its business is to be offered a bowl of lemons, choose one, put it back, put on a blindfold and then find the lemon that they have just chosen.

The point was that every customer is different – individual – and First Direct wants to treat you that way. It encourages staff to use all their senses to understand the customer more personally, particularly because they are dealing with them by telephone or online.

Today it has 1.2 million customers, 885,000 using Internet banking, 390,000 using text messaging, and 43% of new customers coming through these channels. One in three customers join through personal recommendation and 80% of all customer contact is electronic. It also takes 235,000 telephone calls each week, including 3500 from other countries. It has been profitable since 1995 and according to MORI/NOP has been the most recommended UK bank in each of those years.

First Direct was founded in October 1989 by the Midland Bank, then one of the UK's largest banks and now part of HSBC. With more than 1000 calls in the first 24 hours and 100,000 customers in less than two years, it has never looked back.

It targeted the time-poor, money-rich professional customer that valued the 24/7 direct channels and highly personal service. The bank's interest rates have never been particularly competitive, but customers have stayed loyal because of its service. At a time when most customers have become disillusioned with their banks, First Direct is one of the few to maintain a loyal customer base.

Through a mixture of pioneering technologies and human touches it has continued to make its customer life easier and banking a little more fun. In 1995 it reached half a million customers and started trialling Internet banking. In 1999 it launched mobile banking (by SMS text message), alerting customers to their balances and transactions.

In 2004 it launched 'First Directory', adding a range of services to a current account such as travel and personal insurance, and 'Internet Banking Plus', which combined information from a customer's range of banks and accounts in one convenient place. 'First Direct Interactive' offered personalized advice and services online. In collaboration with the *Financial Times* it included blogs and podcasts on topics such as financial planning, tax-free savings allowances and how to survive and thrive in the so-called 'credit crunch'.

The bank even created a 'virtual forest' as a more tangible representation of its sustainability efforts: it encourages paperless transactions by planting a virtual tree for every customer opting for e-statements and plants a real tree for every 20 virtual ones. The fun is not forgotten in banking either, with a 'magic bus' reaching out to communities and customers.

New CEO Chris Pilling, a relationship marketing expert previously with British Airways and Wal-Mart, is continuing to add zest into the bank with the lemons. In 2007 he relaunched the range of customer accounts, with the '1st Account' replacing existing current accounts, and offered new services including new savings mechanisms and linking to an off-set mortgage product to further integrate people's financial portfolio in one place.

More controversially, he also identified his good and bad customers. In relaunching the new accounts with associated annual fees, he made it much less attractive for less profitable customers to stay with the bank. His background told him that volume is not everything and that you cannot serve everybody with a niche proposition.

He went further, introducing new performance metrics to support the service and relationship culture. Building on Fred Reicheld's 'ultimate question', he targeted the everybody in the business on his so-called 'magic number'. Until this time, First Direct had focused on 'very satisfied' or 'extremely satisfied' customers, correlating this to customer retention, with a score that already averaged 91%.

Pilling's new 'magic number' was about action, not feelings. He wanted to measure advocacy, the positive recommendations of existing customers to others like them. He recognized that this was a much better indicator of existing customers' loyalty, a predictor of profitable growth through existing customer purchases and those of their recommended friends. Reicheld's approach asked customers if they *intended* to recommend the brand, Pilling asked them if they *actually* did. An astonishing 96% of customers answered 'yes'.

10.3 BUSINESS IMPACT

Surprisingly few companies connect the value that they create for customers with the value they create for business. Which has more impact of profitability, advertising or customer service? What is the more significant driver of growth, customer satisfaction or customer advocacy? How much budget should you allocate to brand-building compared with customer relationship programmes?

The result is dislocation between business priorities and customer action.

We shout ever louder at customers, bombarding them with direct mail because we don't know what else drives revenues. Like headless chickens we focus on quarterly results because we can't articulate longer-term impacts. We foolishly cut costs in brand development or customer service improvements because we don't know where else to gain efficiency. And we resort to price discounting rather solving customers' problems better for a premium, and end up with promiscuity rather than loyalty.

Few companies connect customers with shareholder value. In fact, most performance is not articulated in either the language of customer or shareholder: it focuses on short-term revenues and looking backwards. It therefore drives 'inside out' tactical decision-making.

Business performance is ultimately about creating long-term business value, or 'shareholder value' as it is often termed. According to research by PA Consulting, 97% of CEOs say that creating long-term shareholder value is their primary objective.

Of course, the business could choose to distribute the value it creates in any proportion: to invest more back in the business, share more with staff or give more to broader society. The point here, however, is to make the connection between what we do for customers and the value that business accumulates through doing this.

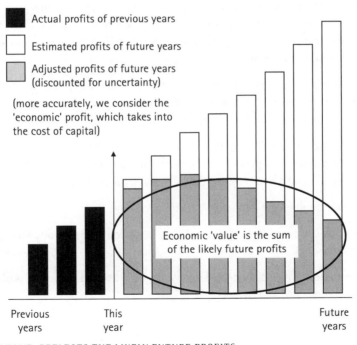

ECONOMIC VALUE: REFLECTS THE LIKELY FUTURE PROFITS

The value of a business can be calculated internally as the sum of economic profits, discounted for the uncertainty in them being delivered:

- Economic profits are profits less the cost of capital. Investors would expect a minimum level of return on their capital investment and therefore only count the additional profit beyond this. Customer activities directly affect this through additional revenues, either from price premiums or more purchases and lower costs of sale.

- The sum of future economic profits is discounted to reflect the uncertainty in this happening. Only contracted revenues are certain; others depend on market demand and broader conditions, and costs may change too. A discount rate reflects this. Customer activities directly affect this through strong brands and relationships, and better innovations and networks that make future profits more certain.

The economic value of a business as calculated internally should approximate to the market value of the business if analysts have a similar view of the future to the managers internally and this is reflected in the demand for shares.

If they are more optimistic, the share price goes up and everybody feels good – until, years later, the profits don't materialize. If they are pessimistic, the share price underperforms, requiring better communication and a better understanding of what really drives business.

Business value has tangible and intangible components:

- **Tangible value** is driven by physical assets, i.e. what could be sold off, such as property, equipment and stock.

- **Intangible value** is driven by non-physical assets, i.e. reflecting the future profit potential of brands, relationships and patents.

Edvinsson and Sveiby define three categories of intangible assets: customer capital, human capital and structural capital. New international accounting standards provide new categories for reporting intangible assets and post-purchase allocation.

'Customer capital' gives us a simple, more inclusive language to focus on what matters in business, particularly in a company that seeks to be a customer business. It articulates the importance and impact of customer-related investments and customer activities, connecting customers and shareholders, balancing short term and long term, and focusing across the organization on what matters most.

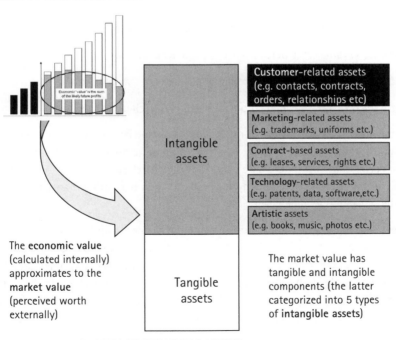

Economic 'value' is the sum of the likely future profits

Intangible assets

Customer-related assets (e.g. contacts, contracts, orders, relationships etc)

Marketing-related assets (e.g. trademarks, uniforms etc.)

Contract-based assets (e.g. leases, services, rights etc.)

Technology-related assets (e.g. patents, data, software,etc.)

Artistic assets (e.g. books, music, photos etc.)

The **economic value** (calculated internally) approximates to the **market value** (perceived worth externally)

Tangible assets

The market value has tangible and intangible components (the latter categorized into 5 types of **intangible assets**)

INTANGIBLE VALUE: CATEGORIES OF INTANGIBLE ASSETS

Customer capital can be expressed as:

- *Basket* – a collection of customer-based measures tracked over time.

- *Equity* – a weighted index of the most important customer-based metrics.

- *Value* – a sum of uplift in likely future profits due to customer-related activities.

This 'basket' of customer measures might well differ by company, depending on what has most impact on business results in their business model. But imagine a company where these were the core targets:

- *Customer preference* – the percentage of people who like us.

- *Customer volume* – the percentage of people who buy from us.

- *Customer retention* – the percentage of people who stay with us.

- *Customer referral* – the percentage of people who tell others about us.

'Customer equity', often discussed but rarely defined, should be considered as a weighted index of the metrics based on their relative importance as value drivers – ideally finding through statistical correlation how much more important each is relative to others in driving business value. This will be specific to a company and produce a number (rather than a monetary figure) that can be tracked as an index over time.

'Customer value' means the value of customers to the business rather than the perceived value to customer – as discussed within the context of customer value propositions, for example. You could argue that all the revenue and profit of a business comes from customers, and therefore customer value equates to business value. However, we are more interested in the incremental value: the uplift in future profits due effective management, the added value due to better propositions, increased perceived value of the products and services, and improved retention and advocacy.

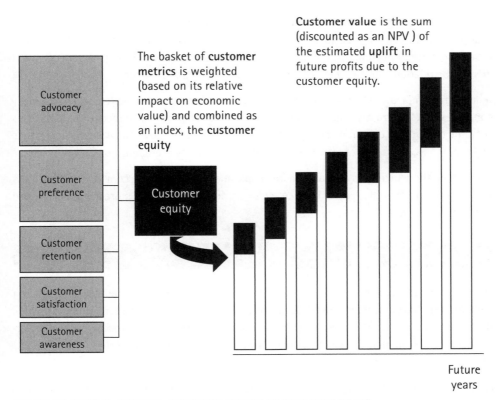

The basket of **customer metrics** is weighted (based on its relative impact on economic value) and combined as an index, the **customer equity**

Customer value is the sum (discounted as an NPV) of the estimated **uplift** in future profits due to the customer equity.

Customer advocacy

Customer preference

Customer equity

Customer retention

Customer satisfaction

Customer awareness

Future years

CUSTOMER CAPITAL: METRICS, CUSTOMER EQUITY OR CUSTOMER VALUE

Everybody in the business can feel motivated to come to work to create customer capital and understand what behaviours helped to deliver each. No boardroom director can argue that these factors are worthy of regular review and every analyst could directly use these to help understand whether this company is more or less likely to outperform its peers in the future.

However, measurement is just the outcome – it's what you do that matters. Growing your customer capital requires you to make customers the foundation of everything you do – your customer strategy and propositions, aligning your business to deliver the best experiences, and driving the relationships that deliver short- and long-term performance.

Indeed, the Tomorrow's Company report *Restoring Trust: Investment in the Twenty First Century* concludes that 'the trust and confidence of investors has been damaged recently' and believes that 'the current system is not serving customers well – a failure to align with customer needs and timescales, and a lack of transparency and accountability is eroding trust in the system'.

Not only do these measures appeal to more people and cut through the complexity of business to what matters, they also present marketing's contribution in a much more collaborative and positive manner too.

Insight 41: GE

When Jeff Immelt became chairman and CEO of GE in September 2001, he took control of an already finely tuned machine. Whilst GE had always had an innovative culture, from its famous Blue Book days of the 1950s, Jack Welch had instilled a formidable bottom line discipline on the business too. Immelt turned to two of GE's strengths – process and execution – and set out in pursuit of organic growth.

At GE's meeting of top managers at Baton Rouge in January 2006, Immelt told his leaders that if they continued to grow existing businesses at current rates, the company would not survive. 'Another decade of 4% growth and GE will cease to exist,' he said, 'but if we can spur our growth rate without losing our productivity edge, GE will keep being the most admired companies into the next century. We're now in a slow growth world. Things were different 25 years ago. Today's global markets are driven by innovation, and stock market premiums are based on companies who can generate their own growth.'

Immelt described further his belief that a culture of productivity and relying on expansion and acquisitions for growth is not enough in an interview with *Harvard Business Review*. Innovation must be at the heart of organic growth and value creation.

He believes this approach will enable GE to deliver average revenue growth of around 8%, double the last decade (and two to three times faster than the world's economy is growing), and that this will deliver 10%+ earnings and 20% returns.

To grow faster than the global economy, GE has turned organic growth into a process rather than just a goal: 'If you run a big multinational, multi-business company like GE, and if you are trying to lead transformative change, then that objective has to be linked to hitting levers across all businesses, and it must keep that up over time.'

Immelt illustrated the challenge and opportunity in a letter to all his shareholders:

> 'A reliable growth company must have the courage to invest and the discipline to deliver. It took courage to invest over $1 billion in a new jet engine, such as the GE90, with minimal returns for more than ten years. Today, because of these investments, GE enjoys exceptional success in commercial aviation. The GE90 engine should generate $40 billion of revenues over the next 30 years.'

He went on to encourage investors to 'think about the company over 10+ years the way an owner would think about it' and to get a sense of the strategic investments rather than short-termism that is required to build the business that is now delivering results: 'We are builders of businesses ... We have a team that is focused on building a company that has enduring value and makes the world a better place.'

GE now focuses on establishing the capabilities that will create and sustain this organic growth – most crucially a focus on customers, innovation and globalization. The 'Execute for Growth' process is mapped out as a circle, with no clear start or finish. It embraces new approaches and techniques, language and behaviour.

- *The 'Growth Playbook'* redefines the strategic planning process, recognizing that it should be a creative rather than financially driven process, encouraging collaboration and rethinking rather than incremental box-filling budgeting.

- *'Customer Dreaming Sessions'* bring together influential and creative people from across the industry to dream its future and through difference of perspective and opinion, to inspire new ideas and strategies.

- *'Imagination Breakthroughs'* focus senior management on the best ideas that will drive new revenue streams, irrelevant of where they come from.

- *'Innovation Labs'* support business strategy, product development and other initiatives with specialist resources and materials to drive and structure innovation of products, businesses and markets.

- *'At the Customer, for the Customer'* is about opening up and transferring its own management approaches into customer companies, helping them solve their own business problems rather than just providing products and services.

- *'CECOR Marketing Framework'* ensures that customers and market opportunities drive innovation and growth, standing for 'calibrate, explore, create, organize and realize' strategic growth.

- *'Growth Traits'* are the attributes expected of future GE business leaders. There are five factors to get on in the company: external focus, clear thinking, imagination, inclusiveness and specialist expertise.

The new approach is not full of lengthy written proposals and PowerPoint slideshows. It's about people working together – people with diverse experiences, skills and perspectives (Immelt gets involved in around eight breakthrough sessions per month) – focusing on the best ideas and opportunities, capturing the essence of ideas in pictures and prototypes, communicated in short summaries and practical action.

The high-flying CEO reflects on his new, highly motivated, fast-growing GE:

> 'This is not a place for small times. Working at GE is the art of thinking and playing big. Our managers have to work cross-function, region and company. And we have to be about big purposes.'

He reminds people that if they fail, the worse that can happen is that they will leave and find a bigger job somewhere else. But if you win at GE, 'you get to be in the front seat of history, creating the future.'

The results are impressive. Over the last two years, organic growth has averaged 8%, higher than competitors and twice GE's historical average. There is now a pipeline of 40 '$1 billion revenue products' to be introduced in coming years, 60 'Imagination Breakthroughs' generating $25 billion and many more on the way. Non-US revenues are now exceeding domestic figures and are predicted to grow at 15% annually. More effective management of the installed base should generate decades of service-based growth.

PART 3

The customer champions

In the final part we reflect on how to create, inspire and sustain a 'customer business' and ensure that it really does deliver superior, lasting value for both customers and shareholders. What does it take to create a customer revolution? Where to start? How to lead and inspire? Where to balance empowerment and control? What kind of culture and structure to adopt? How to ensure it really does improve business performance? And what will keep it going?

Leadership ... leading a customer revolution

" *Business is ultimately about people. And that's why I can tell so much from the leader of a business. I see him or her on television, maybe even meet them in person, and it is their style, attitude and passion, as well as their words, that tell me so much about the business that they lead. Do I want to support this kind of business or not? Am I proud to be their customer or not? Would I be happy to recommend them to my friends?*

Some leaders are anonymous corporate workers, introverted and internally focused, probably obsessed with their balance sheets. Others have a vision. They talk about how they want to make life better for me, they share their ambitions for the future, speak up for me and communicate their commitment and energy. They are open and friendly, they want to know what I think, and care if something goes wrong. Their passion becomes infectious not only in their own people but in people like me, their customers, too. "

6.1 INSPIRING PEOPLE

Leaders inspire people to 'come to the edge' and launch themselves into a near world – to take a new perspective or embrace a new way of working. They inspire followers.

Leaders are 'heads up' people. Managers are 'heads down' people.

'Heads up' people are able to describe a more compelling vision for the business because they see the world from the outside in rather than the inside out. They can bring it to life in practical terms and sell the benefits to each person. They demonstrate what it takes through their own attitudes and actions. They are prepared to make commitments and sacrifices, to let go of the old ways.

Leaders inspire followers.

When Steve Jobs walks to the stage at MacWorld each year, the whole technology sector holds its breath. He leads his business, his industry and his market.

The role of a leader in a customer business is internal and external.

In a successful customer business, customers want the business to succeed – they want to be part of the journey, to participate and share, and even define themselves by it. They look to the business leaders for inspiration and direction, confidence and confirmation, just like employees do.

In fact, a leader must be a leader and manager, executive and entrepreneur. Look at the most successful CEOs of today and you immediately see these collective traits. From Ray Davis to Jeff Immelt, Alan Lafley to Genentech's Arthur Levinson, Meg Whitman at eBay and Xerox's Anne Mulcahy – great leaders and managers, entrepreneurial and successful, at the top of the world's largest and most successful companies:

Heads down	Heads up
Inside out	Outside in
Leading by control	Leading by inspiration
Managing the steady state	Managing sustained growth
Ensuring consistency	Catalyst of change
Reserved and controlling	Passionate and energizing
Cautious and corporate	Open and personal
Overseeing work	Doing work
Managing hierarchically	Facilitating communities
Process and tasks	Knowledge and innovation
Doing what's always done	Embracing ideas from outside
Enforcing regulations	Reinventing the rules
Products and transactions	People and relationships
Evaluating past performance	Supporting future performance
Generating more sales	Creating extraordinary value

Ray Davis has transformed the fortunes of Umpqua Bank from a little lost bank for lumberjacks, with only six branches, deep in Oregon's Umpqua Valley to what they self-confidently describe as 'the world's greatest bank'.

In his book *Leading for Growth: How Umpqua Bank Got Cool and Created a Culture of Greatness,** Davis describes what he believes are the secrets of how he created a great business. He identified ten personal traits:

*The following extracts are reprinted with permission of John Wiley & Sons, Inc.

- Never-ending discipline. Leaders need to realize that growth is not a project or quick fix. You must have the discipline to realize you never have it made.

- Have positive passion. Be relentless about your vision. Know what you stand for. We call ourselves 'The world's greatest bank' – it helps us stand out with our customers. But, more than that, it creates positive passion within the company.

- Snap the rubber band syndrome. Each of us has a rubber band attached to our backside, connected to tradition. Keep snapping it.

- Support your people, and hold 'em accountable. Leaders have many roles. But, support and accountability are essential, and they go hand in hand.

- Give them the power. In the past, the leader was the guy with the answers. Today, you have to empower the people closest to the action to come up with their own answers.

- Rise above the battlefield. Leaders need to rise above the battlefield to give you a strategic view.

- Explain your movie. Leaders cannot delegate the job of explaining their vision for the company – what I call the 'movie that's playing in my head'.

- Be real. If you can't be yourself, you can't lead. It's as simple as that.

- Be there. Maintaining a culture is like raising a teenager – you're constantly checking in. 'What are you doing?' 'Where are you going?' 'Who are you hanging around with?'

- Keep your balance. Leading for growth is a highwire act and there are many dimensions to keeping your balance.

Umpqua Bank is a phenomenal place, more of a coffee shop than a bank, and a bit of Ritz-Carlton and Facebook thrown in. There are no barred screens between you and the cashier, just a concierge desk, as well as leather sofas, funky music and cappuccinos. This is a bank that sells merchandizing, caps and T-shirts because customers are so proud of their bank.

Davis also identified ten collective traits of organizations where leadership is customer-centric and thereby more effective operationally and commercially too:

- Know what business you are really in. Umpqua Bank really started taking off when we realized we were in the retail business, not just the banking business, and started learning from great retailers such as Nordstrom.

- What's going on behind your back? Having the right strategy is meaningless unless you can execute it flawlessly on the ground. You need systems in place to inspect the execution of strategy at the lowest level.

- Who do you want on your bus? Jim Collins in his book *Good to Great* says a leader must get the right people on the bus. I think that is exactly right, but you need to be clear on who are the right people.

- Keep your board strong and informed. Companies can't move fast if the executive team has to drag the board of directors along with it.

- Intangibles matter most. In a service business like ours, the metrics that matter most measure intangibles.

- Find the revolution before it finds you. Revolutions are going on all the time in consumer preferences, technology, marketing and other areas. We do a number of things at Umpqua to find those revolutions before they overwhelm us.

- Your brand is you. People don't like faceless bureaucracies. They like real people, real personalities. We've achieved remarkable success by being true to ourselves. Some people say we are corny, but it's who we are – and people respond.

- Serve the customer. Our Universal Associates program ensures that each associate in our stores is trained to handle any task a customer requires. This sharply sets us apart from the competition. What are you doing to set you apart?

- Put design into everything you do. Design encompasses much more than just the physical layout of stores or products. When design is used effectively, it brings every aspect of your business into alignment so that everything reinforces and supports everything else.

- Remember who you are. The biggest danger in relentless growth is that your very growth will undermine the qualities that created that growth in the first place. You've also got to know what not to change – what to maintain if you want to stay on track.

Management and leadership are the 'yin and yang' of large organizations. Whilst management is more heads down, focus and control, leadership is heads up, vision and connections. Leaders provide the inspiring vision that make people want to follow them. They pull rather than push, they engage and energize people, in a higher purpose, an inspiring vision, in seeing what is possible.

As individuals, leaders are the first to anticipate and respond to change proactively and effectively – they are flexible and adaptive, open to alternatives, and willing to take risks. They are change agents rather than managing the status quo. And they don't just propose change – they make it happen. In many ways, therefore, entrepreneurs are the right people to lead organizations.

Managers and leaders are not different people, but as complementary attributes of the same person. Whilst more senior managers will focus more on leadership aspects, they still need to provide focus and control. And whilst nobody is likely to have the perfect mix of all attributes, teams should be built so that they appreciate the differences that each member brings and the collective strengths in combining those talents.

Insight 42: ECZACIBASI

'Are you a driver or passenger?'

That was the challenge from Dr Erdal Karamercan to his team of senior managers. He is the CEO of one of Turkey's largest conglomerates, Eczacibasi Group, and seeking to bring a new focus, culture and success to the family-owned business.

The business was founded in 1942 by Dr Nejat Eczacibasi, whose father had been given the name 'Eczacibasi', meaning chief pharmacist, by the government of the time. Nejat began by manufacturing vitamin D in his Istanbul laboratory and gradually established the brand in every Turkish home.

The company's heritage and ambitions are reflected in its mission 'to be a pioneer of modern, high quality and healthy lifestyles'. Eczacibasi works towards this goal with a diverse group of businesses and makes significant contributions to its local communities through education and welfare support, culture and arts sponsorship, public policy and scientific research, women's sports, and founding Istanbul's leading modern art museum. Ethics and responsibility are important to the business and can sometimes even put it at a disadvantage in markets where not everybody plays by the rules.

The business is perhaps best known for its VitrA brand, a leading player in bathrooms and tiles around the world. It is also a major exporter of tissue paper, electronic smart cards and financial services. The two major business areas are:

- **Consumer products**: embracing 33 brands such as Egos hair gel, OK condoms and Selpak tissues, as well as licensed brands such as Nivea and Schwarzkopf. They succeed in particular through their strong distribution networks, forming close relationships with leading retail chains, but also personal relationships with smaller shops, like hairdressers.

313

- **Building products**: from industrial raw materials, including some of the world's finest clays and feldspars, through to welding electrodes. They address the construction boom locally and beyond. Alongside VitrA, the business recently acquired a number of German brands – Burgbad, a luxury bathroom furniture business, and tile-makers Engers and Villeroy & Boch Fliesen.

However, the generic pharmaceutical business is no longer part of the group, having been sold to Zentiva in 2007. Selling the family business was a bold move by Karamercan, who had recently been promoted to CEO and set about bringing a more commercial discipline to the management of the business.

He embraced 'value-based management' as a core principle for delivering performance, focusing his efforts on the activities and investments that would create the best future streams of economic profit (the real profit of a business after taking into account the cost of capital – that is, the minimum expected returns to shareholders).

Karamercan set a goal to double the 'value' of the business every five years. This didn't mean just focusing on maximizing existing revenues but working out which markets and sectors would be capable of delivering most profits in the future.

With the rapid emergence of new biomedicines and nanotechnologies, he recognized that a traditional pharma business was living on borrowed time and decided to sell whilst it still had a reasonable value. The business was shocked, but listened to his logic.

They were even more amazed when he started to spend the cash on property development, a booming sector now in Istanbul. On the site of Nejat's old factory he built Kanyon, an extravagant new shopping mall, and went on to win awards at the 2008 World Retail Congress. He built a skyscraper office and apartment block alongside it, which included the new head office of the group, with many other property development projects likely to follow.

It was an icon of transformation, a model for the future, recognition internally that change was inevitable as customers and technologies evolve, and a symbol externally that Eczacibasi was modern and innovative, ready for growth in local and international markets.

Karamercan had succeeded in doubling the value of his business in four years, and immediately declared his intent to do the same again. This time, of course, it would be harder. However, he realized that corporate strategy and structural change was not enough – acquisitions helped, but organic growth was important too.

An example of this new creativity was recruiting international designers like Ross Lovegrove and Matteo Thun to add style and desirability to VitrA's bathroom ranges, and the addition of Artema kitchen and accessories, Burgbad's furniture, and V&B's prestigious tiles in order to turn products into richer lifestyle concepts and customer solutions.

Karamercan is also a great storyteller. He reminded people of his own career as an engineer who loved technologies, the intricate details of products and how to make them better. That all changed when he took the bold step to learn about marketing. His attitude to business changed – he discovered the world of customers, the challenge of competitiveness, the need for deeper insights and stronger differentiation, the role of communication and distribution, and the power of brands.

He now urges every one of his people to follow the same path, to think opportunities rather than capabilities, to be driven by customers rather than products.

Today, Eczacibasi is a fast-growing international business, still located in Istanbul, but with customers and businesses flourishing around the world. At the beginning of 2008 the group had 42 companies with around 9900 employees, delivering a net turnover of $3.2 billion.

6.2   NEW BUSINESS LEADERS

Ritz-Carlton's Horst Schulze says that leaders should 'put their egos in their pockets'. Leaders don't do the real work, he claims – that's what his people do, and his job is to support them.

'At every new hotel, I give the introductory session myself. I've done 45 hotels so far. From the busboy to the housekeepers to the room service chefs, I line up the new hires and say to them on important question: who's more important to this hotel, you or me?' He then tells them that it's them. He argues that if he doesn't go to work on Monday morning, nobody knows. Nobody cares. But if they don't turn up, the food doesn't get served, the beds don't get made. 'You are far more important than me,' he claims.

Marcus Buckingham, co-author of *First Break All the Rules*, argues that business leaders drive business by defining the ways of working around them, the culture of their business. Speaking at the recent *European Customer Service World* conference, he said 'all culture is local – companies don't have one culture but many, driven by local ways of working in each location or department'. He therefore believes that there are as many cultures in a business as there are managers. At the same time, he argues, 'people don't quit businesses, they quit managers.'

Asked what makes a great manager, he argues that it's somebody who 'is able to turn one person's talent in a unique contribution to business performance'. However, he warns that this is not necessarily about being soft or trying to be nice. 'They challenge and push you, they're your harshest critic but they never stop believing in your talent, they may even have fired you, but because they believe it's the right thing for you.' The most important thing you need to do as a manager, he suggests, is 'to find out what is unique about each person and capitalize on it'.

The successful business leader of the twenty-first century, in big companies and small, share some common characteristics – combining the passion and directness of the entrepreneur with the rigour and discipline of the corporate executive. They personify these characteristics:

- **Communicator** *of vision*: articulating a clear and inspiring direction for the business, living the values and personality of the brand, engaging all stakeholders in active dialogues. Externally they will be ambassadors of the brand, engaging stakeholders, partners and the human face of the business to the media.

- **Connector** *of people*: bringing the best people and best ideas together – internally as well as from other companies and specialists – to generate bigger and better ideas and solutions. They will focus on building great teams, the right people in the right jobs for today and planning for future succession.

- **Catalyst** *of change*: constantly seeking new possibilities, challenging the business to think differently, to be more innovative and effective, faster and with more impact. This might be in the form of provocative ideas and disruptive challenges, prepared to play devil's advocate rather than being a rule-maker.

- **Coach** *of high performance*: working with and supporting all levels across the organization and even with peers in other companies. The leader adds their own specialist skills to the business – their brains, technical knowledge, previous experiences, insights and instincts.

- **Conscience** *of business*: deciding what is right and wrong, considering the big picture of the company and its role, and how it can help create a better world. They champion business ethics and corporate responsibility, cultural diversity, equal opportunities, staying true to the business purpose, and brand values.

Observe the way Richard Branson lights the fire in his people by encouraging them to challenge the status quo, have a bit more fun and make life just a little bit better for all the people who both work for him and buy his products. Look at the way Jeff Immelt dives into GE meetings, be they about future dreaming, technical innovation or collaborating with customers on specific solutions – like a juggler, he makes new connections, helps people see things differently and have the confidence to dream.

Insight 43: P&G

A.J. Lafley is in the midst of engineering a remarkable turnaround. The first thing Lafley told his managers when he unexpectedly stepped up to the CEO job in 2000 was just what they wanted to hear: to focus on what they did well – selling the company's major brands such as Crest, Tide and Pampers – instead of trying to develop the next big innovation.

Now, old staples of the P&G stable have done so well that it is again the envy of the industry. So is the share price, which climbed 58% to $92 a share in the six years since Lafley started, whilst the overall stock market declined 32%. Profits are almost $6 billion on sales of $44 billion, having outgrown most rivals for the past five years.

Maybe softly spoken Lafley was the antidote P&G needed after 18 months of Dirk Jager, the previous CEO who had flown into Cincinatti from the Netherlands on a mission to shake up the company. He stuck up 'Old World, New World' posters, asking people which world they were in. The share price plummeted. He rammed through an agenda of change and – although he was absolutely right that the business need a new and much more external culture – he ripped apart everything that P&G's insular culture was built on and alienated almost everyone. Instead of pushing P&G to excel, his torrent of slogans and initiatives almost brought the company to its knees.

Lafley, in his twenty-third year at P&G, was supposed to bring some stability back to the business. Having managed Tide and spent a decade running the Japanese business, he had recently returned to head up North American operations. He recognized the need for change, more speed and agility, a deeper understanding of consumers, and a more radical approach to innovation. But he also understood that P&Gers – some of the best-trained, brightest managers in the world – would only embrace such change in a P&G way.

Lafley pushed through Jager's agenda even faster and more radically than his predecessor had dared hope. However, he did it in a way that engaged people, building on what they had spent their careers doing and offering hope and personal gain rather than despair and pain. In his short time in charge, P&G has not only experienced transformation internally but has absorbed some of its largest competitors too – buying Clairol for $5 billion in 2001, followed by Wella ($7 billion) and Gillette ($54 billion) in 2005. He has replaced at least half of his most senior managers and cut 10,000 jobs. However, this is just the beginning – if one unguarded memo is believed, 25,000 more jobs could soon go, based on the idea of turning P&G into a virtual brand-owning company with marketing as a its core business and most other activities – from innovation to manufacturing – done in partnership with others.

Lafley's rallying call is incredibly simple, almost embarrassingly so, as he reminds people in meeting after meeting that 'the consumer is the boss'. With this phrase he is turning P&G inside out – or more precisely, outside in.

He symbolically removed the walls of the executive offices, including his own. He moved people about, for example seating marketing and finance people together to drive faster, more collaborative and commercial, customer-driven ways of working. He spent hours talking to real consumers in their homes around the world – about how they live, cook and clean. When his managers came to him with an idea, he was ready to respond with a consumer's mindset.

He is a listener and sponge, and when he communicates he does it in very simple *Sesame Street* terms – but people love him because they believe he is trying to do the right thing. He only ever writes one-page memos and most meetings are scheduled for 20–30 minutes rather than the conventional hour. He brought in Meg Whitman, CEO of eBay, as a non-executive director and hung out with GE's new CEO, Jeff Immelt, as well as joining GE's board.

Innovation, in particular, has come under the microscope. Despite battalions of scientists and engineers, P&G hadn't delivered a real innovation in decades, despite millions of dollars being pumped into internal ventures. When they tried to innovate, it was always based on a technically advanced product offer rather than something consumers actually wanted.

He insisted that at least 50% of new products should come from outside, compared with 10% at the time. This would require a seismic culture change, and putting your future in the hands of others would be risky too. The new 'connect and develop' approach is about collaboration with partners who have specialist skills that P&G doesn't, and with consumers.

Lafley's own eyes were opened to the need for change when he worked in Asia. P&G was a minnow compared with the might of Unilever and Nestlé in that market. Brand names long on American heritage and short on real difference just did not sell. Indeed, what sold in the US market was never likely to excite the Indian consumer, as even the likes of Coca-Cola found the hard way. P&G lacked insight, relevance, differentiation and creativity. Performance was respectable, but not sustainable.

Changing a global business is not easy. He recognized that he couldn't do everything. He quickly focused his change agenda on 'the core' business – the select few markets, categories, brands and capabilities that defined the business. 'Core' meant being a global leader, leading economics, high growth and strong cash flow. Other areas would have to wait, telling them to 'just keep doing a great job'.

He was clear and direct with people: 'These are our core business – fabric care, baby care, feminine care and hair care'; and 'Everything is non-core'. He wanted to unclutter the thinking.

His approach was hands-on in the early years but he has increasingly stepped back to become more of a coach and facilitator. He wants his managers to learn to make their own choices and embrace his passion and focus in their own ways, as he can't possibly manage everything. However, he demands a strategy from every team – including a 'to do' and 'not to do' list – and every decision must be based on a sound consumer insight, not just some manipulated financial projection.

He regularly reminds people of their enduring purpose: 'to improve the everyday lives of people around the world with P&G brands and products that deliver better performance, quality and value'. He points out that this has not changed, nor have the values and principles of the business.

One thing Lafley has carefully avoided is setting out a vision statement. He doesn't believe it is necessary – that the purpose of the business is sufficiently clear and otherwise it is about the consumer, not the business. He calls it managing from the 'future back' – his eyes and ears on today's world, and his back to the future, believing that the consumer is his best navigator.

Today, 42% of P&G products have an externally sourced component, whilst revenues grew by 8% in 2007 to $78 billion and profits climbed at twice that rate to $11 billion. It seems that P&G, with the customer as its leader, is doing very well.

6.3   CUSTOMER CHAMPIONS

Who is the 'chief customer officer' in a business?

Is it a sales and marketing task, or a customer service task? Should it be a new role, like finance and talent, managing a fundamental resource that runs horizontally through the business? Or should it be everybody's challenge, in the same way that innovation and corporate responsibility are part of everybody's job description?

Everybody should be a customer champion. Customers are why we do business, they are what the whole business process and structure is centred around, and emotionally it is the need to serve them that engages and energizes employees.

A 'customer champion' is a leader who:

- Immerses themselves deeply and personally in the customer's world.

- Collates and disseminates customer insights across the business.

- Focuses the business on the right, compelling value propositions.

- Constantly seeks to innovate in ways that improve customer solutions.

- Encourages people to work together to deliver a seamless experience.

- Is flexible and responsive to the needs and aspirations of individuals.

- Treats employees fairly and individually, in the same way as customers.

- Focuses on attracting, retaining and growing the best customers.

- Measures their performance using customer and financial metrics.

- Inspires their teams, peers and bosses to do the same.

A customer champion thinks, works and succeeds from the outside in. They fight for the customer in boardroom or team meetings when everybody else is talking numbers or processes. They bring the customer voice to the table and argue passionately on their behalf.

The CEO must be a customer champion. If in a customer-centric business there are departments and managers who have a customer mindset, but the ultimate leaders have their heads stuck in their spreadsheets, then the business will not succeed. If some are aligned around customers and others around products, technology or finance, there will be conflict – or at least a less good experience for the customer.

The CEO can uniquely bring a customer vision to life. Not just internally, but externally too – for customers, partners, media, analysts and investors.

They, more than anybody else, reflect the personality of the brand, the attitude of the organization, the conscience of its people. They speak to the news media, introduce the brochures and shows, and are brought in to woo the key accounts.

The enlightened CEO can be the driving force of a customer revolution.

Imagine if these were some of the ways you did business – encouraged, or sometimes insisted upon, by a customer-thinking CEO:

- Annual reports started with a review of customer activities and performance.

- Performance reports starting with customer impact and then financial impact.

- Investor relations briefings started with customer rather than financial news.

- Board meetings discussed the source of money rather than just counted it.

- Customer representatives on the governance board or executive committee.

- Performance targets based on both customer and financial success.

- Investors basing market valuations of the future profit streams from customers.

- Profitability measured by customer segment, not product category.

- Recruitment based on customer-thinking attitudes, with other skills secondary.

- Reminding people in meetings to think from a customer perspective.

- Demanding not just a business case but a customer case for doing new things.

- Too busy for management meetings – need to be out meeting more customers.

Of course, it's not just the CEO who must think this way – revolutions usually start with the people, not a lone individual. But if they are a good leader who inspires others to follow, then it's a good place to start transforming the business around customers.

Business leaders become customer leaders too.

Insight 44: MAC COSMETICS

This is the story of two Franks, partners in life and business. Frank Toskan was a fashion photographer and make-up artist, and Frank Angelo was a celebrity hairdresser and entrepreneur.

The flamboyant Angelo had a successful chain of hair salons across Toronto when he met Toskan in the early 1970s. Their mutual interest was to search for better make-up that would withstand the rigours of fashion shoots. They set about developing their own range of lipsticks, powders and eyeliners that had a much denser pigment, a non-oily finish and a diverse colour range.

They sold their niche products to friends in the fashion industry, but word soon got around to the celebrities who were made up and from them to the magazines they featured in. In 1984 they sold their previous businesses and set up Makeup Artist Cosmetics (MAC), with Toskan as Creative Director and Angelo as Marketing Director. They moved out of their kitchen and went into full-scale production.

MAC built its reputation at fashion shows and by showcasing the likes of Madonna. The brand became hot and hip – if celebrities loved it, every other girl wanted it too. They claimed to be for everyone – 'all sexes, all races, all ages' – but their cool and sexy image focused on upmarket young women who would pay anything for the perfect look.

Angelo was convinced that there was a different way to sell cosmetics and hated the 'blonde 19-year-old' image of every other brand, the evocative advertising and the constant free gifts that seemed to be on offer with every purchase. Instead he relied up word-of-mouth marketing, focusing on the 'extreme' users (make-up artists) and then relying on a reputation that would spread without the need for gimmicks – a pull rather than push strategy. Describing his approach on CNN, Toskan said 'I always believed in earning your customer, not buying her'.

MAC looked different too. Black pants and T-shirts distinguished their make-up artists from the sales assistants of other brands, who all seemed to want to be wearing white coats. It blasted out hip hop music, Toskan's favourite for getting models in the mood for a photo shoot, rather than the banal tranquillity of other brands. MAC people were paid a salary rather than commission – this reduced the pressure to sell, which encouraged customers to come back.

The two Franks struggled to keep up with demand and address the international market. They recognized that they were artists and, having succeeded in creating a cult brand, they now needed the help of business professionals to go global. In 1994 Estée Lauder bought a 51% stake in MAC for $38 million, although the founders insisted that the deal should be secret, concerned about their customers' response to MAC being owned by such a large, mainstream brand. At first the partnership worked well, until the untimely death of Angelo in 1997. Toskan was inconsolable and felt useless without his soulmate. He sold the remainder of the business to the cosmetics giant for a reported $60 million the following year.

Estée Lauder has continued to drive the growth of MAC, retaining its unique culture and image, and continuing to donate all the profits from its Viva Glam range to AIDS research.

Culture ... creating passion in people

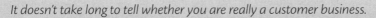

It doesn't take long to tell whether you are really a customer business.

It's not about answering my phone call in three rings (I can wait a little longer) or smiling at me even when you feel miserable (that's just fake). It's not just the mission statements or slogans above the door (anybody can write them). It's certainly not just about customer databases, loyalty cards and sending me lots of personalized mails (don't get me started!). It's not even about giving me good products, great service and excellent value for money. You could do all of this, and still care more about making money. And when I feel like that, I realize that I'm just a statistic to you and you're just a price to me.

It's when I meet your people – the shop assistant, cabin crew, service engineer – and they really care about me, what I really want, how I want it and what more they can do for me. They're real people, doing their job but clearly loving it too, doing what they're trained to do but in a way that is special for me. They take time to listen, understand my problem and see things from my perspective, and they do something about it. They become my champion, even my friend or confidante. They can make me smile or even laugh in the most difficult situations. It's those people, as individuals and together, that make an organization special for me.

Culture is 'the way we do things'.

Whilst people tend to focus on the softer side of developing a culture, it is both hard and soft.

A 'customer culture' needs the right values, aligning the goals of business and customer, a collective desire to do more for customers, a willingness to work together to achieve it, and a personal attitude that never questions whether to 'go the extra mile'.

But it also needs the hard components that encourage and support these attitudes and behaviours. The organizational structure and operational processes, the information and resources available to staff, the performance measures and rewards.

7.1   ENGAGING YOUR PEOPLE

Getting the most out of people – applying their talents and recognizing and growing their potential – is a subtle art. It is about emotions and influence rather than process and instruction. It means we must think of each employee as a unique individual, an emotional and complicated human being.

However, this does not happen in a vacuum. It works best from the 'outside in'. Attracting, serving and retaining the best customers is only possible if you attract, serve and retain the best employees.

As leaders our challenge is to engage, enable and energize people with unique ideas and talents, who build reputations and relationships, and share their passion and energy with others. A motivated, energized business is tremendously powerful. As Walt Disney once said, 'In my organization there is respect for every individual. Whatever we accomplish is due to the combined effort. I feel there is no door which, with the kind of talent we have, could not be opened, and how we can continue to unlock these barriers'.

Employee engagement can sometimes be taken for granted by leaders who live and breathe the organization, and are intimate with the challenges and objectives. This is often not the case further down the organization. As tasks get more specific and regular, there can seem to be less of a 'cause' for the business – less of a need to change, improve or perform better.

In the US, a Gallup survey revealed that only 29% of employees feel actively engaged and committed at work. Yet according to research by the Corporate Leadership Council, if people are committed to the organization they work for, they try 57% harder, perform 20% better and are 87% less likely to leave. On the other hand, employees with lower engagement are four times more likely to leave their jobs, according to the Corporate Executive Board.

The financial impact of employee engagement and business performance can be quantified using value driver analysis to articulate the cause-effect impact of people's attitudes on behaviours, customer service and satisfaction, retention and advocacy, and profits and growth. Although the effect will differ for each company, depending on its markets and structures, there is a common flow that can simply be described as the 'people–service–profit' chain.

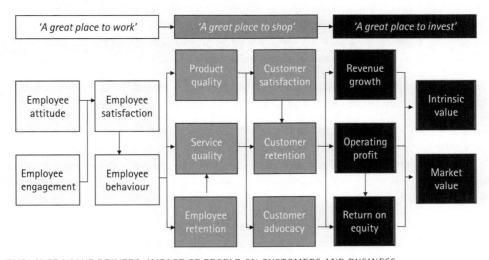

EMPLOYEE VALUE DRIVERS: IMPACT OF PEOPLE ON CUSTOMERS AND BUSINESS

Sears Roebuck, the international retailer, was one of the first to evaluate this impact, and articulated its 'people–service–profit' chain in its own way: 'a compelling place to work' creates 'a compelling place to shop', creates 'a compelling place to invest'. According to research by Rucci, Kirn and Quinn in *Harvard Business Review*, Sears found that a 5% increase in employee attitude drove a 1.3% improvement in customer perception, which drove a 0.5% increase in revenue growth.

A marginal increase in the satisfaction and engagement of your people – an extra smile each day, starting work with a buzz, or a few percentage points' improvement on the employee satisfaction index – could be worth, in large companies, $100 million to the bottom line.

There are many different structural ways to improve the life of your employees – better workplaces, development or rewards – but the biggest and simplest way to make a difference is through better leadership. A study in 2006 by the Hay Group found that an improved relationship with the leaders of the organization would deliver a 30% improvement in productivity.

Insight 45: PRET A MANGER

Pret is a sandwich shop – although its aluminium interiors, accessed through a doorway heralding that it is 'passionate about food', make it feel unlike a normal sandwich shop.

College friends Sinclair Beecham and Julian Metcalfe set up Pret A Manger in 1986 with woefully little experience in the world of business. They created the sort of food they craved but couldn't find anywhere else. They have succeeded, too: the chain has since grown to 4000 shops serving more than a million customers and generating annual turnover of just over £200 million.

'It's important our sandwiches and sales taste better than anyone else's': to achieve this, Pret builds a full kitchen at the back of every store. Suppliers are required to deliver fresh ingredients late every night; early the following morning Pret's chefs get busy making the best sandwiches, wraps, pastries and cakes. There are no 'shelf life' or 'display until' dates on Pret sandwiches, as everything is fresh and made on the day, for the day.

'Pret creates handmade, natural food, avoiding the obscure chemicals, additives and preservatives common to so much of the "prepared" and "fast" food on the market today' says a label on every egg and cress sandwich, crayfish and salad baguette, or mini lemon cheesecake.

Passion lies at the heart of the brand: for the food the company makes and people it employs. Indeed, go to the website, and the 'Passion Facts' describe its passion for natural quality foods free from additives and preservatives, for freshness by ensuring that all food is made fresh in the shop, and for improvement, constantly seeking to make a better sandwich with the help of customers.

The Pret Chocolate Brownie, for example, has changed 34 times, each change small but significant in terms of improving the flavour. Similarly, the Fruit and Oat Slides are, unusually for today, stirred by hand rather than a mechanical mixer, which tends to turn ingredients into pulp rather than retaining a nutty texture.

Despite a minority investment in the business by McDonalds, Pret rejects the conventions of most fast food brands. Not only does it not offer 'with fries', but it also rejects the mass-marketing concepts such as advertising, franchising or even focus groups. Pret has learnt by trial and error what works best. In the US, for example, it found no demand for its All Day Breakfast sandwich and had to swap butter for cream cheese with smoked salmon. However, the British Coronation Chicken with mango chutney sandwich was a big hit in the Big Apple.

Pret offers good jobs to great people who want to make and sell fabulous food. It invests in its people through training, incentives and rewards, paying them well above the average wage for the sector. Working at Pret is fun. They work as a team, enjoy what they do, play funky music all day, wear their own jeans and love what they sell. There are even silver stars, specially produced by Tiffany & Co., for the most outstanding service.

The service passion of Pret is established by a culture that treats and rewards employees as equals. Walk into a Pret store at 8 a.m. on a Monday morning and the music immediately captures the mood of the staff. The service is frantic but friendly and personal. Staff take orders, brew coffee and take the latest bread and pastries out of the oven simultaneously. It's a great buzz that's contagious for customers too, and one that continues throughout the week to the infamous staff Friday nights out – although customers aren't invited to those.

The Pret culture isn't scripted or engineered. It is just real and human, frantic and fun.

7.2   ALIGNING PEOPLE AND CUSTOMERS

The business already has a wealth of developed structures, skilled resources and scientific techniques to engage people. Yet because they are largely deployed only to engage customers in the business, the brand and its products, managers forget that such rigour and approach can equally be applied internally.

There has been much written about creating an 'employee brand'. The reality is that there is only one corporate brand and it is far better to develop the single brand in a way that has relevance to all stakeholders, including employees and shareholders, rather than with single mind for customers.

A core brand idea that defines the organization and captures its purpose and personality, can then be delivered in different, relevant ways to each audience internally and externally, just as it is already adapted to different customer segments. If the big idea is to 'humanize technology' (like Apple), engaging employees in this goal means that they are far more likely to be motivated, and focused on engaging the customers that they serve, too.

The brand effectively acts like a 'magnet', engaging each audience in a core idea – in a way that is visible, emotional and energizing. The brand facilitates a relationship with and between each stakeholder. In the employee's case, this means that people deliver great work in return for a range of benefits, serve customers with a common cause and also understand the role of shareholders.

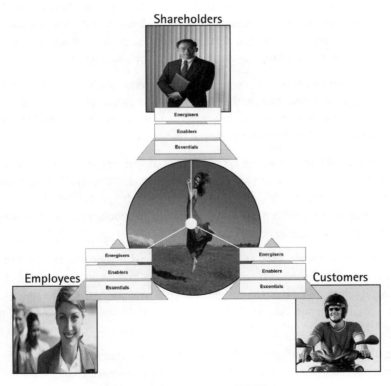

CONNECTING PEOPLE: ALIGNING EMPLOYEES AND CUSTOMERS

The magnetism is based on an idea that engages each audience emotionally. Earlier, we explored how to engage customers through the 'energizer pyramid'; this can be applied to employees – what are their essential needs and wants from coming to work? What is enabling to them, helping them to achieve their goals? What energizes them?

Obviously not all employees are the same, just as customers are not the same. Not all employees are of equal value (not an easy thing to say, sometimes), just as there are good and less good customers. Therefore, segmentation of employees based on physicality (function, level, geography), motivation (needs, wants, ambitions) and value (their specialist skills, potential and performance) helps us to target and tailor our approach appropriately.

Each target segment of people can then be addressed distinctively by developing 'employee value propositions' that take exactly the same format as customer value propositions. They identify what matters most to the particular group and then describe the most important and relevant benefits of working for the company to that audience.

The proposition conditions the whole approach to each segment. It becomes reality through 'products and services': the role and activities, contracts and salary, targets and rewards, environment and management relationship that collectively deliver the 'employee experience' – what it's like to work for the company. The processes and structures deliver a personal, compelling and memorable experience for customers.

Internal communication becomes an ongoing dialogue with your people, founded on their issues and focused on the benefits to them. Like external communication, it should embrace the most appropriate media (such as business television, magazines, websites, blogs, physical events and online communities), enabling people to initiate dialogue quickly and openly. It should facilitate openness between managers and employees, and between employees.

The needs of a diverse workforce can be engaged in very different and much more relevant ways. Personalization of contracts, benefits and work experience is then entirely possible through effective management/employee relationships.

Customer needs
and motivations

Employee needs
and motivations

Customer
proposition

Employee
proposition

Customer
experience

Employee
experience

Customer attitudes
and behaviours

Employee attitudes
and behaviours

ENGAGING PEOPLE: EMPLOYEE PROPOSITIONS AND EXPERIENCES

Insight 46: INNOCENT

In the summer of 1998 three friends came up with the idea of making fruit smoothies at a rock festival. Armed with £500 worth of fresh fruit, a fruit press and a pair of wellies, Richard Reed, Adam Balon and Jon Wright set off to have some fun.

They also took a sign asking 'Do you think we should give up our jobs to make these smoothies?' The 'Yes' bin filled up far quicker than the 'No' bin, and they resigned from their advertising jobs the next day

Innocent, the fast-growing 'tasty little drinks' company from London, has grown rapidly to become a £100 million business within a decade, with over 200 fruit-squeezing, fun-loving employees in eight European offices. It has a huge 68% of the UK smoothie market and around 12,000 retailers spread across Europe.

Since natural fruit is the heart of its business, being natural and down-to-earth – or 'innocent' – informs every aspect of what it does: from the choice of stationery to its offices at Fruit

Towers, to the cheery person who greets you if you call the Banana Phone. Every customer is encouraged to give them a call if they have something to say about the smoothies or are simply feeling bored.

As its business has grown, Innocent still focuses on the detail. 'Sell by' dates on bottle tops are replaced by 'Enjoy by' dates, and the ingredients on the bottle are also an opportunity to have a laugh – my banana and mango smoothie apparently being made of one big banana, two juicy mangoes and a rubber duck. Of course, in a world of scrupulous trading standards, such fun can sometimes come unstuck – having joked that one type of smoothie included 'two plump nuns', the trading standards officer contacted Innocent to ask for more details. Having explained that it was just a joke, the company was asked by the officer to either remove the detail or start using plump nuns!

As well as constantly experimenting with new flavours, its range has diversified too. Large two-litre cartons can now be found in supermarkets and small multi-packs are ideal for a picnic. Also introduced were 'Thickies', a combination of yoghurt and fruit drinks, and 'Juicy Water' water and fruit juice. There is even a range of kids' smoothies that many schools now sell at subsidized prices, encouraging children to eat more fruit.

The similarities to Ben and Jerry's, the ice cream pioneers from Vermont, are all there – delivery vans dressed as cows and grass meadows, a charitable foundation into which it pours 10% of all its profits, a live jazz festival called 'Fruitstock' and a 'Village Fete' in London's Regent Park.

Innocent has made great strides over the last ten years, resisting the temptation to sell out, recognizing that they have a great purpose (and maybe a more valuable business to create). However, the culture has changed little since the early days. The same fun-loving, down-to-earth guys are still running the business. Despite all their success, they have not forgotten their sense of humour, describing their decade growth as below:

	1999	2008
Number of employees	3	275
Number of different recipes on sale	3	30
Market share	0%	72%
Number of retailers	1 (on day one)	More than 10,000
Furthest stockist	Wimbledon	Shetland Islands, Paris, Amsterdam, Salzburg and Copenhagen
Number of smoothies sold	20 (on day one)	Two million a week
Shoe size (Richard)	10	11
Number of Innocent T-shirts (Jon)	1	4
Waist size (Adam)	Too rude to disclose	One bigger

7.3 STRUCTURES, SYMBOLS AND STORIES

'Outside in' cultures are obsessed with customers and solutions, not business and process, delighting their customers rather than their bosses. Traditional organizational structures divert the energy and attention of employees away from customers towards products and hierarchy. People will work harder to please their bosses than their customers, 'put on their best show' for the visit of senior management rather than every day for customers.

Ritz-Carlton, for example, has addressed this problem by inverting the pyramid. The head office acts as a service centre and the main role of the hotel manager is to support frontline staff rather than being elitist, commanding and controlling.

Some of the other difficulties in making the customer business work include:

- **Customer 'focus'**: Paying lip service to customers when times are good, but immediately cutting the costs to serve and support them when times are less good – these are seen as nice to do but not essential to survival.

- **'Internal' customers**: A legacy of quality management and its efficient and standardized processes was to get people focused on their own immediate 'customers' internally but lose sight of the real customer externally.

- **Customer 'satisfaction'**: Believing that an average-to-good score is good enough, which we now know is not. Satisfaction is a mere hygiene factor – customers need more than that to make them stay and want to do more with you.

- **'Market' share**: Believing that all customers are good for you, the more the better – whereas we now know that there are profitable and unprofitable customers. You are probably better off with fewer, not more, and serving the best ones better.

- **'Customer' obsession**: The customer is not king, as it is often easy to say. Working intimately to customize solutions for every customer is a sure way to go bust, particularly if they don't perceive the added value and pay more. Again, it's about finding the balance.

- **People 'first'**: Putting customers first, by definition, puts everyone else second – which is not the best motivator to your employees. Instead it's about a more grown-up, thoughtful, caring approach to customers and employees, achieving success together.

- **'Sheep dipping'**: You don't create a customer-centric company by putting everyone through a one-day corporate programme with slogans, posters and five magic steps. It takes time, hard work, structures and processes, and leadership and rewards.

One of the most common divides within organizations is between operations and customer service staff, for example the cabin crew and the ground staff in an airline, the receptionist and the engineers at a car garage, the shelf stackers and information desk in a supermarket. To the customer, they are all equal brand representatives; internally, they may perceive very different roles.

Virgin Atlantic practises 'holistic' customer service, where all staff are trained in service techniques and are accountable through service-based performance measures. CEO Steve Ridgeway explains: 'We spend time with engineers, for example, demonstrating how if one video screen fails to work on a plane, it leads to a significant drop in satisfaction scores, regardless of how good the rest of the inflight service might be.'

Culture is not just soft and fluffy – it needs nuts and bolts too.

'Outside in' organization structure and performance measurement are probably the two most significant enablers of a customer-centric business. Get it right and it will probably work – the culture will follow. Get it wrong and even the most passionate people will fail.

Structures are typically aligned around the ways in which performance is measured. The traditional organization made products, and profit and loss could fairly easily be attributed to individual units. The organization was product-centric, with product managers reporting to the CEO.

However, moving to a customer-centric structure is not instant, or black and white.

Just like entering a new market or sector, the organization sticks its toe into the water before jumping in. This might be through an experimental structure – maybe introducing a special team for the best customers (the account management team that brings together sales, marketing, finance, service and support roles for a particularly important customer), or by introducing a new cross-functional role (such as 'customer experience managers') who work within a product-centric business but start to encourage new ways of thinking and working, and a blueprint to formalize in future years.

The customer business is designed around customers, segments or markets. Profit and loss must therefore be attributed by segment, and segment leaders then report to the CEO. Products, typically cross-functional, then play a more supporting role, as do other shared or corporate functions.

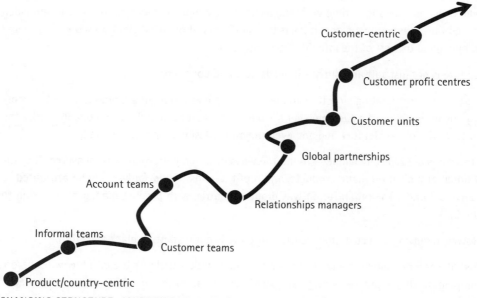

Customer-centric

Customer profit centres

Customer units

Global partnerships

Account teams

Relationships managers

Informal teams

Customer teams

Product/country-centric

CHANGING STRUCTURE: JOURNEY TO A CUSTOMER-CENTRIC ORGANIZATION

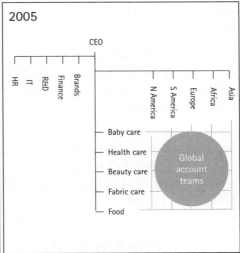

CUSTOMER ORGANIZATION: EXAMPLE OF STRUCTURAL CHANGE AT P&G

And once the structures are in place, the culture is brought to life – through leadership and teams, new roles and processes, and new measures and incentives. However, most important is the emotional connection – just like customers, employees are engaged in the same higher purpose that is emotional, relevant and memorable. With a strong purpose in place, stories and symbols can bring this to life internally.

In the same way that we remember the characters and lessons from childhood tales, stories are a great way to capture 'the way we do business round here', engaging partners and new recruits in a distinctive culture. An example in Xerox is their snowmobile story.

A number of years ago, Xerox Scandinavia ran a promotion promising that if you ordered one of its copiers within the Stockholm postal district, then you would receive it within 24 hours.

And if not – just like Domino's promise with their pizzas – you would not have to pay for the machine.

An order came in from a Stockholm post code, but – by a quirk of the coding system – the house was actually halfway up a nearby mountain, in a forest. And there was deep snow at the time. The Xerox dispatcher knew that the copier would take many days by normal means, so he and a colleague went out and hired a snowmobile.

As they drove through the forest, the narrow road got steeper, and the snow thicker. Eventually they abandoned their snowmobile and continued on foot. Eventually, cold, tired and in the dark, they stumbled upon the house. They had missed their promised deadline by 15 minutes. The customer answered the door and was amazed to receive his new copier and to hear that it really was free. The dispatchers apologized for not meeting their promise and headed off into the night. Dejected after their efforts, they returned the snowmobile and headed to a local bar.

A week later, a large order for copiers arrived by fax from the same house on the mountainside. As CEO of a large Swedish business, he was so impressed with the dispatchers' dedication that he had decided to switch all his company's copiers to Xerox.

Insight 47: TOYOTA

'Yoi kangae, yoi shina!' means 'Good thinking means good products!' and is emblazoned on a giant banner hanging across Toyota's huge assembly plant near Nagoya in Japan. The plant delivers six different models of cars from start to finish in 20 hours. The combination of speed and flexibility is repeated in more than 30 sites around the world.

Toyota is now the world's leading car manufacturer. At the heart of its success is the relationship with employees and customers. Lacking the scale and capital resources of some others, Toyota looked inside to find its advantage – focusing on improving value for customers through deeper insights, continuous improvement and more creative thinking made possible by highly engaged employees.

Yoshio Ishiazaka, Executive Vice President, describes the culture:

> 'I have learned, based on my experience, that everything is dominated by the market. So whenever we are struck by obstacles or difficulties, I always say to myself: "Listen to the market, listen to the voice of the customer." That's the fundamental essence of marketing. Always, we have to come back to the market, back to the customer. That is the Toyota way.'

Toyota's 'lean thinking' approach is less about operational efficiency, more about having a clear and unflinching philosophy to serve and add value to customers. This focuses on customer rather than shareholder value as the immediate objective, working through every aspect of the business to ruthlessly focus only on what adds value to customers and eliminating anything that doesn't. This creates more flow in the organization, encourages more thoughtful problem-solving and improves the customer experience and business performance.

At the most fundamental level, Toyota sees the company as a means to add value to customers, society and community, and its partners. This has its roots in founder Kiichiro Toyoda's desire to invent power looms that made life simpler for women in the farming community where he grew up. From this basis, the business has developed a way of working that is principled and rigorous, and related to the four Ps:

Philosophy is the foundation of everything.

Processes, the right ones managed well, determine the results.

People and partners add value to the business.

Problem-solving drives an improving, learning organization Masoe Inoue is a chief engineer and one of the brains behind the hybrid engine technology that has helped Toyota to create real difference from competitors and a new level of trust with customers. Although Toyota might seem to be about efficient processes, disciplined management and measurement, it is actually a human business where car making is an emotional art:

> 'The feel of a car often comes down to the small things, like the feel when you actually touch the leather or wood. This is a new kind of thinking, thinking of how things feel to the customer. To make my decision, I must always ride in the car. There are many things that you cannot find from data that you discover when you ride in a car. There is nothing, no machine that can replace the human body. It is the best sensor.

> 'When you turn the steering wheel, sometimes you can just feel a sound. So faint you can't really measure it, but the feel of it is there. Also things like the glove box, or the cup holder. When you open and close them they create their own sounds. And there are often faint sounds that can really irritate the person who is driving a car. The aim is to create a stillness that you can't actually measure but figures in the normal sense, and this is done by feeling and touch.'

Transformation ... the journey to customer-centricity

> *I don't expect you to become a different business overnight. I realize that it takes time.*
>
> *In fact I don't want quick fixes or superficial changes. I want to work with you to create an organization that we are all happy with, get real value from and are proud of. I recognize that you can't change your organization, your processes and structures, overnight. What's more important is that you're going in the right direction.*
>
> *As a starting point, why don't you get all your top people to come a have a chat with customers like me? Not just the pleasantries, but really spend time understanding my world. Let's have a coffee, or come shopping with me, stay at my house, see what my life is really like. If you can get this attitude, then I'm sure it won't take long for people to start acting differently too. They'll start to understand why I'm more than a sales volume. They'll start to understand why they actually come to work each day. But it's got to be across the whole business – all the different areas, all your people, activities and technologies. And when you get there, it will be amazing for you and me.*

347

8.1 CREATING A CUSTOMER REVOLUTION

In Japanese, change is more about 'kaikaku' (radical reform for a specific purpose) rather than 'kaizen' (continuous improvement because it's good for you). Change is driven from the 'outside in', responsive to changing markets and the changing world.

Andy Grove, chairman of Intel, calls significant market change, such as the arrival of the Internet, wireless mobility and social networks 'strategic inflection points' that occur when '10×' forces alter a market with '100×' impact. He recalls how Intel almost missed the Internet and ignored the rise of Japanese microprocessor manufacturers.

He now realizes that reacting to external change is not enough and argues that organizations will regularly have to make one of three choices:

- Not to change.

- To change only when forced to.

- To take charge of your destiny and seek to change before, or differently from, others.

Business leaders therefore need to become change agents: sensing the need to change, then galvanizing, leading and managing the process of change in their organizations as essential to future growth and before it becomes essential to their survival.

Change is a journey that leaders will need to persuade, cajole, inspire, support and manage their organizations through. It should be driven by market and business strategy, staying true to the compelling purpose and direction of the business, but also recognize that little else is sacred.

Change requires decisive leadership and rapid action. Everything in the organization should be open to challenge and, if necessary, change. It might require innovation, but even more important will be to decide what to stop doing. It will take time and sometimes be painful, hence the need to do it quickly. It must be driven and managed, with clarity of purpose and actions, and continuous dialogue with all stakeholders.

The result of change, getting from 'old world' to 'new world', is rarely an end point. The benefits need to be realized, which means the change needs to stick. It would be easy to regress back into old ways or even to remain stuck between the two worlds. Change becomes regular and maybe even continuous, as in the world of Intel where the market is driven by relentless innovation.

Every business today is essentially customer-focused – researching needs, articulating benefits, delivering service and measuring satisfaction. It is nothing special; it is a basic hygiene factor.

However, you can do all of this from your ivory tower, from the inside out, where products still drive the business, financials drive the decisions and managers know better than customers.

Becoming a customer-centric business requires more significant change: to the purpose and strategy, priorities and metrics, structure and processes, as well as activities you do directly for customers in marketing and sales, and operations and customer service.

So how do you create a customer revolution?

'The most emotionally wrenching and terrifying aspect' of any major organizational change is getting people to realize that change is essential. Professor Noel Tichy is author of *Control Your Destiny or Someone Else Will,* the story of GE's transformational journey over recent decades. His most significant insight is that every time, GE has struggled to wake people up to the need to change.

Everybody likes the status quo – it is familiar, comfortable and we find a way to succeed within it. But then change comes along and pulls the rug from under our feet, threatening our jobs, projects, bonuses and careers. We don't like change.

Making the case is much easier when there is a crisis. But then it's too late.

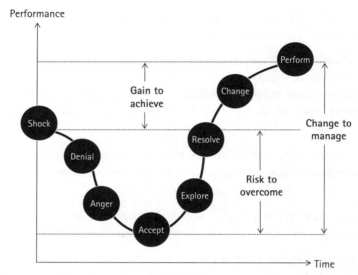

CHANGE CURVE: MOVING FROM FEAR TO DESIRE FOR CHANGE

As Charles Handy will remind you, a frog that jumps into a bucket of boiling water will jump out, but a frog that sits in cold water that is gradually heated to boiling point will not sense the danger until too late. There are plenty organizations and executives who are happy to sit tight and hope things don't get too hot – at least before they move on to their next job.

Change therefore needs leaders and managers. Leaders must inspire people to take the brave step into the unknown, define an inspiring vision and guide them on the journey. Managers must coordinate and control what can often be an incredibly complicated process of transitioning a multibillion dollar enterprise from one state into another.

'Change' is about transforming the way the business works both in terms of its 'harder' structures and processes, and its 'softer' attitudes and behaviours. It can be complex and hard work, and could easily go wrong – 'Why break an organization when it's not broken?', particularly when you need to sustain and grow revenues at the same time as making the change happen.

'Change management' is the process for doing it effectively. Change used to have more of an internal focus, to improve the quality and efficiency of whatever the business does; today, change is much more externally driven, typically with factors beyond the organization's control driving the need for change and a clarity of purpose and priority driving the direction of change.

One simple but effective way to think of making the case for change is in the following formula, demonstrating what is required to overcome people's natural resistance:

Change will happen if $A \times B \times C > D$

Where:

A = an inspiring vision of what the future organization will be like.

B = the reasons why the current organization cannot continue.

C = the first practical steps to get towards the future organization.

D = people's resistance to change and preference to stay as they are.

The case for change should be made simply and definitively. The vision should be personally engaging so that people can quickly recognize the benefits to themselves. The reasons why today is not sustainable might be financial or logical (declining share, rising cost base, new competitors), and how, if extrapolated, it would severely restrict the business's future.

John Kotter in *Leading Change* has some even more direct tactics for overcoming the resistance of your people to change, including:

- Cleaning up the balance sheet to take a significant loss in the next quarter.

- Moving the head office to disrupt old habits and symbolize a new start.

- Telling business units they have 24 months to become number one or two in their market or face closure.

- Toughening up the performance targets of senior managers to provoke 'honest' discussions.

Insight 48: AVON

Would you trust a glitzy advertising campaign or are you more likely to believe a real person like yourself? Would you prefer to think about your personal beauty and buy the things that matter to you in a busy store with sales people all around you or for the business to come to you, with a more friendly and familiar face on your doorstep?

Avon harnessed the power of networks long before Tim Berners-Lee created the World Wide Web. Indeed, the cosmetics company – which reaches 135 countries with sales of $9.9 billion in 2007 – is little about technology and all about people.

With a name inspired by the river that runs through the town of his favourite playwright, William Shakespeare, David McConnell founded Avon in 1886. The 28-year-old was actually a door-to-door book salesman and conjured up the idea of giving away rose petal perfume as an incentive. He realized that women were much more interested in the perfume than the books and so set up the California Perfume Company in New York.

McConnell hired his first representative: Mrs P.F.E. Albee from Winchester, New Hampshire, who sold her neighbour some perfumes and became the first 'Avon lady'. This was a pioneering step, particularly considering it was 34 years before women were even allowed to vote in America.

'Avon' was adopted as the company's name in 1939 at a time when sales had already reached $2 million. By 1954, with the 'Avon calling' campaign popular around the world, sales had climbed to a staggering $55 million, demonstrating the exponential power of network selling. By 1979, as Greta Waitz ran through Central Park to win the incredibly popular women's-only Avon 10,000m race, the company was celebrating $3 billion sales.

Avon today sustains its model by focusing propositions on both sets of so-called 'customers' – its millions of representatives and many more people who buy from them, typically their neighbours and friends. For representatives it offers the opportunity to establish their own business with potentially unlimited rewards. For those who buy the products, it offers that emotionally critical choice of beauty products on your doorstep or in a party among friends.

By 1990 the business was starting to struggle. The Avon lady and her catalogue needed a serious makeover. Sales were down, there were threats of a hostile takeover and the business had a fundamental image problem with modern women.

Canadian-born Andrea Jung joined Avon's marketing team in 1994, having learnt her retailing at Bloomingdale's department store. She fell in love with the Avon concept, the internal culture and the opportunities she could see ahead. Within five years she was CEO.

Her makeover strategy addressed the whole business, from supply chain to distribution channels, product portfolio and pricing structures. She demanded new products and more glamorous, glossy advertising programmes – and definitely no more 'Ding-dong, Avon calling'.

At the Women's Wear Daily Beauty CEO Summit she said: 'You have to be bold, thoughtful and calculated so the financial markets remain calm. But I think you have got to drive enough change to deliver double-digit growth. Nothing else will stick.' She gave herself three years, achieved it in 18 months and became known as 'the mistress of the turnaround'.

Avon continues to thrive. In Russia it has established itself as a glamour brand with a more personal touch. Elena Degtyareva, Avon's CEE marketing director based in Moscow, says 'there is no more exciting or competitive market for cosmetics in the world at the moment than Russia, which Avon has been able to approach in a fresh and tailored way'. After a 1998 ruling banning door-to-door sales in China, Avon began selling in beauty salons. The network expanded quickly across the immense country, with around 10,000 locations and complemented by a franchising concept with China Post.

The brand has also diversified into new areas. 'Mark' targets younger, student-aged women who want to make their mark in the world today. It has an award-winning 'magalog' to talk in a different way to a younger audience and recruits young representatives who want to start making money and be their own boss. Similarly, 'M' is Avon's first ever men's range of grooming products and accessories, and there is a range of soaps and toys for children too.

Avon continues to be a powerful icon for the women of the world. The Avon Running series is incredibly successful in getting women on the streets and getting fit together, raising considerable sums for breast cancer charities. The brand also speaks out on a wide range of issues from domestic violence to female empowerment.

However, it is the network – a human network of like-minded people – that has made Avon one of the most successful cosmetics brands in the world.

8.2   MAKING CHANGE HAPPEN

Creating a customer-centric business requires a structured and managed process of change. It can't happen overnight and is much more than a statement of intent. The change must be driven by business leaders, mitigate risks, release energy that mobilizes people, make a difference to customers and deliver results quickly to give confidence and, long term, to drive a step-change in performance. There are four phases to the change process:

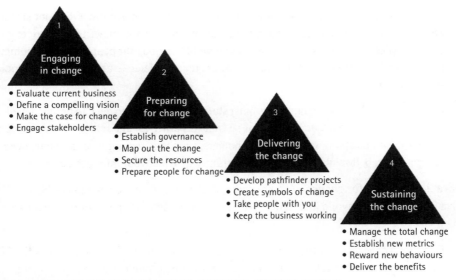

CHANGE MANAGEMENT: FOUR PHASES OF CUSTOMER-CENTRIC CHANGE

Phase 1: Engaging in change. All stakeholders need to understand and hopefully support the change – why it is needed, what it will involve and how it will happen.

- Evaluate the current business – how effective is it currently, and compared with best practices competitively and more broadly? Where are the strengths and weaknesses? What needs to be sustained, changed and eliminated? Benchmarking, strategic alignment and gap analysis will be important in achieving this.

- Define a compelling vision for the future – this may already exist through the strategy process, but may need articulating in simpler, clearer ways. How does it support the core purpose of the business? What will be different and why will it be better? Employee groups might help to define the 'as is' and 'to be' states in practical ways.

- Make the case for change – as above, articulating why the current world is not sustainable and the consequences of no change compared with the benefits of change – the opportunities this would open up and how it would be good for people too. This communication will take time, careful communication, regular dialogue at all levels and ongoing reinforcement.

- Engage stakeholders in change – this must start with leaders who need to design it, believe in it and want it. It must be bottom-up, so that it is practical and relevant, and top-down so that it is consistent. Sponsors, shareholders, suppliers, regulators and unions need to be engaged too. It might even be an opportunity to signal your intent to customers.

Phase 2: Preparing for change. Mapping out a programme of change horizons – how will we move from to the new world in practical steps, with what actions and resources required and when?

- Establish a governance structure – who will sponsor the change? Ideally it will be the CEO. By mapping out stakeholders you can shape a steering group to oversee the project, lend support and keep them engaged. Define a project leader and manager, and recruit a project team with representatives from across the business. Define roles and responsibilities.

- Map out the change – balancing the financial imperatives with what makes more sense for people. Developing horizons of change, so that the change becomes less daunting, more manageable and simply articulated. The 'change plan' should include milestones, timelines and 'quick wins' – business results that will build confidence.

- Bring together the resources for change – acquire the budgets, people and other resources to support the change. You may need specialist external help – either technically or to provide a fresh, independent view. Consider the legal implications, including employee rights. This will require business cases and their approval.

- Keep preparing people for change, with ongoing communication – don't just say there will be a restructuring, with new job roles and reporting lines. Engage employees in the wider reasons and opportunities, maybe letting them define what new processes or behaviours should be like, and then discuss the choices and changes required to implement their ideas.

Phase 3: Delivering the change. Making the change happen comes down to people and effective management sustaining the momentum of change to overcome resistance and barriers.

- Develop pathfinder projects that introduce the change in chosen areas first. Then build on this as an example, transferring skills from one area to another, and showing people practically what it will be like. Learn from the 'pilot' cases to do it faster and better next time, evolving the change as you go, making it real and simple.

- Create symbols of change. Identify small or significant parts of the programme that reflect the bigger idea. As CEO, decide to give up your large office and move to an open workspace, deliver a new service to customers, consider refreshing the corporate brand at the same time, launch new learning and development programmes so that people know they matter.

- Take people with you. Letting go of the old world and overcoming fears of the new is not easy. Focus on hearts and minds, making change in culture and process at the same time so that people have the tools to do what they now believe is right. Keep talking to them, encouraging dialogue, addressing their concerns and sharing your own – be their coach.

- Ensuring that the business keeps working. The worst aspect of change can be that the organization grinds to a halt; unsure of their futures, employees stop working or at least slow down. This could be the death of the business. Functional managers need to stay focused on today, weaving in new process and behaviours as soon as appropriate.

Phase 4: Making it stick. The change must be seen through to completion, sustaining commitment for it and ensuring that it becomes the new 'business as usual' as quickly as possible.

- Managing the change, with a dedicated change team that is taken out of business as usual. The programme, built up of many supporting projects, needs active coordination and delivery: actions and resources, budgets and risks. Steering groups need to review progress frequently, making adjustments as required.

- Sustaining the change momentum by developing sustaining mechanisms to reinforce the new ways of working. Introduce a new approach to strategy and decision-making; state clearly the new priorities and measures of success. Encourage new habits and rituals. Tell the story of how the organization moved from old world to new world and find reasons to celebrate success.

- Reward the new behaviours by restructuring people's KPIs, career progression, capability frameworks, benefit packages, incentives and rewards to reflect and encourage the new behaviours. What gets measured gets done, but what drives an individual's bonus will quickly become their new priority.

- Ensure that the change delivers business impact, a step change in business performance, more effective and efficient ways of working, bringing to life a new brand or competitive position, and delivering a better customer experience. Communicate the success, reinforce the messages of the better world and keep adjusting and improving.

The emerging organization becomes a compelling place to work. It creates a fresh start to build a new reputation in the outside world, drive innovation and new levels of service, change the opinions of analysts and investors, and creates potential for someone to shine as a business leader.

Insight 49: SKODA

In 1894, Václav Klement was a young bookseller in the Czech town of Mlada Boleslav – at the time, part of the Austro-Hungarian Empire. However, his first passion was cycling. After an accident whilst riding his beloved Seidel and Naumann bike, he couldn't find the spare parts to get it repaired and wrote (in Czech) to its German manufacturers asking for help. They replied that unless he wrote in German, they would not help him. Outraged, he decided to make the parts himself.

After the First World War, Václav and his partner Václav Laurin moved into manufacturing trucks; however, they needed more resources for their business and so merged with Skoda Works, then the largest manufacturer in Czechoslovakia. The company used the Skoda brand and had its first significant hit with the Popular model in the late 1930s, a name that would be seen frequently over future decades. Skoda continued to develop under communism of the late 1940s and 1950s: the cars were tough and reliable, although design and comfort were afterthoughts.

In the 1960s and 1970s, Skoda's rear-engined models were laughed at for their dated and ugly looks, yet they won their class in the RAC Rally for 17 consecutive years. The soft-top Skoda Rapid was often called 'the poor man's Porsche' and became popular across Europe in the 1980s. Most significant was the 1987 launch of the Favorit in partnership with Italian designers Bertone.

However, the cars were also the butt of many jokes. 'Why do you need a heated rear window on a Skoda?' went one. 'To keep your hands warm when pushing it' came the semi-comic answer.

Czechoslovakia's 'Velvet Revolution' brought great changes, and the government sought a foreign partner to invest in the car manufacturer. It chose Volkswagen because of its willingness to manufacture locally. Volkswagen recognized that Skoda had been a great car maker and could be great again. It added expertise and investment – particularly in style and engineering – but appreciated the quality of its Czech makers. It retained the brand's independence, developing new models that sometimes shared the same platforms as the Golf and Passat, but designed in its own quirky way.

The brand used ironic advertising lines, such as 'It is a Skoda, honest' and images of the factory line where workers are uncertain about placing the Skoda badge on the cars that looked so good that they 'surely cannot be Skodas'. The message addressed the image issue head on and succeeded – not with everybody, but then no brand needs to. For its target 'low-price but quality' audience Skoda offered great value and symbolized the progressive 'new Europe'.

The brand was even ranked second to Lexus in the JD Power customer satisfaction survey. It was different and inspired great loyalty amongst customers. It continued to launch new models, including an MPV and a three-door city car. As demand grew it opened new manufacturing and assembly plants in Bosnia to serve Southern Europe and India to tap into the fast-growing Asian car market. In 2006 it produced more than half a million vehicles for the first time.

Theodora, a brand advocate from Romania, described her 'lovemark' as follows: 'I love Skoda. Our first family car was a Skoda ... Even though it took a whole day to travel to the seaside, I never experienced more fun in my life than the adventures we have had with our Skoda'.

Perhaps most significant is Skoda's performance in relationship to the rest of the successful Volkswagen Group, which also includes brands such as Seat, Audi, Bentley and Bugatti. After 16 years as part of the Volkswagen Group and a $14 billion investment, sales in 2007 were $5.6 billion and profits $492 million – 8.3% of the group's total revenue and 15.4% of its operating profit.

8.3   VIRGIN INSPIRATION

He is one of the world's most famous entrepreneurs: the champion of customers, continually looking to create businesses that do more for them.

Richard Branson is one of the most successful business people of our generation. No one can argue with his survival instincts. From a cash crisis in his businesses to ballooning in the jet stream at 180 mph without enough fuel, he talks about 'setting myself huge and apparently unachievable tasks, and trying to rise above them'.

Born in 1950 in London, Branson excelled at sports although his mild dyslexia meant that he struggled academically. His first business ideas were formed in the school library and involved Christmas trees, budgerigars and writing stories about his sexual conquests. They didn't take off, but then in 1967 his idea for a magazine called *Student* did. He sold advertising space from the telephone box outside his school during break times and was soon able to publish the first issue. He used to ask the telephone operator to connect him to potential clients, making it appear that she was his secretary. With the help of star interviews with the likes of Mick Jagger, using the operator trick, the magazine became a hit.

He left Stowe School at 15 with his headmaster predicting that he would either go to prison or become a millionaire. He did both.

He became an entrepreneur out of the need to earn money to keep *Student* afloat. He had long ago used the £7 'investment' from his mother and he hatched his next business plan from his London squat. He started selling discount records by mail order through the magazine, a novel concept at the time. He named it Virgin Mail Order, 'because it was run by a bunch of business virgins' and the brand was born. Orders streamed in, although at the age of 21 he was briefly arrested and jailed for exporting records without paying the correct taxes. He did a deal with Customs and was released.

Virgin launched its first record store in 1971 in London's Oxford Street. Then Branson built a recording studio in Oxfordshire and launched his own record label. Mike Oldfield (who made Branson his first million by recording *Tubular Bells*) and the Sex Pistols (who got him into jail again briefly, for bad language) were his first signings, followed by Phil Collins, Boy George and Janet Jackson.

When an American lawyer approached him with the idea of starting a new airline in 1984, Branson really got excited. Setting up Virgin Atlantic was his most risky and lucrative achievement. 'My proudest moment', he says, 'taking on the world's airlines with one Jumbo, and not much idea of what to do next.'

Today there are around 450 Virgin companies, most of them being joint ventures, operating independently with their own boards. Collectively they generate more than £10 billion revenues annually and are part of 'the largest private company in Europe' he adds, proudly.

In 2008. I interviewed Branson in front of 2500 people at the London Business Forum. I asked him how he managed so many businesses and stayed close to all their customers.

'It's important to think about what business really is. People think it's about balance sheets, profit and loss. But really it's about creating things, having a vision, creating something extremely special, then getting all the little details right – something that you can be really proud of and others can be too. The actual business and its financial aspects are something to mop up at the end. If you've created something really special then people will come to it, pay for it, and that gives you the money to pay salaries and invest in creating an even better business.

'If you just call in the accountants, you'll get one company who predict you'll make lots of money and another who say it's a ghastly idea. Basically they have no idea. It's up to you and your team to create something really special, that people will really want. Don't let the accountants in until afterwards.'

The Virgin Group is more like a venture capital firm, using funds from existing companies to build new ones, making use of existing assets and resources. Branson has seven close 'right-hand men' who sit on the boards of each Virgin business and come together to share ideas, nurture the brand and ensure that the group is not missing a trick.

Meanwhile the 50,000 Virgin employees love their leader and many get the chance to join him for a weekend on Necker Island. He loves to spend time with his people, whether at work or at a party with them. Although he is relaxed, informal and always looking for fun, he is always listening too – for an idea, a suggestion or the next adventure.

Later I asked him what his secret was. His response came without hesitation: 'I love people. I love listening to people, being with people, and achieving things with people.'

He only spends a third of his personal time on his businesses these days. This is split between creative thinking – what to do next, why not to do things – and being the public face of his brand. In the latest ad for Virgin Media he plays a plastic surgeon, offering to enhance the assets of Spice Girl Mel B, whilst it's hard to forget that he promoted an Australian venture by pretending to be fellated in a jacuzzi (just think 'down under').

Branson is inspirational and exceptional. He provides a role model to every business person for daring to do the extraordinary. He never stops championing the cause of customers and trying to make life better for them.

The Genius Lab

The pursuit of high performance involves a multitude of challenges whether you are the leader of a small or large business. If we take one definition of genius as the ability to hold two conflicting ideas in your head at the same time, you probably feel like you need to be a genius many times over.

From entrepreneurship and growth, strategy and innovation, customers and propositions, to change and performance, we have explored the essential challenges for business.

I truly believe that a small business can take as many ideas away as a large business, and whilst they might seem like 'big company' ideas, smaller organizations can often make them happen quicker and better, to seize an advantage over lumbering giants who struggle to turn their organizations around.

For more information and regular updates, go to www.customergeniuslive.com.

The CUSTOMER BUSINESS ROADMAP

Ten dimensions containing 30 tools and 150 actions to implement in your customer business.

- Customer Toolkit 1: Customer Vision
- Customer Toolkit 2: Customer Strategy
- Customer Toolkit 3: Customer Insights
- Customer Toolkit 4: Customer Propositions
- Customer Toolkit 5: Customer Solutions
- Customer Toolkit 6: Customer Connnections
- Customer Toolkit 7: Customer Experiences
- Customer Toolkit 8: Customer Service
- Customer Toolkit 9: Customer Relationships
- Customer Toolkit 10: Customer Performance

Customer Toolkit 1: Customer Vision

Customer Purpose Defining a more engaging reason for doing business that adds value to society.		1. Consider what your existing mission, vision or strategy does for customers, how they benefit. 2. Engage business leaders and customers in a 'big talk' conversation about their aspirations. 3. Create a 'mosaic' vision of how the business will make society and people's lives better. 4. Evaluate the implications, opportunities and sacrifices that the vision would demand. 5. Shape and articulate this as a 'customer purpose' describing how we make peoples' lives better.
Customer Brand Articulating the brand based on customer aspirations, what you enable them to do.		1. Define the audience for the brand, which might be a corporate, product or subsidiary brand. 2. Explore what people seek to achieve through the brand, and what it enables them to do. 3. Consider the alternatives for customers and how the brand enables them to achieve more. 4. Articulate how customers would feel about the brand, and the 'one word' that captures this. 5. Creatively develop a brand blueprint that defines how you will deliver the 'big idea' practically.
Customer Alignment Bringing all the stakeholders together, making the purpose relevant and energizing.		1. Map out all the stakeholders internally and externally – customers, employees, shareholders. 2. Consider the aspirations and priorities of each group, and segments within them. 3. Develop relevant communication based on how the purpose links to their motivations. 4. Ensure coherence across the diverse stakeholders, and how they mutually support each other. 5. Bring the purpose to life through symbolic leadership and customer deliverables.

CUSTOMER VISION: PRACTICAL TOOLS AND ACTIONS

Customer Toolkit 2: **Customer Strategy**

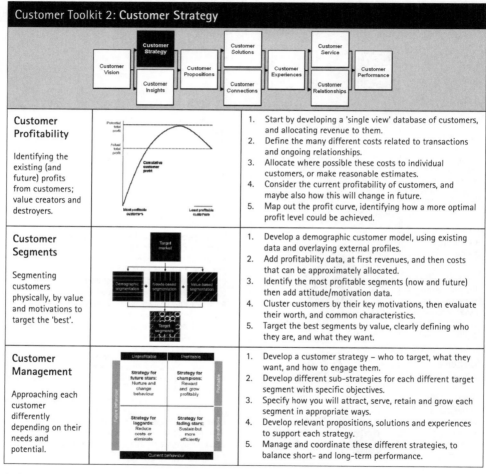

Customer Profitability Identifying the existing (and future) profits from customers; value creators and destroyers.		1. Start by developing a 'single view' database of customers, and allocating revenue to them. 2. Define the many different costs related to transactions and ongoing relationships. 3. Allocate where possible these costs to individual customers, or make reasonable estimates. 4. Consider the current profitability of customers, and maybe also how this will change in future. 5. Map out the profit curve, identifying how a more optimal profit level could be achieved.
Customer Segments Segmenting customers physically, by value and motivations to target the 'best'.		1. Develop a demographic customer model, using existing data and overlaying external profiles. 2. Add profitability data, at first revenues, and then costs that can be approximately allocated. 3. Identify the most profitable segments (now and future) then add attitude/motivation data. 4. Cluster customers by their key motivations, then evaluate their worth, and common characteristics. 5. Target the best segments by value, clearly defining who they are, and what they want.
Customer Management Approaching each customer differently depending on their needs and potential.		1. Develop a customer strategy – who to target, what they want, and how to engage them. 2. Develop different sub-strategies for each different target segment with specific objectives. 3. Specify how you will attract, serve, retain and grow each segment in appropriate ways. 4. Develop relevant propositions, solutions and experiences to support each strategy. 5. Manage and coordinate these different strategies, to balance short- and long-term performance.

CUSTOMER STRATEGY: PRACTICAL TOOLS AND ACTIONS

Customer Toolkit 3: Customer Insights

Customer Canvas Bringing together all your customer jigsaw in one place, and making sense of the bigger view.		1. Identify and collate all the different sources of customer information, internally and externally. 2. Develop a wall-sized blank 'canvas' divided into four quadrants – who, why. what and how. 3. Post the key data and insights from documents against the appropriate quadrants. 4. Engage project team in finding connections between different pieces of data. 5. The team develops a deeper, broader picture of the customer, that can be regularly updated.
Customer Immersion Diving deep into the customers world, their lives and dreams, their real goals and needs.		1. Hypothesize key issues and ideas (using canvas) to explore in more detail with customers. 2. Engage project team (incl. business leaders) in spending time talking to individual customers. 3. Discuss their broader lives, what they seek to achieve, what matters most, what influences them. 4. Probe each of the issue and idea areas in detail, seeking parallels and practices across sectors. 5. Summarize your one to one experience in writing, share with team, make it real, tell the story.
Customer Energizers Finding what really motivates customers rationally, and particularly emotionally.		1. Interpret existing and new customer information, from immersion and other research techniques. 2. Identify the factors that matter most to the individual, or segment of customers. 3. Define the essential items, which are prerequisites for addressing their challenge. 4. Define the enabling items, the things they cannot currently do, but seek rationally to be able to do. 5. Define the energizing items, the more emotional factors, maybe small, that really excite them.

CUSTOMER INSIGHTS: PRACTICAL TOOLS AND ACTIONS

Customer Toolkit 4: Customer Propositions

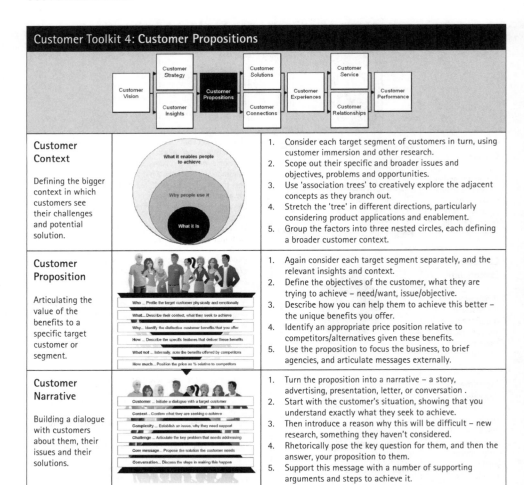

Customer Context Defining the bigger context in which customers see their challenges and potential solution.		1. Consider each target segment of customers in turn, using customer immersion and other research. 2. Scope out their specific and broader issues and objectives, problems and opportunities. 3. Use 'association trees' to creatively explore the adjacent concepts as they branch out. 4. Stretch the 'tree' in different directions, particularly considering product applications and enablement. 5. Group the factors into three nested circles, each defining a broader customer context.
Customer Proposition Articulating the value of the benefits to a specific target customer or segment.		1. Again consider each target segment separately, and the relevant insights and context. 2. Define the objectives of the customer, what they are trying to achieve – need/want, issue/objective. 3. Describe how you can help them to achieve this better – the unique benefits you offer. 4. Identify an appropriate price position relative to competitors/alternatives given these benefits. 5. Use the proposition to focus the business, to brief agencies, and articulate messages externally.
Customer Narrative Building a dialogue with customers about them, their issues and their solutions.		1. Turn the proposition into a narrative – a story, advertising, presentation, letter, or conversation . 2. Start with the customer's situation, showing that you understand exactly what they seek to achieve. 3. Then introduce a reason why this will be difficult – new research, something they haven't considered. 4. Rhetorically pose the key question for them, and then the answer, your proposition to them. 5. Support this message with a number of supporting arguments and steps to achieve it.

Customer Toolkit 5: Customer Solutions

Customer Co-creation Collaborating with customers to develop better solutions for individuals and generally.		1. Invite and encourage customers to take part in designing or improving products and services. 2. Explore their priorities and preferences, working together to design the right solutions. 3. Develop the physical solution rapidly, testing and modifying with customers as you progress. 4. Implement the solution together, helping them to apply it effectively and get the most out of it. 5. Capture the learning from individual co-creations to turn into better standard solutions.
Customer Innovation Innovating every aspect of the business and the customer's experience profitably.		1. Clearly define the objective of the innovation, the issue or opportunity to be addressed. 2. Creatively explore how to achieve this, using customer insights, disruptions, and parallels. 3. Fuse together the best ideas into distinctive concepts, visualizing and enhancing them. 4. Focus on the best few concepts, evaluated through rapid, intuitive assessment of the project team. 5. Accelerate the best ideas, also innovating the ways they will be delivered and used by customers.
Customer Solutions Building molecular solutions that solve customers real challenges distinctively.		1. Encourage a customer solution mentality – so that everybody thinks like a problem solver. 2. Recognize the many components that go into solutions – multi-branded products and services. 3. Articulate these clustered solutions as 'molecules' and define the broader concept they reflect. 4. Focus on these distinctive, richer molecular solutions in your communication and sales. 5. Support customers in implementing and applying the total solutions rather than just your products.

Customer Toolkit 6: **Customer Connections**

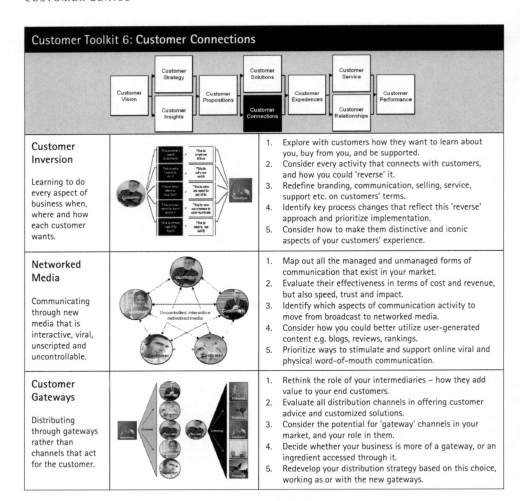

Customer Inversion		
Customer Inversion Learning to do every aspect of business when, where and how each customer wants.		1. Explore with customers how they want to learn about you, buy from you, and be supported. 2. Consider every activity that connects with customers, and how you could 'reverse' it. 3. Redefine branding, communication, selling, service, support etc. on customers' terms. 4. Identify key process changes that reflect this 'reverse' approach and prioritize implementation. 5. Consider how to make them distinctive and iconic aspects of your customers' experience.
Networked Media Communicating through new media that is interactive, viral, unscripted and uncontrollable.		1. Map out all the managed and unmanaged forms of communication that exist in your market. 2. Evaluate their effectiveness in terms of cost and revenue, but also speed, trust and impact. 3. Identify which aspects of communication activity to move from broadcast to networked media. 4. Consider how you could better utilize user-generated content e.g. blogs, reviews, rankings. 5. Prioritize ways to stimulate and support online viral and physical word-of-mouth communication.
Customer Gateways Distributing through gateways rather than channels that act for the customer.		1. Rethink the role of your intermediaries – how they add value to your end customers. 2. Evaluate all distribution channels in offering customer advice and customized solutions. 3. Consider the potential for 'gateway' channels in your market, and your role in them. 4. Decide whether your business is more of a gateway, or an ingredient accessed through it. 5. Redevelop your distribution strategy based on this choice, working as or with the new gateways.

CUSTOMER CONNECTIONS: PRACTICAL TOOLS AND ACTIONS

Customer Toolkit 7: Customer Experiences

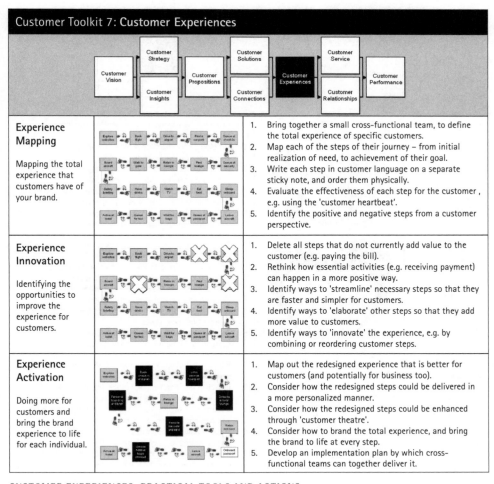

Experience Mapping Mapping the total experience that customers have of your brand.	1. Bring together a small cross-functional team, to define the total experience of specific customers. 2. Map each of the steps of their journey – from initial realization of need, to achievement of their goal. 3. Write each step in customer language on a separate sticky note, and order them physically. 4. Evaluate the effectiveness of each step for the customer, e.g. using the 'customer heartbeat'. 5. Identify the positive and negative steps from a customer perspective.
Experience Innovation Identifying the opportunities to improve the experience for customers.	1. Delete all steps that do not currently add value to the customer (e.g. paying the bill). 2. Rethink how essential activities (e.g. receiving payment) can happen in a more positive way. 3. Identify ways to 'streamline' necessary steps so that they are faster and simpler for customers. 4. Identify ways to 'elaborate' other steps so that they add more value to customers. 5. Identify ways to 'innovate' the experience, e.g. by combining or reordering customer steps.
Experience Activation Doing more for customers and bring the brand experience to life for each individual.	1. Map out the redesigned experience that is better for customers (and potentially for business too). 2. Consider how the redesigned steps could be delivered in a more personalized manner. 3. Consider how the redesigned steps could be enhanced through 'customer theatre'. 4. Consider how to brand the total experience, and bring the brand to life at every step. 5. Develop an implementation plan by which cross-functional teams can together deliver it.

CUSTOMER EXPERIENCES: PRACTICAL TOOLS AND ACTIONS

Customer Toolkit 8: **Customer Service**

Customer Service		
Customer Service Delivering the customer promise in a effective, reliable and appropriate way.		1. Consider the key moments to serve customers across the total customer experience. 2. Develop a service strategy based on all service points and channels e.g. people, phone, Web etc. 3. Define service values in clear and simple terms, the three aspects that make your service special. 4. Map out the core service activities at each delivery point, maybe defined by service people themselves. 5. Deliver service through principles, teamwork and leadership, rather than scripted processes.
Individual Service Serving customers more personally through natural intuition and judgement.		1. Explore with your team what makes them special, and how they engage best with people. 2. Encourage them to apply their own personalities, addressing customers as real individual people. 3. Consider also how to combine this with better use of personal data, and customization tools. 4. Give people more space to use their own judgement and express their only styles. 5. Be more intuitive, in judging how to service each customer in a more individual and inspiring way.
Service Recovery Turning disasters into delight by showing what you can do when things go wrong.		1. Recognize problems as an opportunity to do more, and complaints an opportunity to learn. 2. Establish fast and personal processes for address (and anticipate) occasional service failures. 3. Build service recovery as a key service skill, being ready and prepared for when things go wrong. 4. Focus on the customer first, solving the problem, compensating as needed, then fixing it for future. 5. Use the situation to stimulate a better relationship or generate new insights for innovation.

CUSTOMER SERVICE: PRACTICAL TOOLS AND ACTIONS

Customer Toolkit 9: **Customer Relationships**

Customer Relationship

Building customer relationships of mutual commitment and value.

1. Identify the target customers that you would like to retain and grow profitably over time.
2. Explore with them what they seek from you, beyond products and services.
3. Reflect on how relationships are built elsewhere, personally, in other activities, or businesses.
4. Develop a relationship plan based upon committing to, contributing to and championing each other.
5. Encourage more informal dialogue with customers to learn what more you can do for (and sell) them.

Customer Community

Harnessing networks as communities of customers with a common passion or purpose.

1. Identify social networks (physical and virtual) that your customers are most likely to be part of.
2. Understand the common purpose or motivations that bring your target customers together.
3. Explore how you could enable these networks to work better, to better achieve their purpose.
4. Build an affinity between the brand and the relevant communities, adding value in some way.
5. Collaborate with communities, engaging them in new ideas and innovations that do more for them.

Customer Loyalty

Retaining customers, selling more, costing less, and driving advocacy.

1. Identify your portfolio of direct (business-customer) and indirect (customer-customer) relationships.
2. Deploy your customer strategies to grow the profitability of each customer in appropriate ways.
3. Target specific actions to encourage retention, cross-buying, costing less and customer advocacy.
4. Provide incentives and rewards as part of the relationship, such as exclusive benefits.
5. Measure the impact of each factor on the customer profitability or 'customer lifetime value'.

CUSTOMER RELATIONSHIPS: PRACTICAL TOOLS AND ACTIONS

Customer Toolkit 10: Customer Performance

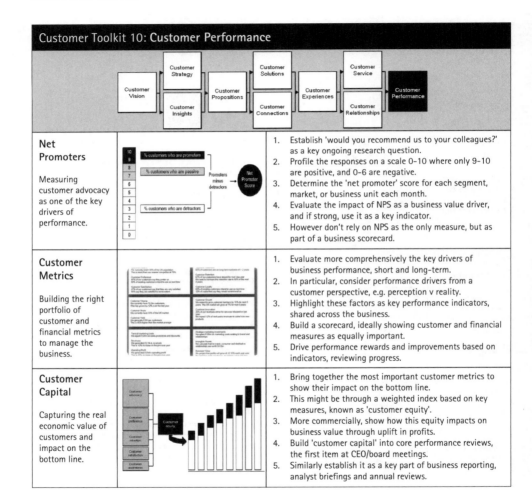

| Net Promoters

Measuring customer advocacy as one of the key drivers of performance. | 1. Establish 'would you recommend us to your colleagues?' as a key ongoing research question.
2. Profile the responses on a scale 0-10 where only 9-10 are positive, and 0-6 are negative.
3. Determine the 'net promoter' score for each segment, market, or business unit each month.
4. Evaluate the impact of NPS as a business value driver, and if strong, use it as a key indicator.
5. However don't rely on NPS as the only measure, but as part of a business scorecard. |

| Customer Metrics

Building the right portfolio of customer and financial metrics to manage the business. | 1. Evaluate more comprehensively the key drivers of business performance, short and long-term.
2. In particular, consider performance drivers from a customer perspective, e.g. perception v reality.
3. Highlight these factors as key performance indicators, shared across the business.
4. Build a scorecard, ideally showing customer and financial measures as equally important.
5. Drive performance rewards and improvements based on indicators, reviewing progress. |

| Customer Capital

Capturing the real economic value of customers and impact on the bottom line. | 1. Bring together the most important customer metrics to show their impact on the bottom line.
2. This might be through a weighted index based on key measures, known as 'customer equity'.
3. More commercially, show how this equity impacts on business value through uplift in profits.
4. Build 'customer capital' into core performance reviews, the first item at CEO/board meetings.
5. Similarly establish it as a key part of business reporting, analyst briefings and annual reviews. |

CUSTOMER PERFORMANCE: PRACTICAL TOOLS AND ACTIONS

More GENIUS

Inspirational ideas and action every day
A book is just a beginning. It will hopefully introduce new ideas, make you think differently and inspire you to do them in extraordinary ways. There is a range of other 'genius' resources to help you.

Genius LIVE

Updates on the best ideas from around the world
From Amazon to Baidu, business is a living, shifting story. Be inspired by the new genius: the new ideas as they emerge, the best practices as they evolve, the people and stories that inspire you think differently. Visit www.thegeniusworks.com for live updates.

Genius blog
The best 'yin-yang' anecdotes from around the world. A real-time diary of new experiences from unusual business places. Remember, ideas are found in the margins, not the mainstream. Learn how companies large and small are competing and winning in extraordinary ways.

Genius events
An ongoing programme of inspirational speeches, workshops and retreats in companies and countries around the world. They explore the changing business agenda and how to implement

'outside in' thinking as a source of innovation and inspiration, survival and success, and how you can be a customer business too.

Genius downloads

More than 250 free downloads including the latest research and trends, case studies and reports, all together in one place – one of the best collections of leading-edge papers on strategy and leadership, customers and marketing, growth and innovation, people and performance.

Genius WORKS

Practical support in making your ideas happen

It's not easy to stretch your mind, think in new ways, or challenge your conventions from the inside. You need the right environment, processes and support to do it. A number of practical 'genius' approaches can help you address business issues and opportunities in more powerful ways. See thegeniusworks.com for more information.

Genius Lab

A one- to three-day creative event that that inspires your people to think creatively – to challenge and shape, innovate and focus business strategies and customer propositions. The Lab is built on a high-energy interactive environment where people work fast and collaboratively to reach beyond normality.

The Fast Track

Explore the very latest ideas and best emerging practices in the areas of strategy and leadership, customers and innovation – a series of one- or two-day development workshops that combine inspirational thinking with practical application.

Zoom Ventures

Working in partnership with leading brands, investors and entrepreneurs to make the best new ideas happen, with a particular focus on 'social entrepreneurship'. We uniquely bring a customer-centric approach to venturing, the allocation of funds, development of concepts and accelerated development.

Genius BOOKS

More insights and ideas to help you think different

You can explore more 'genius' ideas and insights from by Peter Fisk. Each book brings together a more intelligent and imaginative approach to specific aspects of business, exploring the emerging ideas and very best practices from every corner of the world.

Business Genius – how to survive and thrive in changing markets

Fast and connected markets need new business approaches. They demand more innovative strategies and entrepreneurial leaders, more network-based solutions and energized people. The inspired business thinks with right more than left brain, guided by the future back as opposed to now forward, works from the outside in rather than the inside out, and ensures that radical ideas become practical reality. With Diesel and Red Bull, Shanghai Tang and Natura, the book explains how.

www.businessgeniuslive.com

Marketing Genius – how to compete with your left and right brain.
Marketing is the most important and exciting part of business today; brands and relationships are the most valuable assets, engaging customers and delivering differentiation. From Apple to Coke, Jones Soda to Virgin, we explore how to shape new markets in your vision and build brands and customer solutions that deliver extraordinary results.

www.marketinggeniuslive.com

Creative Genius – how to innovate from the future back.
Strategic innovation transforms business and markets, harnessing the power of creativity and design. We explore the four creative zones of business and how you can combine the intelligence of P&G with the imagination of D&G, the creative culture of Google with the innovative practices of Zara to make your best ideas happen.

www.creativegeniuslive.com

Credits

Nothing in work, or life, is possible without the inspiration, advice and support of the people around you. That is why business must learn to work much more collaboratively with its customers, and it matters just as much when you write a book.

It is particularly the case when you seek to do something different: to bring together diverse issues and ideas from different parts of business – customer strategy and insights, customer propositions and innovation, customer service and relationships; and from companies in every part of the world – China and India, Japan and Singapore, Turkey and Mexico, the Czech Republic and Latvia, Denmark and Sweden, France and Spain, the UK and the US.

I would like to acknowledge the contribution of family and friends, colleagues and their contacts, fellow authors and experts. Thank you to them all, and in particular

- My wife Alison, and daughters Anna and Clara

- Simon Benham at Meyer Benham

- Brendan Barns at Speakers for Business

- Holly Bennion and Iain Campbell at Wiley Capstone

- David Cook and Mark Thomas at PA Consulting Group

- Authors Phil Dourado and Elen Lewis, Andy Milligan and Shaun Smith

- Reinier Evers at Trendwatching and Magnus Lindkvist at Pattern Recognition

- Carl Sharples and David Newman at Co-operative Financial Services

- Hugh Burkitt at the Marketing Society and David Haigh at Brand Finance

- Urmas Kõiv, Hando Sinisalu and Alina Lisina in the Baltics

- Alper Utku and Tanyer Sonmezer at Management Centre Turkey

- Deniz Uzuncarsilioglu and Bilge Gunes Cetin in Eczacibasi

Additionally some of the resources that I find most useful and enlightening are:

- *Authenticity: what consumers really want* by James Gilmore and Joe Pine

- *Blink: the power of thinking without thinking* by Malcolm Gladwell

- *Chief Customer Officer* by Jeanne Bliss

- *The Cluetrain Manifesto* by Rick Levine and others

- *Complicated Lives* by Michael Willmott and William Nelson

- *Converting Customer Value* by John Murphy and others

- *Creating a Company of Customers* by Malcolm McDonald and others

- *Customer Experience Management* by Bernd Schmidt

- *Designing the Customer-Centric Organization* by Jay Galbraith

- *The Disney Way Fieldbook* by Bill Capodagli and Lynn Jackson

- *Enterprise One to One* by Don Peppers and Martha Rogers

- *The Experience Economy* by Joe Pine and James Gilmore

- *Leading for Growth* by Ray Davis and Alan Shrader

- *The Long Tail* by Chris Anderson

- *The Loyalty Effect* by Frederick Reicheld

- *Lovemarks: the future beyond brands* by Kevin Roberts

- *Moments of Truth* by Jan Carlson

- *Purple Cow: transform your business by being remarkable* by Seth Godin

- *Relationship Marketing for Competitive Advantage* by Adrian Payne

- *Right Side Up* by Alan Mitchell

- *See Feel Think Do* by Andy Milligan and Shaun Smith

- *The Toyota Way* by Jeffrey Liker and David Maier

- *Uncommon Practice* by Shaun Smith and Andy Milligan

- *We are Smarter than Me* by Barry Libert and Jon Spector

However the biggest inspiration of all is to go and spend time with real people, the wonderful people we call customers. Watch how they behave, talk to them about their ambitions, and start thinking like they do.

About the author

Peter Fisk is a best-selling author and inspirational speaker, an advisor to leading companies around the world and an experienced business leader.

He grew up in the remote farming community of Northumberland, in the North East of England, and after exploring the world of nuclear physics, joined British Airways at a time when it was embarking upon becoming 'the world's favourite airline' with a cultural alignment around customers.

He went on to work with many of the world's leading companies, helping them to grow more profitably by becoming more customer-centric in their structure, operations and leadership. He works across sectors, encouraging business leaders to take a customer perspective, and learning from different types of experiences. His clients include American Express and Coca-Cola, Lastminute.com and Marks & Spencer, Microsoft and O2, Orange and Red Bull, Shell and Virgin, Vodafone and Volkswagen.

He was also the transforming CEO of the Chartered Institute of Marketing, the world's largest marketing organization. He led the strategic marketing consulting team of PA Consulting Group where he developed an integrated consulting approach called *Customer Breakthrough*, was managing director of specialist measurement firm Brand Finance, and partner of The Foundation.

Peter now leads the Genius Works, a strategic innovation business that works with senior management to 'see things differently' – to develop and implement more inspired strategies for customers, innovation and marketing. *The Genius Lab* is a facilitated innovation process for developing new business and customer strategies based on deep customer insights and creative thinking, *Zoom Ventures* bring together business investors and social entrepreneurs, and *The Fast Track* is a coaching and personal development programme that combines leading edge learning with fast practical solutions for implementation.

He was recently described by *Business Strategy Review* as 'one of the best new business thinkers' and is in demand around the world as an expert advisor and energizing speaker.

Peter's best-selling book *Marketing Genius* explores the left- and right-brain approaches to competitive success, and has been translated into more than 25 languages. *Business Genius* describes the challenge for business leaders of sustaining business profitability and growth through turbulent times. This will be followed by *Creative Genius* on a more sustainable approach to innovation, and *The Good Growth Guide* which explains how to grow your business, whilst doing good ethically, socially and for the environment.

To find out more, see his website: www.theGeniusWorks.com

To contact him, email: peterfisk@peterfisk.com

Index

advocates 274–9
Air Asia 18–19
alignment 103–5
Amazon 74–8
American Express 224
Anderson, Brad 81–4
Anderson, Chris, *The Long Tail* 206
Angelo, Frank 324–5
Apple Computer 94
Armstrong, Lance 57–8
Arnold Communications 200–201
association trees 158
Aveda 101–103
Avon 352–4

Baidu 33–4
Bain & Co. 276
Balon, Adam 335
Bank Account 241–2
Banyan Tree Hotels and Resorts 25–7
Beecham, Sinclair 330

Bell, David 153
Berners-Lee, Tim 38
Berzina, Zane 40, 42–3
Berzins, Janis 40, 42–3
Best Buy 81–4
Bezos, Jeff 74, 77–8
Blitz, Gerard 120
Boeing 787
   Dreamliner 39, 191–2
Bosch, Margareta van den 145–6
Bowerman, Bill 115
brands 98–101, 216, 231–2, 268, 275
   comparative 101
   core 332–3
   emotional 101
   gateway 211
   ingredient 211
   rational 100
   tattoo 275
Branson, Richard 19, 317, 360–63

British Airways 186–7
Buckingham, Marcus, *First Break All the Rules* 316
Build-a-Bear Workshop 232–5
business impact 294–300
business portfolios 19
business value 78–81, 294–300
   intangible 296–7
      customer capital 297–300
      human capital 297
      structural capital 297
   tangible 296
business-to-business relationships 262–3
businesses
   consolidation 37
   intangibles 37
   investment 38
   resources 38
   transparency 37, 77–8

Camper brand 48–51
CARER (capable, accessible,
        relevant, effective,
        responsible) 238–9
Carlson, Jan 216
Cemex 106–7
change drivers 36–9
change management 347–52
    delivering change 357
    engaging in change 355–6
    making it happen 354–8
    making it stick 358
    preparing for change 356–7
Chase, Robin 68
chief executive officer (CEO)
        322–4
Choo, Jimmy 174–5
Clark, Maxine 233–5
Club Med 120–21
co-creation 177–81
    co-defining 179
    co-delivering 180
    co-designing 179
    co-developing 180
Co-operative Group 272–4
Coca-Cola 148
communication 10, 196–201
communities 267–71
    application 270
    characteristics 270
    connectors 271
    mavens 271
    participants 270
        devotees 270

insiders 271
minglers 271
tourists 271
see also networks
complaints 136, 250–54
connections 195–213
    gateways 209–13, 372
    inversion 196–202, 372
    networked media 203–8,
        372
consumers 13
context 156–60
conversations/narrative 170–73
    challenge 171
    complexity 171
    context 171
    core message 172
Covey, Stephen 241
crowds 39
culture 77, 327–44
    aligning people/customers
        332–5
    engaging your people
        328–30
    four Ps (philosophy,
        processes, people,
        problem-solving)
        343–4
    outside in 337–42
        customer focus 338
        customer obsession 338
        customer satisfaction
            338
        internal customers 338

market share 338
people first 338
sheep dipping 339
structures 337–42
symbols/stories 341–2
Current TV 39
customer agenda 43–50
customer behaviour 37–8
customer blueprint 86
customer business 71–3
customer canvas 139–40
customer capital 297–300
    basket 298
        customer preferences
            298
        customer referral 298
        customer retention
            298
        customer volume 298
    equity 298
    value 298
customer champion 321–4
customer focus 73, 338
customer heartbeat 220–21
customer immersion 136,
        142–5, 150–51
    deep dives 144–5
    thin slicing 142
customer kaleidoscopes 34–9
customer knowledge 3–6, 12
customer lifetime value (CLV)
        113–15
customer management 121–7
    all-to-one 127

attract 122, 123
champion and grow
        profitability 124, 125
grow 122
identify 122
markets 126
niches 126
nurture and change
        behaviour 124, 125
one and one 127
one-to-one 126
reduce costs/eliminate 124,
        125
retain 122, 123
segments 126
serve 122, 123
sustain but more efficiently
        124, 125
Customer Power Profile 65–7
customer relationship
        management (CRM)
        125, 260, 264
customer satisfaction 54, 338
customer value 78–81
customer-centric business
        73–8, 83–4
    building 84–8, 340–42,
        347–52
    difficulties 339–40
customization 12

Damasio, Anthony, *The Feeling
        of What Happens:
        Body and Emotion*
        *in the Making of
        Consciousness* 30–31
Danielson, Antje 68
Davidson, Arthur 265
Davis, Jim 279–80
Davis, Ray, *Leading for Growth:
        How Umpqua
        Bank Got Cool and
        Created a Culture of
        Greatness* 309–12
Dawkins, Richard 172
Degtyareva, Elena 354
D'Estaing, Henri Giscard 120–21
Disney Corporation 95
Disney, Walt 243, 244
Disneyland 232, 243–4
distribution channels 209–11
Dove 140–42
Drucker, Peter 71

Eczacibas, Dr Nejat 313
Eczacibasi 313–15
EFQM (European Foundation for
        Quality Management)
        Excellence Model 86
Elliot, Ben 212–13
emotion 30–31, 54
employee brand 332–3
employee engagement 328–30,
        334
employee value propositions 334
energizer pyramid 150–51, 334
    enablers 150
    energizers 150
    essentials 150
Enterprise car rental 286–8
Estée Lauder 325
Evers, Reinier 36
experiences 215–35
    activation 229–35, 373
    coaching 227
    educational 227
    elaborating interactions
        224
    entertaining 227
    extraordinary 229–32
    guiding 227
    innovation 222–8, 373
    mapping 216–22, 373
    streamlining interactions 224

Facebook.com 13–15, 267
Fader, Peter 15
Fernandez, Tony 18–19
First Direct 246–7, 292–4
Fluxa, Antonio 50
Fohboh 267
Friedman, Thomas, *The World is
        Flat* 39

gateways 209–11
GE (General Electric) 279,
        300–303, 317, 348
    Execute for Growth 301
    At the Customer, for the
        Customer 302
    CECOR Marketing
        Framework 300

Customer Dreaming
   Sessions 302
Growth Playbook 302
Growth Traits 302
Imagination
   Breakthroughs 302
Innovation Labs 302
Geek Squad 83
genius lab 365–6
   blog 377
   books 379–80
   downloads 378
   events 377–8
   fast track 377–8
   inspirational ideas and
      action 377
   roadmap 367–76
   support 377
   updates 377
   zoom ventures 379
Gladwell, Malcolm 142
   The Tipping Point 271
global village 16–18
Grazia, Sebastian de, *Of Time,
   Work and Leisure* 51
Green, Jack 61
Griffith, Scott 69
Grove, Andy 348

H&M 145–7
Handy, Charles 349
Harley, William 265
Harley-Davidson 216, 265–7,
   271
Harrah's Casinos 151–3

Hayek, Nicolas 187–8
Hayon, Jaime 50
heads down people 307, 309,
   312
heads up people 307–8, 309
Heinz 148
Heinz, Henry 181
Heinz Tomato Ketchup 181–2
Ho Kwon Ping 25, 27
Humanicity 241–2

Immelt, Jeff 279, 300–301, 303,
   317–18, 319
information sources
   brain scanning 136
   census information 136
   cool hunting 34, 136
   customer complaints 136
   customer feedback 136
   customer immersion 136
   customer panels 137
   customer surveys 137
   external reports 137
   focus groups 137
   mystery shopping 137
   omnibus surveys 137
   personal intuition 137–8
   previous collaborations 138
   staff anecdotes 138
   third party databases 138
   transactional databases 138
   vox pops 138
Innocent 335–7
innovation 63, 73, 183–7
   design 185–6

development 186
discovery 184–5
Inoue, Masoe 343–4
inside out approach 64–7, 294
insights 131–53, 369
   canvas 139–40, 369
   distinction with insight
      147–8
   energizers 147–53, 369
   hypothesis generation 148
   immersion 142–7, 369
   obstacles 150
   techniques 148–9
   transparency 77
Intel 348
intelligence (information)
   132–40
   decision making 133–4
   research 132–4
   sources 134–9
Internet 38, 39
Ishiazaka, Yoshio 343

Jiangzhong, Wu 202
Jimmy Choo 174–5
Jobs, Steve 308
John Lewis 104
Jung, Andrea 353

Kano diagram 149
Karamercan, Dr Erdai 313–15
Kederlen, Johannes 228
Kelleher, Herb 254
key account management
   263–4

Klement, Václav 359
Knight, Phil 115, 172
Koch, Christof 275
Kotter, John, *Leading Change*
        351–2
Kristiansen, Kjeld Kirk 96
Kristiansen, Ole Kirk 96

Lafley, A.J. 143, 318–21
Lance Armstrong Foundation
        57–8
Lawson, Rene 161
leadership
    inspiring people 308–12
    market 104–5
    new 316–18
    organizational traits 311–12
    personal traits 310
    successful 316
        catalyst 317
        coach 317
        communicator 317
        connector 317
        conscience 317
Lego 96–8
Lewis, Joe 61
Li, Robin 33–4
Libert, Barry, *We Are Smarter
        Than Me* 39
Lindkvist, Magnus 35
Lindstrom, Martin, *BrandSense*
        275
loyalty 4, 54, 60, 274–9
    buy more 276
    cost less 276

pay more 276
programmes 274–5
stay longer 276
tell others 276

MAC (Makeup Artist Cosmetics)
        324–5
McConnell, David 352
Mackay, John 161–2
managers 307, 312
market leadership 104
    customer intimacy 104
    operational excellence 105
    product 104
market research 134–9
market structures 37
    competition 37
    corporations 37
    fragmentation 37
    globalization 37
    regulation 37
marketing 58, 59–61
    affinity 199
    interruptive 59–60
    one-to-one 126
    permission 60
Maslow, Abraham 36
Mason, Tim 144
Mellon, Tamara 174–5
meme 172–3
Metcalfe, Julian 330
Metcalfe, Robert 15
metrics 288–90, 339
    business performance
        scorecard 291

customer capital 297–300
    Return on Customer (ROC)
        290
    short-and-long-term
        actions 289–90,
        300
    value 290
Midland Bank 292
mission statements 42, 92,
        94–6, 107, 233, 287
Myamoto, Shigeru 221

Net Promoter Score (NPS)
        276–9
networked media 203–8, 372
networks 14–15, 39, 203–7
    collectors 204
    commentators 204
    connectors 204
    creators 204
    curious 204
    non-participants 204
    see also communities
neuroscience 136
New Balance 279–81
Nike 115–17, 183
Nike Women 115–17
Nintendo Wii 221–2

Oldenburg, Ray 268
O'Neill, Heidi 116
outside in approach 64–7, 110,
        162, 178, 196, 260,
        284, 319–20, 337–42
Oxfam Unwrapped 168–70

Parker, Mike 115–16
partnerships 259–64
    advocacy 261
    commitment 260–61, 263
    connecting 261
    partnering 262
passion 9, 331
people-service-profit chain
    329–30
Peppers, Don, *Return on
    Customers* 290
Pepsi Challenge 134
perceived value 159
performance 283–303
    capital 294–303, 376
    effectiveness
        customers 284
        drivers 284
        value 284
    metrics 288–94, 376
    net promoters 284–8, 376
personal agenda 29
Persson, Erling 145
Pilling, Chris 293–4
power 54–7
Pralahad, C.K. 16
Pret A Manger 95, 330–32
Proctor & Gamble (P&G) 143,
    318–21
product availability 4
product-centric business 86
profit 92, 110–15, 124, 277
Progressive Insurance 61–3
promise 94–6
promise gap 56

propositions 156–75, 162–8,
    216, 370
    context 156–62, 370
    how much? 166
    narrative 170–75, 370
    what not? 166
    what? 166
    who? 166
    why? 166
pull-push 59–61, 64, 312
purpose 92–6
    statement 94
push-pull 167

Quintessentially 212–13

Rechelsbacher, Horst 101–3
Red Bull 199
Reed, Richard 335
Reicheld, Fred 293
    The Loyalty Effect 276
relationships 260–81
    building 3–6, 260–67,
        375
    community 267–74, 375
    loyalty 274–81, 375
research 232
rewards 288
Ridderstrale, Jonas, *Funky
    Business* 54
Riley, William 279
Rin Li 34
Ritz-Carlton Hotel Company 95,
    157, 231, 252, 254–7,
    316, 338

Roberts, Kevin 275
Rogers, Martha, *Return on
    Customers* 290

Saatchi & Saatchi 275
St Lukes' agency 263–4
Scandinavian Airlines 216
Schulze, Horst 157, 316
search engines 33–4
Sears Roebuck 330
segmentation 82, 117–19
    competitive positioning
        117
    engaging customers 117
    strategic prioritization 117
service 238–57, 287–8
    customer 78
    defect reduction 78
    delivery 238–42, 374
    holistic 339
    individual 245–9, 374
    recovery 250–54, 374
        apologize 251
        compensate 251
        fix 251
        improve 251
        recognize 251
    repeatable processes 78
shareholder value 294–5
shareholders 81
Simpson, Aaron 212–13
Singapore Airlines 18, 229,
    247–9
Skoda 359–60
Smart car 187–8

social networks *see*
        communities;
        networks
solutions 178–213, 189–92,
        371
    agree 180
    analyse 180
    co-creation 178–82,
        371
    design 180
    explore 180
    identify 180
    implement 181
    innovation 183–8, 371
    molecular 189–0
    review 181
Sony 104
Southwest airline 253–4
Specter, Jon, *We Are Smarter
        Than Me* 39
Spiral of Positivity 242
standardization 12
Starbucks 238, 269
Stenders Soap Factory 40–43
Stephens, Robert 83
strategic inflection points
        348
strategy 110–29, 368
    business 121
    customer 122–7
    management 121–9, 368
    market 121
    profitability 110–17, 368
    segments 117–20, 368

Surowiecki, James, *The Wisdom
        of Crowds* 39

TAG (talk, act, grow) 253
Tagish 253
Tapscott, Don, *Wikinomics: How
        Mass Collaboration
        Changes Everything*
        39
targets 117–19, 288
Tata Motors 127–9
Tata, Ratan 127, 128
Taylor, Jack 286
technology 10, 36
    convergence 36
    digitalization 36
    networks 36
    robotics 36
    speed 37
Tesco 144, 267
TGI Friday's 95, 217
theatre 222–7
third place 268–9
Tichy, Noel, *Control Your Destiny
        or Someone Else Will*
        348
Toskan, Frank 324–5
touchpoints 216–21
Toyota 105, 342–4
traditional media 206
trends 43–4, 58
    me 44
        authentic 45
        desire 45

        individual 45
    my world
        anchors 46
        expression 46–7
        participation 46
    the world
        connection 47
        responsible 48
        simplicity 47
trendspotting 34–6
tribes 19–24
    active boomers 22
    assertive women 22
    Chinese dreamers 22
    deep believers 22
    designer gays 23
    economic migrants 23
    green consumers 23
    growing south 23
    Indian entrepreneurs 23
    intrepid explorers 23
    living elders 24
    luxury seekers 24
    new Europeans 24
    pyramid masses 24
    serial singles 24
    talented youth 24
Trigano, Gilbert 120

Umpqua Bank 309–12

value added 224–7
value drivers 284–6, 289
    inputs 289

outputs 289
throughputs 289
value-based management 314
Virgin Atlantic 339, 362
Virgin Group 104, 224, 360–63
virtual communities 13–15
vision 91–107, 367
    alignment 103–7, 367
    brand 98–103, 367
    purpose 92–6, 367
    workshop 93–4
Vodafone 148

Volkswagen 200–201
Vom Fass 228

Wal-Mart 95
Wenzhong, Dr Zhang 202
Whitman, Meg 319
Whole Foods Markets
        160–62
WINet 152–3
wonderful people 10–13
World Wide Web 38
Wright, Jon 335

Wu, John 33
Wumart 201–202

Xerox Scandinavia 341–2
Xu, Eric 33

Zambrano, Lorenzo 106–7
Ziemer, James 265
Zipcars 68–9
zone of difference 149
Zopa 39, 207–8
Zuckerberg, Mark 13–15